How to Get Published in the Best Tourism
Journals

How to Get Published in the Best Tourism Journals

Edited by

Chris Cooper

School of Events, Tourism and Hospitality Management, Leeds Beckett University, UK

C. Michael Hall

Department of Management, Marketing, and Tourism, University of Canterbury, New Zealand; Eminent Scholar, College of Hotel & Tourism Management, Kyung Hee University, Korea; and Docent and Visiting Professor in Geography, University of Oulu, Finland

Cheltenham, UK • Northampton, MA, USA

Published by
Edward Elgar Publishing Limited
The Lypiatts
15 Lansdown Road
Cheltenham
Glos GL50 2JA
UK

Edward Elgar Publishing, Inc.
William Pratt House
9 Dewey Court
Northampton
Massachusetts 01060
USA

A catalogue record for this book
is available from the British Library

Library of Congress Control Number: 2024930595

This book is available electronically in the **Elgar**online
Geography, Planning and Tourism subject collection
http://dx.doi.org/10.4337/9781035300600

MIX
Paper | Supporting
responsible forestry
FSC
www.fsc.org   FSC® C013604

ISBN 978 1 0353 0059 4 (cased)
ISBN 978 1 0353 0060 0 (eBook)

Printed and bound by CPI Group (UK) Ltd, Croydon, CR0 4YY

Contents

List of contributors   vii

PART I   INTRODUCTION

1   Publishing in tourism   2
      Chris Cooper and C. Michael Hall

2   The tourism journal landscape   6
      Bob McKercher

3   The view from journal editors: contributions from the
      editors of top tourism journals   20
      Chris Cooper and C. Michael Hall

PART II   THE PAPER

4   Crafting a refereed journal paper   55
      Chris Cooper

5   The Herculean task of making a contribution to the
      scholarship of tourism   65
      Freya Higgins-Desbiolles

6   Getting the methods right   79
      Rodolfo Baggio

7   Writing a literature review   91
      Noel Scott, Hafidh Al Riyami and Mohammad Soliman

8   Positioning the paper for publication   108
      Girish Prayag

9   Publishing in special issues   122
      Dallen J. Timothy

PART III   PUBLISHING ISSUES

10   Research and publishing ethics and integrity   133
      C. Michael Hall and Yael Ram

11   Gender and publishing   149
      Donna Chambers

12   Writing for English language versus other language journals   168
      Serena Volo

PART IV   PUBLISHING AND ACADEMIC CAREERS

13   Crafting a publications career   177
      Garry Wei-Han Tan and Dimitrios Buhalis

14   A perspective on official research performance evaluation
      in tourism   189
      Rhodri Thomas

15   Journal rankings: tourism management's *idée fixe*   202
      Nigel Morgan and Annette Pritchard

16   Careers, citations, bibliometrics, and impact: perspectives
      of new and emerging researchers   211
      Bailey Ashton Adie, Alberto Amore, Richard S. Aquino,
      Tim Baird, Dorothee Bohn, C. Michael Hall, Fahimeh
      Hateftabar, Sara Naderi Koupaei, Tyron Love, Lan Lu,
      Hamed Rezapouraghdam, Samaneh Soleimani, and Chris Zhu

PART V   CONCLUSION

17   Publishing lessons, futures and emerging issues   240
      Chris Cooper and C. Michael Hall

Index   244

Contributors

Hafidh Al Riyami is an Assistant Professor at the Tourism Department, Sultan Qaboos University, Muscat, Oman. He holds a doctorate in Tourism Management from UQ Business School, the University of Queensland, Australia. His research interests include tourist behaviour, Arab/Muslim tourism, sustainable tourism development, tourism experience and risk-taking behaviour.

Alberto Amore is an Assistant Professor in Tourism Geography at the University of Oulu, Finland. His main research interests are on resilience, urban planning, urban tourism and urban regeneration. He has more recently focused on post-disaster urban governance and destination resilience. He has published authored and edited books, peer-reviewed journals and chapters on topics such as urban tourism, urban governance, spatial planning and urban development.

Richard S. Aquino is an early career researcher and lecturer based at the Department of Management, Marketing and Tourism, UC Business School, University of Canterbury in Christchurch, New Zealand. His research interests are social entrepreneurship through tourism, sustainable tourism planning and development, community development, sustainable tourist behaviour, and decolonising tourism knowledge production.

Bailey Ashton Adie is a postdoctoral researcher in Spatial Resilience at the University of Oulu. She is also Chair of the Leisure Studies Association and the Director of Communications for the Recreation, Tourism and Sport Specialty Group (RTS), part of the American Association of Geographers. She has a PhD in Management and Development of Cultural Heritage from IMT Lucca, Italy. Her research interests include community resilience, second homes, community-based tourism, World Heritage, tourism and development, and heritage tourism. She is the author of the book *World Heritage and Tourism: Marketing and Management* (2019) and co-editor of *Second Homes and Climate Change* (2023). She sits on the editorial boards of the *Journal of Heritage Tourism*, *Tourism Geographies*, *Tourism Management Perspectives* and *El Periplo Sustentable*.

Rodolfo Baggio is Professor in the Masters in Economics and Tourism, and Research Fellow at the Dondena Centre for Research on Social Dynamics and Public Policy at Bocconi University, Milan, Italy. He actively teaches and researches on the use of information technology in tourism and on the interdisciplinary applications of complexity and network science methods to the study of tourism destinations.

Tim Baird is a Senior Lecturer in the Department of Agribusiness and Markets, Lincoln University, New Zealand. His research interests lie within the areas of wine and food marketing, particularly in the areas of tourism, sustainability and innovation.

Dorothee Bohn is a PhD candidate in Human Geography at Umeå University, Sweden. In addition to political economy analyses of tourism development and governance, her research interests revolve around financial geography, policy evaluation and human–nature interactions.

Dimitrios Buhalis is Director of the eTourism Lab at Bournemouth University Business School in England. He is a strategic management and marketing expert with specialisation in information communication technology applications in the tourism, travel, hospitality and leisure industries. He is the Editor of *Tourism Review* and the Editor of the *Encyclopedia of Tourism Management and Marketing*. Professor Dimitrios Buhalis was recognised as a Highly Cited Researcher by Clarivate™. For more information, books, articles and presentations see: www.buhalis.com.

Donna Chambers is Professor of Critical Cultural Studies at Northumbria University, Newcastle, United Kingdom. She is a critical tourism scholar interested in how people and places are represented in tourism, decolonial and postcolonial theories, and Black feminism. Donna is an Associate Editor of *Annals of Tourism Research* and a Managing Editor of *Leisure Studies*.

Chris Cooper is the co-editor of *Current Issues in Tourism*. He is a member of the editorial board for leading tourism journals and has authored a number of leading text and research books in tourism, including *Essentials of Tourism* for Sage. He is the co-series editor of the influential Channel View book series 'Aspects of Tourism'.

C. Michael Hall is Ahurei Professor at University of Canterbury, New Zealand; Eminent Scholar, Kyung Hee University; Guest Professor, Lund University Campus Helsingborg, Sweden; Visiting Professor, Linnaeus University, Kalmar, Sweden; Taylor's University, Malaysia; Visiting Professor and Docent, University of Oulu, Finland; and a research fellow at the University of Johannesburg. He is also co-editor of *Current Issues in Tourism* and field editor of *Frontiers of Sustainable Tourism*. His research interests include tourism, regional development, global environmental change, food, sustainability, wilderness, and World Heritage.

Fahimeh Hateftabar is an Assistant Professor at Ferrandi Paris Business School. She has expertise in the application of quantitative and mixed research methodologies, leading her to accumulate research experience in areas such as consumer behaviour, tourism economics and sustainable development.

Freya Higgins-Desbiolles is affiliated with the Business Unit, University of South Australia; the Department of Recreation and Leisure Studies, University of Waterloo, Canada; and the Centre for Research and Innovation in Tourism, Taylor's University, Malaysia. Her work focuses on tourism planning, sustainability issues and human rights in tourism, hospitality and events. She has published in leading tourism journals, written and edited important tourism texts and serves on the editorial boards of leading journals, including the *Journal of Sustainable Tourism*, *Current Issues in Tourism*, *Event Management* and *Leisure Sciences*.

Sara Naderi Koupaei is currently a doctoral candidate in the Department of Management, Marketing and Tourism in the UC Business School at the University of Canterbury, New Zealand. She was formerly in the Tourism Faculty at Eastern Mediterranean University. Her research interests include sustainable restaurant management; sustainable tourism; waste management; local foods; CSR; and new technologies on the tourism and hospitality experience and in destination and business marketing and management.

Tyron Love is an Associate Professor in the UC Business School at the University of Canterbury, New Zealand. Tyron has Māori (Indigenous New Zealand) tribal affiliations to Te Atiawa (Te Whanganui-a-Tara, Wellington), Ngāti Ruanui and Taranaki and has New Zealand Pākehā (non-Indigenous) ancestry. He is an Associate Editor for *Culture & Organization*, *Journal of Industrial Relations*, and *Kōtuitui: the New Zealand Journal of Social Sciences Online*. Tyron's research looks at institutions and Indigenous people's experiences in/of them.

Lan Lu is a Postdoctoral Research Associate in the Chaplin School of Hospitality and Tourism Management at Florida International University. She received her doctoral degree in Adult Education and Human Resource from Florida International University. Her research interests include workplace behaviours and turnover, learning/performance in hospitality business, career management, hospitality education and consumer behaviours.

Bob McKercher has been a tourism academic since 1990. Prior to that he worked in the Canadian tourism industry in a variety of advocacy and operational roles. He received his PhD from the University of Melbourne in

Australia, a master's degree from Carleton University in Ottawa, Canada, and his undergraduate degree from York University in Toronto, Canada. He has published over 300 scholarly papers and research reports and is the author or editor of seven books. Professor McKercher is the past President of the International Academy for the Study of Tourism and a Fellow of the International Academy for the Study of Tourism, the Council for Australian University Tourism and Hospitality Education, and the International Academy of Culture, Tourism and Hospitality Research.

Nigel Morgan is Professor of Social Sustainability at the University of Surrey's School of Hospitality and Tourism Management and a Tourism Reset Research Fellow. He has extensive editorial board experience, including on _Tourism Management_ and _Annals of Tourism Research_ and was a subpanel chair in the Hong Kong 2020 RAE.

Girish Prayag is a Professor of Marketing at the UC Business School in New Zealand. He is the Editor of Method and Practice for the journal _Current Issues in Tourism_. His research interests are related to both the production and consumption of tourism and hospitality. He has published more than 100 articles in peer-reviewed journals.

Annette Pritchard is Professor of Tourism Management at Leeds Beckett University School of Events, Tourism and Hospitality. She was Research Notes Editor of the _Annals of Tourism Research_ from 2010–2020 and a specialist advisor to the Business and Management Panel in the 2008 UK RAE.

Yael Ram is an Associate Professor in the Department of Tourism Studies at Ashkelon College, Israel. Her research interests focus on person–environment relations. She studies sustainable (and unsustainable) consumer behaviours and mobilities, place-driven emotions and cultural tourism. Yael has authored and co-authored academic papers in leading academic journals, co-authored a book on tourism and sustainable mobility, and co-edited a book on walking.

Hamed Rezapouraghdam, PhD, is an Assistant Professor in the Faculty of Tourism at Eastern Mediterranean University. He obtained his PhD degree in Tourism Management from Eastern Mediterranean University. His research interests are in the areas of corporate sustainability, environmental psychology and sustainable development.

Noel Scott is Adjunct Professor in the School of Business and Law at Edith Cowan University, Joondalup, Australia. He provides training and consulting in a number of countries in Asia and the Pacific. His research interests include the study of tourism experiences, destination management and marketing. He has published 18 books.

Samaneh Soleimani is a Lecturer in Marketing and Entrepreneurship at the Australian Institute of Business, Adelaide, South Australia. She has research interests in astrotourism, astronomical tourism, niche product development and digital marketing.

Mohammad Soliman is the Head of the Scientific Research Department at University of Technology and Applied Sciences (UTAS), Salalah, Oman; and Professor at the Faculty of Tourism & Hotels, Fayoum University, Egypt. He has published multiple papers in Web of Science and Scopus journals. He is an editorial board member of several journals.

Garry Wei-Han Tan is a Senior Professor at UCSI University, Malaysia. He has published over 90 papers with 62% of his papers currently ranked 'A*' and 'A', according to the Australian Business Deans Council (ABDC) Journal Quality List. He is currently the Brand Ambassador for Emerald Publishing East Asia and also the Assistant Editor for *Tourism Review*.

Rhodri Thomas is Professor of Tourism at Leeds Beckett University, UK. He is a member of the Economic and Social Research Council's Peer Evaluation College and served as a member of the Business and Economics Panel of New Zealand's 2018 Performance Based Research Fund (PBRF).

Dallen J. Timothy is Professor of Community Resources and Development and Senior Sustainability Scientist at Arizona State University. He is also a Research Fellow at the University of Johannesburg, South Africa, and a visiting professor at universities in China, Spain and Mexico. His tourism interests include geopolitics, heritage, empowerment of marginalised communities and religion.

Serena Volo is an Associate Professor of Marketing at the Faculty of Economics and Management of the Free University of Bozen (Italy). She is the Editor-in-Chief of the *Consumer Behaviour in Tourism and Hospitality* journal. Her research interests include consumer behaviour in tourism, experiences and emotions in tourism, destination image, big data in tourism, visual research methods, and innovation and competitiveness in tourism. She also serves on the editorial board of leading scientific journals in the field of tourism, hospitality and leisure. Serena is the scientific responsible and convenor of the Tourism Research Methods Summer School. She has worked and lived in France, the UK, Ireland, the US and Switzerland.

Chris Zhu is a PhD candidate in the School of Tourism Management at the Macao Institute for Tourism Studies, China. His research interests include smart tourism experience, social media marketing and sustainable tourism. His papers have been published in *International Journal of Tourism Research*,

Current Issues in Tourism, Information Technology & Tourism, Journal of Hospitality and Tourism Technology and elsewhere.

PART I

INTRODUCTION

1. Publishing in tourism

Chris Cooper and C. Michael Hall

Publishing in the best refereed journals has become the key to academic success in the twenty-first century. These publications are the currency of academic life yet the process of what makes a good paper and how to get it accepted for publication is shrouded in mystique, distrust and bafflement. This book aims to demystify this process by providing practical and well-founded advice to tourism scholars based on the experience of seasoned editors, reviewers and commentators. We feel there is a clear and urgent need for such a book, particularly for early career academics, at a time when every individual, paper and journal is assessed by metrics and impact factors. There is nowhere to hide.

When we were asked to compile this book, we approached the best researchers and editors of leading journals to contribute chapters and also in the case of editors to write a short piece on how they view success in writing for their refereed journal. What is remarkable is that throughout all of the chapters and pieces by the editors, there is a simple golden thread running through them – success in refereed journal publishing is about quality writing, contribution to knowledge, perfection in style and positioning the paper in the most appropriate journal. Of course, this is not rocket science but as editors of *Current Issues in Tourism* we can attest to the fact that very few papers actually abide by this. To be successful demands dedication, hard work and the old adage – proof, proof and then proof again. And of course, there are the rules of the game – how to submit, how to respond to referees and how to craft a publication-based academic career. This book takes you through those rules, is clear about what you should and should not do, and provides sound, practical advice about how to get published.

The book is divided into four parts – an introductory set of chapters on the tourism journal publishing landscape, a part on the paper itself, one on issues surrounding getting published and a final one on academic careers.

The introductory part opens with a chapter by Bob McKercher on the tourism journal landscape and how it has evolved to the complex system of today. This chapter examines the current family tree of tourism journals, showing the evolution of and linkages between titles since the first tourism journal appeared in the 1940s. The chapter then documents the historical quest for legitimacy of tourism as a field of study. The section continues with a number of individual contributions from editors of the leading tourism journals, outlining the issues they are experiencing and providing advice for successful submissions. We were not sure what to expect across a diverse range of journals but were surprised at the degree of alignment across the field. There are three themes: first, the range of papers which are now sought ranging from empirical papers, perspectives, research notes and letters, special issue papers and conceptual foundation papers. Second, the maturing of the journal landscape has brought a rise in the number of journals, away from the early generalist journals to a later splintering of journals into sub-sections of tourism – technology, destination marketing and sustainability for example. This creates more of a challenge to potential authors in their choice of an appropriate journal. As always though, it is the contribution that is key, and this comes across clearly in the editors' viewpoints on their own journals. Third, the editors identify a range of challenges that they face in the day-to-day job of editing their journal. These include poor-quality papers where the readability, language or structure of the paper is not up to standard. finding reviewers for papers, and the use of plagiarism software which adds a second layer of complexity to decision-making about manuscripts and journal metrics. Finally, issues such as ethics, author misconduct, open access, and inclusion and diversity render the journal landscape increasingly sophisticated and complex to navigate.

The second part of this book focuses on the paper itself. Chris Cooper looks at how to craft a refereed journal paper, providing hints and tips for successfully publishing in a refereed journal and how to choose the right journal. The chapter continues with an analysis of how to make a contribution and position the paper. The bulk of the chapter covers the various sections of the paper and some dos and don'ts for each. The chapter then covers the actual process of submitting the paper and how to navigate journal publishers' systems. The various parts of crafting a paper are then detailed in the following chapters. Freya Higgins-Desbiolles unpacks the key concept of 'contribution' – so often the cause for rejection. She states that academics are expected to make novel and valuable contributions to tourism's existing body of knowledge through their scholarly work. However, she recognises that exactly what is required to accomplish this can be difficult to ascertain. Rodolfo Baggio is clear-sighted in his chapter on getting the methods right – after all methodology is also a common reason for rejection. The methodology section plays a crucial role in academic papers as it outlines the approach taken to conduct the study, provides a roadmap for replication and serves as a means to establish the relevance, rigour and validity of the research findings ultimately contributing to the advancement of knowledge in the domain. Noel Scott, Hafidh Al Riyami and Mohammad Soliman provide a valuable chapter on writing the literature review – a part of the paper that is often misunderstood. They explain why the literature review is considered a central building block of a paper and clarify the importance of literature review writing skills for academic activities and the skills required to complete a literature review. The chapter deliberates on the structure of the tourism literature and the use of the paradigm funnel model. Girish Prayag examines the tricky area of 'positioning' the paper. He states that positioning is both an art and a science, often requiring adherence to publisher, journal, editor and reviewer expectations. While there is no standard framework that can be readily applied to position a paper for tourism and hospitality journals, there are ways to ensure that a paper transcends the desk rejection and goes under review. Finally, Dallen Timothy examines publishing in special issues as an important outlet for academic research and the advantages and benefits of themed issues for journal publishers, guest editors and individual scholars. He concludes with some of the perceived challenges associated with special issues, including concerns over quality and nepotism.

The third part of the book examines a range of key issues that have emerged across the tourism journal publishing landscape. Michael Hall and Yael Ram examine ethics and integrity in research and publishing, including institutional ethics, professional ethics, publisher ethics and personal ethics. They provide context with respect to the notion of ethics creep and the regulatory scope of ethics before detailing macro and micro ethical issues. Donna Chambers provides a reflexive, critical exploration of gender (in) equality in academic published work generally, and in tourism. The chapter has three key observations: (i) there is a lack of agreement in the general academic community on the nature and extent of gender (in) equality in academic publications and discrepancies about its causes; (ii) limited research exists in tourism on the gendered nature of academic publications and where this exists there is evidence of a gender gap that is deleterious to women, albeit this is decreasing; and (iii) gender remains a relatively marginal subject within published work in tourism which also often fails to manifest the influence of colonialism and the intersection between gender and race. Serena Volo provides a valuable perspective on tourism journal publishing from a non-English language perspective. She focuses on four perspectives – (i) the debate on the relevance that English has in scientific writing; (ii) the difficulties of thinking, writing and disseminating in a non-native language; (iii) suggestions on writing structure, style and clarity; and finally (iv) 'the art of writing' for top English language journals.

The final part of the book turns its focus on academic careers and publishing. Garry Wei-Han Tan and Dimitrios Buhalis show how publishing excellent research plays an essential role in shaping and progressing an academic career through securing jobs and promotions, obtaining grant funding, and creating pathways for career progression. The chapter aims to serve as a guideline for diverse segments of the academic community, ranging from PhD students and early career researchers to senior academics when crafting their publication careers. Rhodri Thomas examines the key area of performance-based research funding systems (PBRFS) and what they mean for academic researchers in tourism. These systems are the hard edge of publication assessment as they effectively allocate public research funds based on the performance of an individual or group. Nigel Morgan and Annette Pritchard look at the second hard edge of publications – journal rankings. Journal rankings have assumed increasing importance in tourism management in recent years as part of the overall shift to a managerialist culture in universities and particularly as a result of increasing external evaluation of research quality outlined in Rhodri Thomas' chapter. The chapter critically reflects on journal rankings, discussing their methodologies, flaws and subjectivities. Most importantly, it considers how a fixation with journal rankings is shaping the field's development and the careers of its scholars and concludes with some advice for new scholars negotiating their way through journal rankings. The penultimate chapter is written by Michael Hall and twelve early career researchers and PhD students and stresses the increasing pressure to publish in ever higher ranked journals and the strain that this creates for achieving an acceptable work–life balance. In the concluding chapter, we summarise the key issues faced by researchers publishing in top journals and examine some future challenges including AI, higher education policy and open access.

2. The tourism journal landscape

Bob McKercher

INTRODUCTION

Academic journals have been, and will continue to be the dominant platform to disseminate knowledge (Martínez Ruiz, 2016), for they are the most important medium available to circulate both theoretical and applied research (Zehrer, 2007, p. 139). The main reason is that the refereeing process represents a critical quality assurance step, whereby the reader knows the publication has gone through a rigorous review process to ensure its legitimacy. This issue is especially prescient in a field like tourism, hospitality and events where a huge array of material is available on the web, without any guarantee of its quality, accuracy or veracity. As a result, Crouch and Perdue (2015) commented that tourism researchers have increasingly turned to refereed journal articles to inform their research. In addition, at a more pragmatic level, one's journal publication record plays a key role in securing first jobs, getting tenure and being granted promotion (Roberts & Shea, 2005).

Tourism, hospitality and events studies have undergone a seismic shift over the past 30 years, as the number of programmes has expanded exponentially, initially in developed economies (Craig-Smith, Davidson & French, 1995) and more recently in rapidly developing Asian and African economies (Airey et al., 2015). While some consolidation is occurring in some places, the field is still expanding in many others. It is estimated, though impossible to verify, that about 4,000 universities and institutes of higher education worldwide offer degree programmes in tourism and hospitality studies and that these programmes employ upward of 40,000 teaching and research staff.

The expansion of academic journals has mirrored the growth of programmes. Based on records kept by the author (McKercher, 2022, p. 2), in 2021, some 316 tourism, hospitality and events journals were active, of which some 188 published in whole or in part in English; 39 in whole or in part in Portuguese, mostly originating out of Brazil; 27 in Spanish; and the rest in other languages. In total, more than 12,500 papers were published, with most, 8,253, in English.

This chapter examines the state of play in our academic journals. It is divided into four parts. The first part describes the rise and fall of journals, while the second part examines the evolution of journal titles over time. The third part discusses the quest for legitimacy which has faced the field. The final part discusses the consolidation of titles among a small number of multinational publishers and identifies some issues facing the field in the future.

RISE AND FALL OF JOURNALS

The author has maintained a database of tourism, hospitality and events journals that has been updated at regular intervals and published on the International Academy for the Study of Tourism website (http:// www .tourismscholars .org/ journals .php). The database includes the names of journals, economy of origin, publisher (if known), websites (if active), the year the journal was launched and the last year it was published. The information presented below was accurate as of January 2023. Over that time, some 432 journals have been identified. An analysis of their websites suggests that 296 were still active, while it appears that just under another 140 were no longer active. This figure represents a decline of some 20 journals from the 2021 figure presented in the introduction to this chapter.

Figure 2.1 documents the emergence and disappearance of the number of titles by year, where full information is available. The birth of our field can be traced to the 1940s with the launch of *The Tourism Review* as the official publication of the International Association of Scientific Experts in Tourism *(*Association Internationale D'Experts Scientifiques Du Tourisme – AIEST). It was followed soon afterward by the debut of *Tourism/Tourizam* out of the Tourism Research Centre in Croatia (Kozak, 2020). Both journals were multilingual. The *Cornell Hotel and Restaurant Quarterly*, now simply titled the *Cornell Hospitality Quarterly*, was launched in 1960 and represented the first dedicated hospitality journal.

The expansion of the number of journals was slow in the early years. Indeed, as late as 1980, only 11 titles could be identified, including eight titles in English and three titles in Japanese, Korean and Spanish. Growth remained tentative, as only 14 more titles were introduced in the 1980s, which also included the first journals from China, Poland, Brazil, and Quebec, Canada.

The field began to grow rapidly in the 1990s as tourism and hospitality programmes expanded rapidly in the UK, Oceania and North America, creating both increased demand for knowledge and an increased supply of researchers wishing to publish that knowledge. Typically, five to ten new titles were launched each year throughout the 1990s, including many of the titles that are seen to be leading journals today. The early 2000s saw an exponential expansion of the field, with about 20 or more titles launched each year between 2008 and 2015. While the number of new titles has slowed in recent years, they continue to be introduced, with five new journals launched in 2021 and another eight in 2022.

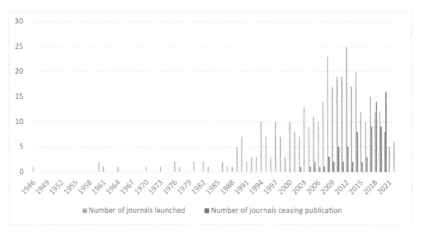

Figure 2.1   Emergence of disappearance of tourism, hospitality and events journals

Growth in new titles was also balanced by the disappearance of a number of journals since the early 2000s, suggesting the field is still evolving. No journals ceased publication throughout the 1990s and early 2000s, but since 2003, we have witnessed the loss of many titles. Indeed, some 16 titles ceased publication in 2020. The author was also not able to verify if another 32 journals were still active in 2022, as their websites have not been updated over that period. No doubt, some of these journals are no longer active, while others are just reticent in updating their online presence.

It would appear that the period of rapid journal growth has now ended and we are entering a consolidation stage, where only the strong titles will survive. Kozak (2020) feels that the field has progressed through three eras. The first era, from the 1940s through the end of the 1980s, was typified by the emergence of journals led by organisations or institutions and largely excluded major publishing houses. The second era, from the 1990s through the early 2000s, saw the emergence of small speciality publishing houses that allowed for opportunities to develop thematic journals. Now, we are in the third era, which is marked by the increasing power of international publishers and the subsequent loss of independence of some journals. We are also seeing a replication of the first era in the Asian, Eastern European and African contexts as a number of institutions and societies in these areas are now launching their own journals in order to give scholars outlets to publish regionally relevant research. To date, the major publishing houses have not shown much interest in acquiring these journals.

The observation that a number of journals have disappeared highlights the risk involved in launching a journal, with independent journals or those produced by institutions and societies being most vulnerable. Jamali, Wakeling and Abbasi (2022), looking more broadly at academic journals as a whole, note that 88% of discontinued journals belonged to educational institutions or societies. This situation appears to be replicated in our field, as just under 90% of the defunct journals were hosted by universities or societies. Another 6% were launched by predatory publishers and failed to attract enough submissions, while only a handful of defunct journals were hosted by publishing houses (McKercher, 2022).

The reasons for failure are manifest. To begin with, journals may not generate enough subscriptions to be commercially viable, leading funding organisations to lose interest and withdraw support (Zeff, 1996). In addition, a change in institutional or departmental leadership causes many organisations to reprioritise their goals, resulting in the decision to discontinue a journal. Jamali et al. (2022) further identified burnout caused by too much reliance on voluntary work on behalf of the editors. In addition, independent journals face a challenge in convincing libraries to make one-off subscription purchases (Lariviere, Haustien & Mongeon, 2015). COVID-19 also tipped many marginal journals over the edge, for the pandemic resulted in the number of submissions drying up (McKercher, 2022).

EVOLUTION OF JOURNAL TITLES

The growth in the number of titles has corresponded with the broadening of the thematic domains covered in the field. Figure 2.2 shows the family tree of title themes in English language journals. It documents the first time a thematic title occurred, but does not show the subsequent launch date of other journals under the same theme. For example, the first journal using 'Marketing' in its title debuted in 1992. Since then, a total of eight other journals have been launched that also have 'Marketing' in their titles. Figure 2.2 makes it possible to trace the lineage of each type of journal, by documenting the emergence of second, third and in some cases fourth generation titles that can trace their lineage directly back to the set of generalist titles that emerged first. More than anything else, it highlights the emergent diversity in journal themes. Once upon a time, our field could be classified into two broad title categories of tourism and hospitality journals, and going back even further, just to tourism journals. By 2023, however, the suite of journals covered close to 50 different title themes and subthemes.

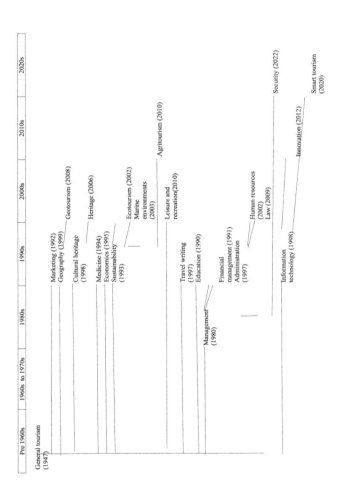

Pre 1960s	1960s to 1970s	1980s	1990s	2000s	2010s	2020s

General tourism (1947)

Marketing (1992)
Geography (1999)
Geotourism (2008)

Cultural heritage (1998)
Heritage (2006)

Medicine (1994)
Economics (1995)
Sustainability (1993)

Ecotourism (2002)
Marine environments (2003)

Agritourism (2010)

Leisure and recreation(2010)

Travel writing (1997)
Education (1990)

Management (1980)

Financial management (1991)
Administration (1997)

Human resources (2002)
Law (2009)

Information technology (1998)

Innovation (2012)

Security (2022)

Smart tourism (2020)

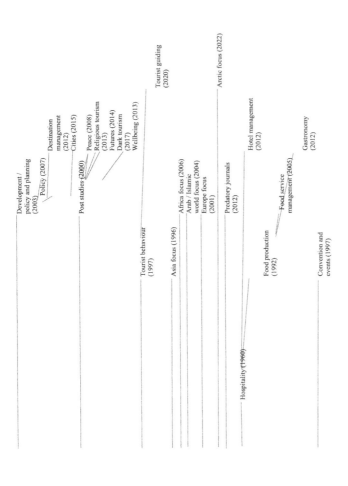

Development /
policy and planning
(2003)

Policy (2007)

Destination
management
(2012)
Cities (2015)

Post studies (2000)

Peace (2008)
Religious tourism
(2013)
Futures (2014)
Dark tourism
(2017)
Wellbeing (2013)

Tourist guiding
(2020)

Tourist behaviour
(1997)

Asia focus (1996)

Africa focus (2006)
Arab / Islamic
world focus (2004)
Europe focus
(2001)

Arctic focus (2022)

Predatory journals
(2012)

Hotel management
(2012)

Food production
(1992)

Food service
management (2005)

Gastronomy
(2012)

Hospitality (1960)

Convention and
events (1997)

Figure 2.2   A family tree of journal themes in English language tourism, hospitality and events journals

The field of study was largely undifferentiated until the rapid expansion of tourism programmes in the 1990s. The few titles that did exist tended to examine tourism as a generic field of interest, although the focus of these journals was quite specific. For example, *Annals of Tourism Research* was positioned as a social science journal, while the *Journal of Travel Research* focussed on destinations in its formative years. The first split occurred in 1960 with the introduction of the *Cornell Hotel and Restaurant Quarterly* which introduced hospitality research as a separate field of study. Likewise, the first 'management' journal, at least by title, was *Tourism Management* that started in 1980.

Generalised tourism and hospitality titles still dominate the field. As an example, 85 journals can be classified as general tourism journals based on their titles, 33 include both tourism and hospitality exclusively in their titles, and 17 focus exclusively on hospitality management. The rest either have a regional focus or include one or more other areas of inquiry in their titles. Generalist journals tend to be based in non-English speaking economies where the field is still emerging. Specialist titles tend to be more common in English, Portuguese and Spanish language journals.

The fracturing of the field began in earnest in the early 1990s and has continued apace. Many discipline-based titles were launched then, including dedicated marketing, geography, cultural heritage, economics and travel medicine journals. Sustainability also rose to prominence in the aftermath of the release of *Our Common Future* or the so-called Brundtland Report (WCED, 1987). Also noted was the divergence from generic management themed titles to the development of more specialist titles focussing on financial management and administration. This era also saw the creation of a small number of journals examining tourism and hospitality education themes. Specialist policy journals did not emerge until ten years later, at about the same time that post-tourism journals began to be introduced.

Sustainability titles produced the perceived need for more specialist titles in ecotourism, marine tourism and agritourism. Geography led to a title in geotourism, while generic cultural heritage and tourism titles produced more titles specialising in heritage and tourism history. Likewise, information technology journals begat journals focussing on innovation and smart tourism, while the first group of policy and development journals spawned the creation of dedicated policy and planning, destination management and city-focussed outlets. Perhaps the greatest evolution was noted in the emergence of post-tourism journals starting in the 2010s, which saw the creation of such specialist titles as peace, religious studies, futures, dark tourism and wellbeing.

Titles with a narrow geographic focus began first in Asia and are now being seen elsewhere. Many of these titles are designed to provide a publishing outlet for academics in emerging economies that have difficulty getting published in dominant English language journals. The first such regional journal was *The Asia Pacific Journal of Tourism Research* which first appeared in 1996. This journal is now complemented by titles focussing on Malaysia, Thailand and Indonesia. In a similar manner, specialist titles have emerged in the Islamic world (*Egyptian Journal of Tourism and Hospitality Studies, Iranian Journal of Tourism and Hospitality*), Europe (*Czech Journal of Tourism, Finnish Journal of Tourism Research*) and Africa (*African Journal of Hospitality, Tourism and Leisure, The Eastern African Journal of Hospitality, Leisure and Tourism*). It is unclear, though, if all titles are still operating.

Much less divergence has been noted in the hospitality and events fields. Hospitality-oriented journals led to journals focussing on food production and service in the early 1990s, with further refinement to food service in the 2000s and a focus on gastronomy in the past ten years. Events journals began by covering both conventions and events but have morphed more broadly into covering the topic of events without reference to conventions.

The emergence of themed journals gave birth to a proliferation of even finer, more focussed titles as the field continued to specialise. Cheng, Li and Petrick (2011) found general titles covered an average of more than six disciplinary areas. Specialist journals debuting up to 1990 targeted merely 4.0 disciplines per journal, while journals started after 1991 had an even narrower focus of 3.4 disciplines per journal. My guess is that the focus of journals started after 2010 is even more constrained.

This proliferation of titles and the increasingly fine division of our field into smaller and smaller subfields presents both opportunities and challenges (McKercher & Tung, 2015). On the one hand, the failure to change with the times places disciplines at risks of intellectual stagnation (Posner, 1987). Instead, they can maintain their vibrancy by moving into new areas of exploration. On the other hand, too much fragmentation can lead to a field losing its focus (Hollingsworth, 1986). This situation has been observed by the type of adjectival creep that has beset geography (Clifford, 2002; Thrift, 2002). Today, geography seems to be defined as much by the adjectives used to describe what type of geography is being studied (economic, cultural, human, physical, etc.) as by the noun itself.

Franklin and Crang (2001) voiced a similar concern about tourist studies more than 20 years ago, when they commented on the risk posed by fragmentation. Time has shown this concern to be largely overstated, for although tourism studies has entered a number of fields, tourism, hospitality and events continue to represent the *raison d'être* for their existence. Rather than losing focus, instead we are seeing a proliferation of approaches to examine tourism that reflects its multidisciplinary origins with Crouch and Perdue (2015) identifying more than 50 broad discipline and fields of study that inform this sector.

QUEST FOR LEGITIMACY

Tourism hospitality and events has had a long struggle to be recognised as a legitimate field of study, and for its journals to be seen as being the equal to journals published in other fields and disciplines. The roots of this challenge can be traced back to the earliest days of tourism studies when it was seen as a peripheral, frivolous, inconsequential (Nash, 1979) and not particularly credible (Dann, Nash & Pearce, 1988; Tribe, 1997) area of inquiry. Most early generation tourism scholars explored this topic from the own disciplinary silos and were subsequently directed to publish their 'serious work' in their home discipline if they wished to be promoted. In many ways, that legacy continues today, for Shani and Uriely (2017) recently commented on two different approaches adopted by institutions. The inward-looking approach argues that our field is mature enough that hospitality and tourism should be recognised as mainstream fields in their own right with many highly reputable outlets. By contrast, a number of institutions are still encouraging an outward-looking approach whereby, in order to enhance the reputation of tourism research, scholars need to publish their work in major mainstream discipline journals dealing with traditional, established research fields.

The legitimacy issue has deep historical roots. Because only a small number of speciality journals and programmes existed, the major journal citation services did not see sufficient demand to create a separate labour-intensive tourism category. Even as recently as 2004, McKercher (2005) reported the Thomson ISI scale (Thomson, 2004), housing the Social Sciences Citation Index (SSCI), assessed more than 8,750 journals including at least 20 accounting and finance titles; another 20 marketing, promotion and consumer behaviour journals; about 40 in the field of general management; and 30 in geography. However, tourism was notable by its absence, as only *Annals of Tourism Research*, *Tourism Management* and *Travel Medicine* were indexed, with each being allocated to a different non-tourism social science, management or medicine category. The net result was that these journals had low impact factors, not because their quality was poor, but because the system did not include the more than 130 relevant titles that cited their work in its citation searches.

In response, tourism academics took it upon themselves to create their own sets of journal ranks, as well as lists of leading academics. Roberts and Shea (2005, p. 4) called for the 'need in many academic institutions to have some sense of quality rankings of the publication outlets that faculty use to share their research … This type of information is often used for tenure and promotion decisions. Such rankings also help guide faculty in the selection of a desired publication venue.' Hall (2011) identified at least ten such projects that were published prior to 2010, with more recent journal ranking lists developed by Gursoy and Sandstrom (2016), even though other more cross-disciplinary metrics have been developed.

While these ranking studies served an important role in helping tourism and hospitality programme leaders and academics identify which journals were leaders in the field, they had a number of weaknesses that limited their applicability outside of tourism. Jamal, Smith and Watson (2008) argued against a universal ranking system, noting the multidisciplinary nature of the field, the emergence of high-quality speciality journals that may not generate as many citations as more generalist titles and the impact our journals may have on other fields. Law, Chan and Zhao (2019) identified a range of more pragmatic issues affecting the efficacy of such ranking systems, including lack of consistency in metrics measured and the limited number of journals analysed in various studies. They concluded 'journal ranking is sensitive to the critical set of journals being selected for analysis. The rankings obtained from these reports and studies, therefore, may not be entirely objective' (Law et al., 2019, p. 754).

The greatest limitation of such self-serving studies (of which this author is guilty of contributing), though, is that the rankings are field specific and are not comparable to system-wide rankings adopted across all disciplines. Thus, while these studies may identify a certain number of journals as being leading journals in the field, the findings cannot be used to gauge their influence vis-à-vis journals in other disciplines. It is a case of comparing apples with oranges and not apples with apples.

Fortunately, or unfortunately as some may argue, technology and the move to the neoliberal metrification of academic research has resolved this problem. Software development has removed much of the manual labour involved in counting citations, enabling the collection of much more varied data in a more cost-effective manner. Tourism and hospitality studies have been one of many beneficiaries. For example, SCImago (https://www.scimagojr.com/index.php) now catalogues over 34,000 titles from more than 5,000 international publishers. As of early 2022, the *Tourism, Leisure and Hospitality Management* portal listed 129 titles, including 75 dedicated English language tourism, hospitality and events journals. Admittedly, the coverage is not complete, but it does represent the most comprehensive, objective set of metrics that are available to the public. Importantly, four of the tourism, leisure and hospitality journals are among the top 100 titles in the 'Business, Management and Accounting' category and 12 appear in the top 200 titles, among the more than 1,580 journals assessed. Likewise, seven titles appear among the top 100 'Geography, Planning and Development' journals, with 14 listed in the top 200.

In addition, the development of various system-wide research assessment exercises, notably among Western economies that are faced with the dual challenge of budget constraints and demand for evidence of impact, has resulted in the creation of system-wide ranking lists that provide some level of cross-disciplinary comparability. The lists are somewhat subjective and therefore controversial (Phillips, Page & Sebu, 2020), but in the UK, Australia and elsewhere, it has reinforced the fact that tourism research has moved from outsider status to being recognised and named as a significant research area (Brauer, Dymitrow & Tribe, 2019).

Hopefully, the fight for legitimacy has been won, or at least is being won, as we collectively dispel the perception that tourism studies is a vocational field that produces cooks, waiters and travel agents, or worse is just a subset of other disciplines, instead of being a vibrant field of intellectual enquiry in its own right that is now starting to produce is own groundbreaking research.

THE FUTURE

What does the future hold for tourism, hospitality and events journals? What is certain is that the only constant is change. As Cohen and Lloyd (2014) noted, whether and how disciplines and fields of studies respond to the inherent dynamism will determine if they remain relevant over time. The other certainty is that academic journals will remain the dominant platform used to disseminate research, even if technology transforms how articles are presented. Clearly the paper-based journal is an endangered species, being replaced by electronic delivery systems. In addition, social media now plays a critical role in raising awareness of our research.

Kozak (2020) indicates that we are now in the third period of tourism publishing marked by the increasing power of international publishers and loss of the independence of journals. My own research (McKercher, 2022) shows that a degree of consolidation is moving ahead at a rapid pace, at least in English language journals. Here the five major publishing houses maintained 61 journals in 2021, accounting for more than 60% of all English language material published. By contrast, the other 127 English language journals identified accounted for less than 40% of outputs. These findings led the author to conclude that independent journals may be an endangered species, just as they are in other disciplines.

Consolidation will likely continue as major publishers either launch new journals or purchase the publishing rights from independent journals to fill gaps in their collections. It will be a mixed blessing. On the one hand, it will deter authors from submitting essentially the same paper to multiple journals, for various similarity checks will be able to identify them. In addition, publishers may be able to bundle more journals in attractive packages for libraries, potentially increasing the reach of papers published in lesser-known outlets. On the other hand, though, we may lose diversity, especially if authors are directed by universities and research evaluation frameworks to target certain journals. Once upon a time, you published in the best outlet for the paper regardless of the journal's so-called impact. Now, we publish papers that certain journals will likely accept, which may lead to a narrowing of both topics explored and methods adopted.

Open access will become the norm, potentially leading to even wider dissemination of our research, but also potentially excluding some researchers from publishing if they cannot secure the funds needed for open access rights.

Another issue relates to predatory journals – journals that will publish your work for a fee, regardless of the quality. These journals are a scourge on many disciplines, for they present themselves as being legitimate outlets, when in fact they bely everything that journal publishing stands for: truth, veracity of research, and confidence that published work has gone through a rigorous vetting process to ensure its validity. Predatory journals are creeping into our field, although with limited success. The database used for this study identified over 30 predatory journals that have been launched since 2012. Fortunately, our field as a collective has largely ignored these types of journals as many have already ceased publication and many others are struggling to attract papers.

A final issue relates to whether we are publishing too many journal articles in too many journals. The trend now is for researchers to slice and dice their research into the smallest publishable level in order to enhance their CVs, without necessarily focussing on producing quality research. McKercher and Dolnicar (2022) raised this issue in a recent commentary – but this is not unique to tourism. Indeed, the issue of publishing as many papers as possible to make résumés look good has been around in other disciplines for more than 30 years (Hamilton, 1990), with one sociologist commenting that almost any paper, regardless of how trivial or flawed, can be published, leading to an ocean of unread and unreadable articles (Hargens, 1991). In fact, Oosterhaven (2015, p. 261) has produced mathematical models that illustrate 'all manuscripts submitted to any journal [could] ultimately be published, either by the first journal or by one of the following journals to which a manuscript is resubmitted' if they are shopped around enough. The net result is that quality is an issue that will become increasingly challenging as the number of journals continues to expand.

CONCLUSION

This chapter introduced the state of play on tourism, hospitality and events journals and presented largely a good news story. Our field is vibrant and growing, although the winds of consolidation are starting to blow. There are now close to 300 journals covering a huge array of topic areas all related to understanding the phenomenon and practice of tourism, hospitality and events. More than that, the journal coverage is global and multilingual, enabling scholars from around the world to find suitable outlets for their work. The future looks encouraging for the field, although, as other authors will raise in this book, a number of issues will also need to be addressed.

REFERENCES

Airey, D., Tribe, J., Benckendorff, P. & Xiao, H. (2015). The managerial gaze: The long tail of tourism education and research. *Journal of Travel Research*, 54(2), 139–151.

Brauer, R., Dymitrow, M. & Tribe, J. (2019). The impact of tourism research. *Annals of Tourism Research*, 77, 64–78.

Cheng, C., Li, R. & Petrick, J. (2011). An examination of tourism journal development. *Tourism Management*, 32(5), 3–61.

Clifford, N. (2002). The future of geography, when the whole is less than the sum of its parts. *Geoforum*, 33(4), 431–436.

Cohen, E. & Lloyd, S. (2014). Disciplinary evolution and the rise of the transdiscipline. *Informing Science, The International Journal of an Emerging Transdiscipline*, 17, 189–215.

Craig-Smith, S., Davidson, M. & French, C. (1995). Hospitality and tourism education in Australia, challenges and opportunities. In Faulkner, B., Fagence, M., Davidson, M. & Craig-Smith, S. (eds.), *Tourism Education National Conference Papers*. Canberra, Bureau of Tourism Research, 144–150.

Crouch, G. & Perdue, R. (2015). The disciplinary foundations of tourism research, 1980–2010. *Journal of Travel Research*, 54(5), 563–577.

Dann, G., Nash, D. & Pearce, P. (1988). Methodology in tourism research. *Annals of Tourism Research*, 15, 1–28.

Franklin, A. & Crang, M. (2001). The trouble with tourism and travel theory? *Tourist Studies*, 1(1), 5–22.

Gursoy, D. & Sandstrom, J.K. (2016). An updated ranking of hospitality and tourism journals. *Journal of Hospitality & Tourism Research*, 40(1), 3–18.

Hall, C.M. (2011). Publish and perish? Bibliometric analysis, journal ranking and the assessment of research quality in tourism. *Tourism Management*, 32(1), 16–27.

Hamilton, D. (1990). Publishing by and for the numbers. *Science*, 250, 1331–1332.

Hargens, L. (1991). Impressions and misimpressions about sociology journals. *Contemporary Sociology*, 20(3), 343–349.

Hollingsworth, J.R. (1986). The decline of scientific communication within and across academic disciplines. *Policy Studies Journal*, 14(3), 422–428.

Jamal, T., Smith, B. & Watson, E. (2008). Ranking, rating and scoring of tourism journals: Interdisciplinary challenges and innovations. *Tourism Management*, 29(1), 66–78.

Jamali, R., Wakeling, S. & Abbasi, A. (2022). Why do journals discontinue? A study of Australian ceased journals. *Learned Publishing*. https://onlinelibrary.wiley.com/doi/ epdf/10.1002/leap.1448.

Kozak, M. (2020). Historical development of tourism journals – a milestone in 75 years, a perspective article. *Tourism Review*, 75(1), 8–11.

Lariviere, V., Haustien, S. & Mongeon, P. (2015). The oligopoly of academic publishers in the digital era. *PlosOne*. https://doi.org/10.1371/journal.pone.0127502.

Law, R., Chan, I.C.C. & Zhao, X. (2019). Ranking hospitality and tourism journals. *Journal of Hospitality & Tourism Research*, 43(5), 754–761.

Martínez Ruiz, X. (2016). The relevance and future of academic journals. *Innovación Educativa*, 16(72), 25–32.

McKercher, B. (2005). A case for ranking tourism journals. *Tourism Management*, 26(5), 649–651.

McKercher, B. (2020). The future of tourism journals. *Tourist Review*, 75(1), 12–15.

McKercher, B. (2022). The rise and potential fall of some tourism journals. *Annals of Tourism Research Empirical Insights*, 3, 100049.

McKercher, B. & Dolnicar, S. (2022). Are 10,752 journal articles per year too many? *Annals of Tourism Research*, 94, 103398.

McKercher, B. & Tung, V. (2015). Publishing in tourism and hospitality journals. Is the past a prelude to the future? *Tourism Management*, 50, 306–315.

Nash, D. (1979). Tourism as an anthropological subject. *Current Anthropology*, 22(5), 461–481.

Oosterhaven, J. (2015). Too many journals? Towards a theory of repeated rejections and ultimate acceptance. *Scientometrics*, 103, 261–265.

Phillips, P., Page, S. & Sebu, J. (2020). Achieving research impact in tourism: Modelling and evaluating outcomes from the UK's Research Excellence Framework. *Tourism Management*, 78, 104072.

Posner, R. (1987). The decline of law as an autonomous discipline, 1962–1987. *Harvard Law Review*, 100, 761–780.

Roberts, C. & Shea, L. (2005). Editorial: Ranking hospitality and tourism journals. *Journal of Hospitality & Tourism Education*, 17(4), 4.

SCImago (2022). SJR – SCImago Journal & Country Rank. Retrieved 9 December 2022 from: http://www.scimagojr.com.

Shani, A. & Uriely, N. (2017). Stand your ground: The case for publishing in hospitality and tourism journals. *International Journal of Hospitality Management*, 67, 72–74.

Thomson (2004). Thomson – about us. Retrieved 19 April 2004 from: http://www.isinet.com/aboutus/.

Thrift, N. (2002). The future of geography. *Geoforum*, 33(3), 291–298.

Tribe, J. (1997). The indiscipline of tourism. *Annals of Tourism Research*, 24(3), 638–657.

WCED (1987). *Our Common Future, World Commission on Environment and Development*. Melbourne, Oxford University Press.

Zeff, S.A. (1996). A study of academic research journals in accounting. *Accounting Horizons*, 10(3), 158–177.

Zehrer, A. (2007). The justification of journal rankings – A pilot study. *Scandinavian Journal of Hospitality and Tourism*, 7(2), 139–156.

3. The view from journal editors: contributions from the editors of top tourism journals

Chris Cooper and C. Michael Hall

INTRODUCTION

When we asked the editors of leading tourism journals to write a short piece about their journal, we were anticipating significant variation across the submissions. However, surprisingly, there is significant similarity in the sentiment and issues addressed by editors.

It is clear that tourism journals have a long pedigree, with the establishment of *Tourism Review* in 1947, followed by *Annals of Tourism Research* in 1974. But the new millennium has seen a maturing of the journal publishing sector, with concentration into a handful of large publishers. This maturation brings with it a range of issues identified by the editors, which we have grouped into three themes.

First, journals no longer confine themselves to empirical papers, book reviews and conference reports. The way that readers access content is no longer through the physical browsing of hard copies, but through search engines. In response journals have reconfigured their contents to include a variety of new sections. These include:

- Empirical papers;
- Conceptual/foundations papers;
- Method papers;
- Perspective papers;
- Research letters;
- Research notes;
- Viewpoints;
- Conference reports;
- Special issue papers; and
- Book reviews.

Second, the maturing of the journal landscape has brought a rise in the number of journals, away from the early generalist journals to a later splintering of journals into sub-sections of tourism – technology, destination marketing and sustainability, for example. This creates more of a challenge to potential authors in their choice of an appropriate journal, but it does provide more opportunity for innovative and specialist papers, as well as multi-method and multidisciplinary papers. As always though, it is the contribution that is key, and this comes across clearly in the editors' viewpoints on their own journals.

Finally, the editors identify a range of challenges that they face in the day-to-day job of editing their journals. A number of editors identify issues around submission of poor-quality papers where the readability, language or structure of the paper is not up to standard. Sometimes language barriers are at fault, but these can be easily addressed by the use of proofreading. Finding reviewers for papers remains a perennial problem, as is the use of plagiarism software which adds a second layer of complexity to decision-making about manuscripts. Journal metrics and use of social media means that there is an increased sophistication in the marketing and management of journals and a number of journals now have their own dedicated social media manager. These metrics are transparent and available for all to see, resulting in an increasingly competitive journal landscape. Finally, issues such as ethics, author misconduct, open access, and inclusion and diversity render the journal landscape increasingly sophisticated and complex to navigate.

The following pages are the contributions from the editors of the top journals in the tourism field.

ACTA TURISTICA: THE BENEFITS OF PUBLISHING IN A SMALL TOURISM JOURNAL, EDITOR: NEVENKA ČAVLEK

Scholars are invariably required to publish in renowned Anglophone journals with high impact factors to be promoted. Yet, since the submissions to these journals are quite steep, they have to be particularly selective, which depletes their acceptance rates considerably. For early career researchers who lack publication experience, especially those from small research communities with limited research funding and English as a foreign language, publishing in renowned journals presents a huge challenge (Majid et al., 2022; Mohammad et al., 2017). Alternatively, small tourism journals from small research communities compete with the established journals to empower research performance and scientific advances at national levels (Gasparyan, 2014).

Croatia could serve as a good example of a country with a well-established publishing tradition (Gasparyan, 2014). High publication standards imposed long ago in natural sciences and biomedical journals with outstanding impact factors inspired the launch of journals in other fields. Hence, Croatia has "the largest number of journals per scientist and per Gross Domestic Product" compared to its neighbouring countries (Utrobičić et al., 2014, p. 31). Many are listed in the Web of Science and Scopus databases. *Acta Turistica* is one of them.

Acta Turistica, a bilingual (Croatian and English) scientific journal published by the University of Zagreb's Faculty of Economics and Business, has been issuing two volumes annually since 1989. It promotes an interdisciplinary and multidisciplinary approach and aims to disseminate the positions on various theoretical and pragmatic topics in tourism and hospitality based on strong scientific research and argument while including a double-blind review process and research paper classification. Having established its international scientific reputation by publishing simultaneously in both Croatian and English, *Acta Turistica* promotes linguistic diversity and contributes to enhancing the Croatian scientific terminology while focusing on multiculturalism.

Acta Turistica's commitment to internationalisation was encouraged by the World Tourism Organization and has since developed a reputable 47-strong editorial board of very diverse scholars with significant international reputations and citation records. Since 37 of them span all continents and 16 are members of the International Academy for the Study of Tourism, the quality of the review process of manuscripts is assured. Furthermore, by article distribution based on new Clarivate Classification Citation Topics on meso level as of 25 August 2023, *Acta Turistica* covers: hospitality, leisure, sport and tourism, management, economics, smell and taste science, transportation, economic theory, robotics, human computer interaction, artificial intelligence and machine learning, sustainability science, communication, religion, political science, and human geography. Classification from the same source based on the UN's Sustainable Development Goals identifies the following most frequent topics in *Acta Turistica*: sustainable cities and communities, industry innovation and infrastructure, poverty alleviation, good health and well-being, decent work and economic growth, reduced inequality, quality education, and climate action.

Research confirms the crucial role of the strong editorial structure which is essential in nurturing new knowledge areas and research approaches (Teixeira & Oliveira, 2018) as members also very often serve as reviewers of and advisors on journal policy. This plays a crucial role in the constant enhancement of *Acta Turistica*'s international reputation as well as its inclusion in the most relevant databases which has enabled the necessary visibility to the widest academic community.

The relevance and specific role of a small journal for the global scientific community can best be illustrated by using bibliometric mapping. The bibliometric analysis based on co-occurrences of keywords (i.e., the article contents) enables identifying the conceptual structure of research topics and recognising the multidisciplinarity of the analysed field (Cobo et al., 2011, p. 148). The co-occurrence analysis of *Acta Turistica*, performed on the assigned keywords and automatically generated in the database and bibliometric network, has revealed four clusters with the most relevant topics: tourism, management, image and model (Figure 3.1). Figure 3.1 shows the layout and interrelation of the connected sub-topics within each cluster.

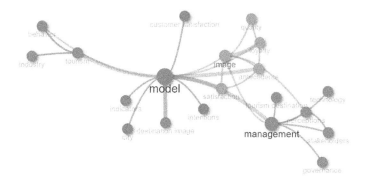

Source: Bibliometric analytic tool Biblioshiney, WoS data-set.

Figure 3.1   Co-occurrence network

The co-citation analysis identifies the most influential journals that are based on the cited publications connecting the documents, authors or journals by appearance on the reference list of other articles (Zupic and Čater, 2015, p. 432). This analysis shows that articles published in *Acta Turistica* are based on the knowledge drawn from the references published in the best tourism journals (Figure 3.2). This confirms *Acta Turistica*'s commitment to top relevance in the global scientific community and the tourism sector.

Since the mission of *Acta Turistica* is to disseminate scientific research on the key tourism issues to benefit authors, the academic community and tourism professionals in Croatia and around the world, it emphasises the review process as the vital factor in preparing a manuscript for publication. If a paper passes the first stage for publication consideration, i.e., plagiarism check, checking the credibility of references, sources of previously published data, adherence with strict publishing standards and procedures with no exceptions, it is sent to the meritorious reviewers for comments. The research papers that apply sophisticated statistical methods are sent to experts for additional reviews.

Source: Bibliometric analytic tool Biblioshiney, WoS data-set.

Figure 3.2   Co-citation analysis – Sources

In summary, the evaluation process in *Acta Turistica* follows the same strict rules and procedures as any other highly reputable tourism journal. Additional guarantees of scientific rigour and quality are the journal's publisher, i.e., the academic institution with its strict rules, and its co-financier, the Croatian Ministry of Science and Education.

The benefits of publishing in *Acta Turistica* are manifold. The authors have greater chances for publication of quality manuscripts due to lower submission pressure compared to most renowned journals. Early career researchers or PhD students with interesting and current or emerging topics can count on an efficient editorial process and more personal review procedures that offer continuous support in achieving the required standards and complying with the academic rigour. Since *Acta Turistica* affirms the importance of publishing the research results which are often of interest to smaller international audiences and therefore might escape the attention of the best-known tourism journals, the research which may be relevant only regionally is more likely to be presented to international audiences there. Thus, *Acta Turistica* serves as a platform for scientific communication among prominent and junior researchers, small research and publishing markets focusing on cutting-edge tourism topics.

References

Cobo, M.J., López-Herrera, A.G., Herrera-Viedma, E. & Herrera, F. (2011). An approach for detecting, quantifying, and visualizing the evolution of a research field:

A practical application to the Fuzzy Sets Theory field. *Journal of Informetrics*, *5*(1), 146–166. https://doi.org/10.1016/j.joi.2010.10.002.

Gasparyan, A.Y. (2014). Editorial: Editing Croatian scholarly journals: Achievements and challenges. *European Science Editing*, *40*(2), 30.

Majid, H., Jafri, L., Ahmed, S., Abbas Abid, M., Aamir, M., Ijaz, A., Habib Khan, A. & Siddiqui, I. (2022). Publication dynamics: What can be done to eliminate barriers to publishing full manuscripts by the postgraduate trainees of a low-middle income country? *BMC Research Notes*, *15*, 249. https://doi.org/10.1186/s13104-022-06138-5.

Mohammad, A.A.A., Shehata, A.M.K. & Ammar, S.A.M. (2017). Challenges to academic research and international publishing in the discipline of tourism and hospitality management in Egypt. *Journal of Association of Arab Universities for Tourism and Hospitality*, *14*(2), 67–78. https://doi.org/10.21608/JAAUTH.2017.48145.

Teixeira, E.K., & Oliveira, M. (2018). Editorial board interlocking in knowledge management and intellectual capital research field. *Scientometrics*, *117*, 1853–1869. https://doi.org/10.1007/s11192-018-2937-x.

Utrobičić, A., Šimić, J., Malički, M., Marušić, M. & Marušić, A. (2014). Composition of editorial boards and peer review policies of Croatian journals indexed in Web of Science and Scopus. *European Science Editing*, *40*, 31–33.

Zupic, I., & Čater, T. (2015). Bibliometric methods in management and organization. *Organizational Research Methods*, *18*(3), 429–472. https://doi.org/10.1177/1094428114562629.

ANNALS OF TOURISM RESEARCH, EDITORS: SCOTT MCCABE AND SARA DOLNICAR

Annals of Tourism Research is uniquely positioned among tourism journals since it champions a broad-based, multidisciplinary approach to the subject, which aims ultimately to develop theoretical constructs and new approaches to advance our understanding of tourism as a field and practice. As such, *Annals* views tourism as a fascinating contextual set of phenomena that can be understood from the perspective of the social sciences. The journal focuses on academic perspectives on tourism. While advancing theory is a priority, it also aims to ensure the research published offers relevant, cutting-edge applications for the tourism industry, wider stakeholders and policy makers. *Annals* has a long and proud history of publishing conceptually driven research articles that have become reference works for scholars, education professionals, and public and private sector organisations. In 2024, it celebrates its 50th anniversary.

Annals invites and encourages research from various disciplines, to provide a forum through which different social sciences' disciplinary perspectives interact, and thus expands the frontiers of knowledge by contributing to the literature on tourism social science. Disciplinary areas include, but are not limited to: service industries management, marketing science, consumer marketing, decision-making and behaviour, business ethics, economics and forecasting, environment, geography and development, education and knowledge development, political science and administration, consumer-focused psychology, and anthropology and sociology. However, papers that take a social science perspective on matters related to tourism from the other branches of science (cross-disciplinary approaches) are also welcome.

Annals of Tourism Research applies strict quality standards to ensure that the research published meets the highest possible criteria for research integrity and ethics. The journal applies these criteria based on the UK's Research Excellence Framework indicators for research: Originality: the study should be able to demonstrate a degree or novelty and uniqueness within the tourism context. Significance: the work should have a very high level of importance to tourism theory development, knowledge, policy or practice, which is transferable to wider contexts. Rigour: research should apply the very latest and/or develop innovative methodologies and be able to demonstrate the application of research ethics guidelines relevant to the context of the study.

More specifically, *Annals* seeks to publish papers that are curiosity driven, and which aim to offer groundbreaking, bold, new approaches and ideas, even if they are unproven. Recognising the academic publishing system is quite risk averse, *Annals* seeks to provide space for highly novel ideas and offer new conceptual or methodological approaches. However, the research or thinking that underpins such approaches must be able to demonstrate the highest standards of methodological and conceptual rigour to be judged as credible among an international social science readership. Therefore, data collection and analysis should be consistent with the leading available methods and authors should ensure that conclusions are verifiable and trustworthy. Since *Annals* encourages research that makes an impact on defined communities of interest – the academy, policy makers, the tourism industry or a local population – the relevance of the research should be immediately evident, and communities of interest should be explicitly referenced in the article.

Annals attracts a broad-based, diverse social science readership. Therefore, the work that we publish should be written clearly and communicate specialist technical ideas and material in a way that is intelligible to a broad and diverse readership, including practitioners. Papers should use the clearest possible language to communicate (see the Plain English Campaign's guide at http://www .plainenglish.co.uk/files/howto.pdf). Authors should avoid academic language that prevents ready understanding of the key problems or questions driving the study, or stops findings being grasped by a multidisciplinary audience, or prevents an understanding of how the results might benefit society. However, articles should be written to the highest standards of English language expression, grammar and syntax. Authors are encouraged to read the aims and scope of the journal.

Annals operates a highly devolved editorial board consisting of around 50 associate editors representing the diversity of social sciences approaches to tourism studies. Each manuscript is initially evaluated by one of the editors-in-chief, who assess whether the article meets the aims and scope of the journal, that it is clearly grounded in social science perspective and theories, and meets our criteria for quality, ethics and integrity. However, the editors-in-chief also consider a duty to encourage submissions from under-represented regions and disciplinary approaches within the field of tourism to ensure against disadvantaging groups and approaches. We also recognise the importance of providing opportunity and feedback to the early career research community and try to support submissions appropriately. Around 65–70% of submissions are desk rejected at this stage. Articles are then passed for further consideration to an expert (associate editor) on the disciplinary or methodological approach used, and a small percentage are desk rejected at this stage, while the remainder are sent out for review.

To ensure the strongest possible chance of success in publishing your research in *Annals of Tourism Research*, it is recommended that contributors read the guide for authors and write their article according to the aims and scope (as well as style and formatting guidelines) of the journal. Each journal is different in this respect, and it is important to ensure your study relates to and is contextualised within the aims and published content of that journal. Ensure that your research has been undertaken in accordance with the standards of research ethics and integrity in your country (or apply established approaches in the UK/EU where these do not yet exist in your country). Finally, ensure that your research paper is written in a way that can be read by a non-specialist in your field/discipline, the aims and research questions are clearly outlined, and your conclusions relate how your study advances knowledge at the conceptual level. *Annals* aims to ensure the academic health of the research undertaken in the field and to support researcher development across the whole field.

CURRENT ISSUES IN TOURISM, EDITORS: MICHAEL HALL AND CHRIS COOPER

Current Issues in Tourism (*CIT*) was established in 1998 as a peer-reviewed journal. It was initially published by the independent publisher Multilingual Matters but subsequently the journal was sold to Taylor and Francis. Since its launch, it has become one of the world's foremost venues for the dissemination of innovative, scientific research related to all aspects of tourism.

Current Issues in Tourism encourages in-depth discussion and critique of key questions within tourism. We publish applied and theoretical work that addresses tourism inquiry, method and practice. Lively and rigorous, *CIT* welcomes contributions from the broad gamut of subjects that make up the stuff of tourism studies. We aim to be accessible to both new and experienced researchers and practitioners on a global basis. The principal aims of the journal are to: encourage the full range of approaches that are available to the study of tourism; bring together researchers from different subject backgrounds for interdisciplinary and post-disciplinary debate; develop the theoretical base on which the study of tourism is built; encourage reflection on prior research and theory, including issues of replication; provide a basis for the development of critical approaches to the study of tourism; disseminate new approaches, concepts, frameworks, methods, models and practices which may be developed in the study of tourism; and promote new research. *Current Issues in Tourism* prides itself on its inclusivity, supporting universal participation in tourism studies and the social sciences overall, regardless of minoritised status. We affirmatively declare our support for an academic research community that is open to, and provides support and safety for, every individual, regardless of ethnicity, cultural identity, nationality, sex, sexual orientation, gender identity and expression, faith, or medical condition.

Current Issues in Tourism offers a readable format for normal empirical papers as well as papers that are designed for four other sections:

- *CIT Research Letters* are short pieces intended as a forum for the rapid publication of novel research that transforms our perspective on important issues relevant to tourism studies. Given the nature of tourism as an applied subject area, research that particularly affects society, business and policy will be especially pertinent.
- *CIT Reviews* provide in-depth critiques of sub-fields of tourism and related areas, designed to spark off further reader response on the key issues and topics. Each review will provide the reader with the development of the relevant literature, keep the reader up-to-date on advances in the fields of tourism research, provide some theoretical or methodological contribution, offer perspectives on future developments and research agendas, as well and provide a useful reference list.
- *CIT Research Notes* are short pieces up to 1,500 words designed to discuss and share preliminary data, exploratory work or aspects of methods such as updates and new approaches.
- *Current Issues in Method and Practice* represents cutting-edge advances in tourism research methods and methodologies. This section responds to the need for the development of a continuous platform designed to disseminate the very latest thinking in tourism research. It acts as a means to facilitate discussions on how tourism research could be operationalised. This includes detailed interrogations of both existing and new methods.

In addition, *CIT* occasionally publishes special issues on topical themes. Recently this has included special issues on COVID-19 and tourism. As well as these special issues, we have introduced *Current Issues in Asian Tourism* (*CIAT*), which are regular specific issues dedicated to papers on tourism in Asia.

Since its launch, *CIT* has experienced a significant growth in submissions, particularly since the purchase by Taylor and Francis. By 2022, submissions were approaching 2,000 annually, and with this rise in submissions we have increased the number of issues per year to 24. Despite this, our acceptance rate now stands at 15%.

Also, the rise in submissions has not necessarily translated into a rise in quality of submissions. The editors are finding that they are having to desk reject an increasing number of papers. This can be for a variety of reasons including lack of a significant contribution, lack of fit for *CIT*, one-off case studies where generalisation is difficult, poorly crafted papers, papers with trivial research questions but with overly sophisticated methods, and papers where the literature cited is dated. Once a paper is accepted for review it undergoes peer review by at least two referees. Here, a significant challenge lies in the difficulty of finding reviewers for papers. Finally, associated with the rise in submissions is the increasing number of submissions from China with the danger of the journal being dominated by a particular set of researchers and research issues.

The increasingly sophisticated journal metrics that are now available is both a curse and a blessing. Of course, they provide detailed breakdowns of submissions, the geography of submissions, and readership and impact. But they also are beginning to skew the type of submissions we receive. We are also finding the use of plagiarism software – in our case Cross-Ref – is picking up more papers, although sometimes the issue is easily resolved. Finally, as the journal landscape matures, marketing is increasingly done through social media and *CIT* now has its own social media editor and analysis of social media metrics is provided by Taylor and Francis.

THE *INTERNATIONAL JOURNAL OF HOSPITALITY MANAGEMENT*: DIRECTIONS FOR FUTURE RESEARCH, EDITOR: MANUEL RIVERA

As we find ourselves in a dynamic and transformative era, the field of hospitality management stands at the crossroads of innovation and evolution. I am delighted to inform our authors about the underlying motivation behind the *International Journal of Hospitality Management* (*IJHM*). My aim is to illuminate the continuously growing research trends that currently shape our discipline and have promising prospects for the future. This commentary serves as a guide for authors, providing valuable tips and strategies to better understand current trends and emerging topics in the *IJHM*. As I approach my 19th year of service to the *IJHM*, I am driven by a deep passion for the hospitality industry, education and research, along with extensive experience in managing journal publications. My goal is to empower authors to navigate the publishing process with confidence and make a significant contribution to the realm of hospitality research.

Recent articles in our journal cast light on the intricate and varied facets of our field. Initially limited to the service industry, the scope of hospitality research has expanded beyond its traditional boundaries. The concept has endured a process of evolution, resulting in a cultural philosophy that permeates all sectors, exerts influence over relationships, and produces transformative experiences. In the coming section, I will examine the primary research streams that have been included in the *International Journal of Hospitality Management* over the recent years. This encompasses the examination of digital platforms such as online reviews, brand communities and social media, with a specific emphasis on their function in facilitating interactions and moulding perspectives. Moreover, this study delves into the concept of collaborative consumption, the dynamics of servicescapes, corporate accountability, staff well-being, human–robot interaction, and the convergence of metaverses and artificial intelligence. These areas of investigation together contribute to the generation of creative insights that aim to improve visitor experiences and industry practices.

The whole fabric of hospitality is interwoven with the realms of online review sites, brand communities and social media. We highly encourage research into how these platforms facilitate and support interaction, build long-lasting connections and shape collective perspectives in this age defined by the importance of connectedness.

Research opportunities also exist in the context of collaborative consumption and servicescapes. The growth of the "collaborative consumption" movement and peer-to-peer connections is here to stay. In addition, the dynamics between customers' physical and emotional environments, and their behavioural shifts, places servicescape and customer experiences as forefront subjects of research. Understanding how these new trends impact business models and joyful experiences remains crucial. As researchers, it is our responsibility to investigate and provide value to all stakeholders.

Two additional factors that must be considered when it comes to research are: corporate awareness and employees' well-being. Corporate social responsibility offers a wealth of opportunities to define and measure ethical corporate practices. Understanding the linkages between businesses and society is becoming essential and not just a choice. At the same time, an opportunity exists to better understand employees' emotional experiences and enhance their happiness and wellness.

A new era of discovery marked by rapid and major advances in technology and robotics was brought in by the COVID-19 pandemic. The growing interest in the dynamics between humans and robots is developing into a fascinating area of research and promising vast opportunities in the future. An opportunity exists to reimagine customer service practices, foster operational efficiencies and identify the ethical implications. Ask yourself, how will the structure and dynamics of hospitality shift when human and technology merge? These issues bring a starting point for novel ideas and research inquiry.

The advancement of technology is also influencing customer interactions. The convergence of metaverses and artificial intelligence in the hospitality sector offers intriguing research prospects. Exploring the blend of physical and virtual realms and the utilisation of automation and machine learning for streamlined tasks provides a promising avenue for ongoing innovation. The effects of these technologies on operational effectiveness, customer connections, customised services and data-guided decision-making offer chances for hospitality researchers to offer valuable insights to industry professionals and pioneers.

The domain of hospitality research is full of expertise, novelty, progress and rigorous scholarly standards. The research published in the *IJHM* confirms that the domain of hospitality research has progressed through four distinct phases: Story Tellers (1930–1950), Profilers (1950–1970), Copy Cats (1970–2005) and Innovators (since 2000). The existing literature demonstrates that academics and researchers in the hospitality industry have progressed towards a more appropriate alignment of theoretical frameworks and practical implementations.

The potential for groundbreaking research and innovation is greater than ever. The *IJHM* is committed to providing a space where research exploration and innovation can flourish. The research opportunities from a "Hospitality Organizational Culture" are tangible and have important implications for the future of our discipline as a whole (Pizam, 2020). Other industries and disciplines can learn from articles published in the *IJHM* if they are interested in enhancing their customer and stakeholder interactions via the implementation of creative concepts and a distinctive corporate culture.

A good example is a special issue on "Hospitality in Healthcare" published by the *IJHM* (*International Journal of Hospitality Management*, 2023). This is a way of thinking that extends beyond the hospitality industry into other sectors like healthcare, technology, education and others (Shoemaker & Yesawich, 2023) and is characterised by empathy, warmth and excellent service. The results of integrating hospitality principles into a company's culture are enhanced customer experiences, stronger relationships and greater employee engagement.

When conducting hospitality research in a different context (i.e., such as hospitals or retail businesses), authors must not overlook the hospitality literature. By integrating hospitality concepts into different contexts, researchers can examine the transferability and adaptability of established theories. The current hospitality literature has much to teach us that is applicable to those in pursuit of infusing a hospitality culture. Overlooking the current body of literature will prevent us from fostering interdisciplinary research and expanding our reach. Reviewing and citing the work of hospitality journals shows appreciation for the expertise gained and formalises the significance of research findings to a wider range of industries.

In summary, future research in hospitality must acknowledge the value of established theories while expanding our understanding of the implementation of a hospitality culture in other sectors. It is possible that this approach will lead to a major advancement. The *International Journal of Hospitality Management* is dedicated to being the impetus behind this revolutionary change.

References

International Journal of Hospitality Management (2023). Hospitality in healthcare. ScienceDirect.com by Elsevier. https://www.sciencedirect.com/journal/international-journal-of-hospitality-management/vol/112/suppl/C.
Pizam, A. (2020). Hospitality as an organizational culture. *Journal of Hospitality & Tourism Research, 44*(3), 431–438. https://doi.org/10.1177/1096348020901806.
Shoemaker, S., & Yesawich, P. (2023). *Hospitable healthcare: Just what the patient ordered!* (1st ed.). Pensacola: Indigo River Publishing.

JOURNAL OF DESTINATION MARKETING AND MANAGEMENT, EDITORS: ALAN FYALL, BRIAN GARROD AND YOUCHENG WANG

Founding Editors' Views from a Niche Journal

Published for the first time in November 2012, the *Journal of Destination Marketing and Management* (*JDMM*) set out to be the "leading" international journal for the study of tourist destinations. Contributors are encouraged to critically explore the marketing and management of destinations from the perspective of their particular "policy, planning, economic, geographical and historical contexts". Considering the centrality of destinations to tourism, both as a phenomenon and as a unit of analysis, it is somewhat surprising that such a journal was not launched earlier. Before *JDMM* was brought into existence, destination-related papers were plentiful but spread among an array of more generic tourism journals.

Early nervousness of launching a new, and primarily niche, journal proved to be misplaced, with a rapid rise in the range and quality of submissions, prompt indexation and a consequent rise in the journal rankings over a short period of time. With a CiteScore of 11.2, Impact Factor of 7.158 and 5-Year Impact Factor of 8.096, within ten years of its launch, *JDMM* has become a force to be reckoned with. Since its launch in late 2012, citations have increased from 41 in 2014 to 4,081 in 2021 with over 5.6 million downloads/views up to and including July 2022. It thus comes as no surprise to report that *JDMM* is today a Q1 journal in the fields of Hospitality, Leisure and Tourism (11/131) and Management (43/391) with an above-average Journal Citation Indicator (JCI) of 1.83, indicating high levels of citation in all journals. With the top ten submission-originating countries including the USA, China, Spain, the UK, Australia, South Korea, Hong Kong, New Zealand, South Africa, Turkey and Italy, the subjects covered are diverse yet consistent, with destination/place marketing/management central to each study. This diversity is evident in the most-cited papers to date, which cover topics such as over-tourism, destination image, experiences, social media and technology, virtual and augmented reality, sustainability, visit motivations, and crisis management.

Despite its success, *JDMM* continues to search for excellence and innovation in the study of destination marketing and management. One lingering frustration is the limited number of submissions that truly draw upon the full breadth of disciplinary and methodological approaches. Papers using quantitative methods greatly outnumber those using qualitative and mixed methods. As is likely to be the case for many journals, the attraction of interdisciplinary papers also continues to be a priority, with papers that embrace the fields of sociology, psychology, anthropology and public administration eagerly sought.

After a decade of editing *JDMM*, we find it interesting to note that some of the challenges experienced at the very beginning of its life remain, albeit to a significantly reduced extent. First, the editors still receive papers that do not clearly match with the journal's aims. Memorable examples include papers on the banking system in Iran and the postal service in Pakistan. These papers are easily rejected but it remains a mystery why the authors should take the time and trouble to submit them.

Second, and perhaps more understandable, a significant number of submissions study tourism in general terms but lack a specific focus on the marketing and management of tourist destinations. In many cases, the destination where the fieldwork was undertaken is mentioned in the text, but it then plays no further role in the theoretical, conceptual or analytical conduct of the research. It is undeniable that all tourism takes place in a destination, but that does not imply that all papers that consider tourism will be suitable for a journal that focuses specifically on destination issues.

A third group of papers that tend, after editorial consideration, to be desk rejected are those that are merely descriptive. These papers often lack a strong methods section, or propose a methodology based on a single-case study approach. While descriptive and single-case studies have the capacity to be valuable as research, there is simply not enough room in the journal to publish them. The same can be said of papers that set out to test new measurement scales. This is valid research, but it is difficult to justify publishing it in a premium journal. Authors of such papers are, however, often encouraged to develop their paper to make it more analytical and submit again, provided the topic is interesting and relevant.

A fourth group of papers that tend to struggle to be accepted in *JDMM* are those that make only a limited contribution to knowledge, have a weak theoretical basis, or lack strong implications for theory, policy and practice. This is something that the editors usually like the paper referees to comment upon, as the editors cannot realistically claim to have expert knowledge across the whole range of topics that papers submitted to *JDMM* are based upon. As such, papers that fall by the wayside on this criterion tend to be rejected post-review. An exception are papers which make mechanistic or formulaic use of statistical methods such as exploratory/confirmatory factor analysis and structural equation modelling, some of which come across as being written using a boiler plate. Unless these papers are well justified in terms of their aims and objectives and provide valuable insights for policy and/or practice, they struggle to find acceptance among reviewers and are often desk rejected by the editors. While most journal editors would be very happy to send out every paper to reviewers, not having to desk reject any, that is simply not possible given the amount of time and energy required to identify suitable reviewers, recruit them, evaluate their reviews and let the authors know the outcome. Unfortunately, journals cannot be used by authors simply to obtain feedback on work in this way. Desk rejection of some papers is inevitable.

Fifth are those cases where the authors are unwilling to fully address the revisions suggested by the reviewers. While it is reasonable for authors to stick to their guns, this must be accompanied by a well-argued rebuttal. It is reasonable to expect authors to stand their ground on some, but not all aspects of their paper, and then they should make it clear to the reviewers why they do not wish to move to the ground the reviewers have suggested. Good arguments are acceptable, obstinacy not.

Sixth are papers that contain so many grammatical and spelling errors or are expressed so poorly that it is unreasonable to expect the reviewers to be confident in what the authors are trying to say. Such papers should be edited for language before they are submitted. Also linked to this are papers that have too much text similarity with previously published materials. The editors are sure that most of these are the result not of attempted plagiarism but of inadequate writing skills on the part of the authors. Perhaps the most surprising instances are when one of the authors is known by the editors to have extremely good writing skills. This leaves the editors wondering whether that author has really had sufficient involvement in the production of the paper.

To conclude, the launch of *JDMM* back in 2012 not only represented a career highlight, but served as the beginning of an incredible academic journey which continues to this day with the new editorial team. Our singular aim at the outset was to provide a forum for exploration of the tourist destination among like-minded researchers and to dissect its importance and impact on the wider tourism system. This, we believe, has been achieved. *JDMM*'s continued relevance, however, depends on the quality of submissions from around the world with adherence to the six observations above by contributing authors ensuring its longevity and overall impact.

JOURNAL OF HERITAGE TOURISM, EDITORS: JENNIFER FROST AND WARWICK FROST

Journal of Heritage Tourism was established in 2006 to create a home for research that sits at the intersection of tourism studies and heritage studies. While cultural heritage tourism is a large focus, the journal also welcomes research about natural heritage, in keeping with the UN World Heritage listing criteria. We are a multidisciplinary journal and publish work derived across a range of fields and geographic locations.

Our editorial board reflects this rich diversity and contains some of the most respected and brightest emerging scholars working on heritage tourism. They act as a sounding board for the editors-in-chief across a range of matters, including assisting with the judging of the Dallen Timothy Best Paper Award, which is given annually to the paper or papers that are considered to make the best contribution to our understanding of heritage tourism.

Like many journals with a specific focus, part of the challenge for the editors is to ensure that the journal does not stray into publishing work that is outside the remit of the journal. To take an example, a paper on conservation of a heritage asset is within the scope of the journal if there is a strong link to the implications for heritage tourism and if the paper furthers our knowledge of heritage tourism, both theoretically and practically. It is not sufficient just to have a heritage context for a study.

The editors recognise the importance of publishing a broad body of work, both geographically and theoretically, within the bounds of heritage tourism. This may necessitate at times asking authors of submissions to revise their work before it can be considered to be sent out for peer review, if there is a kernel of a good idea, but the submission is weak and lacks critical detail, such as a methods section or rigorous and accepted ways of presenting data. This can be a means, in particular, of giving papers prepared by inexperienced scholars or those drawn from the Global South a better chance of receiving a positive peer review down the track and is a learning opportunity for the scholar, even if their paper is not ultimately accepted for publication in the *Journal*.

Papers submitted by PhD candidates or early career researchers are always welcomed, but there are some tips we would pass on based on our experience as editors. First, reading the *Journal*'s aim and scope and guidelines is critical. This might seem obvious but is often observed in the breach. This maximises an author's chance of getting published and certainly of not falling at the first hurdle. While we allow submissions to utilise different formatting of references, prior to final acceptance, the structure of the paper still should conform to the *Journal*'s guidelines and those references should adopt a consistent style.

Second, reading previously published work in the *Journal* and critically engaging with it is a must. This allows authors of submissions to see what sort of work has been published in the *Journal* in the past, to build on this work and to contribute to debates in the field of heritage tourism. Of course, reading should be wider than the *Journal*, but it is a starting point. This review of pertinent literature will form the basis of a literature review section of a paper where the potential theoretical contributions of the study are articulated as gaps in knowledge to be addressed.

Third, think about the originality of the paper. Is it on a topic that has been researched "to death" or is it simply based around a practical issue that does not have any theoretical implications? Try to make a paper stand out in terms of innovation, whether that relates to the study method or the theoretical framework employed and show a reader how this provides new insights into an issue or problem.

JOURNAL OF SUSTAINABLE TOURISM, EDITOR: XAVIER FONT

Understanding the Aims of Your Target Journal: An Example from the *Journal of Sustainable Tourism*

Increasingly, we see authors that select which journal they will submit their work to based on metrics, and who work their way down their selected ranking list as if journals were all interchangeable. They consider the only penalty of indiscriminately targeting inappropriate journals is delay. Instead, we suggest that authors should be crystal-clear about their target journal before they even start writing. This is for two reasons: first, because it is essential to know who your target audience are, so that your content and language, etc. are appropriately crafted; and second, because it is helpful to read the editor's guidelines to know how to structure your paper. Journal editors have specific journal aims and criteria that inform their choices of the type of papers they select. While every journal has in common the criteria of rigour, novelty and significance, there are differences in how these are interpreted. We believe that understanding what a journal is trying to achieve, and how it aims to do so, can help authors to understand whether their article is a good fit with the journal and, consequently, whether they should send their work to the journal's editorial team for consideration.

We shall briefly exemplify the need to understand the personality of your target journal by using the *Journal of Sustainable Tourism* (*JoST*) as our example. The two original aims of *JoST*, from over 30 years ago, remain valid today: to foster sustainable research and practice, and to develop both a theoretical base for sustainable tourism and reliable empirical evidence of its results and impacts (Bramwell & Lane, 1993). Thirty years on, the current editorial team has reinterpreted the original aims in line with a journal that seeks to be *rigorous*, *novel and significant*, *accessible*, *impactful*, *diverse and inclusive*, *and empowering*. A more detailed account of the journal's aims can be found in Font et al. (2023). Let's consider these contemporary aims of *JoST* in more detail from the perspective of its editorial team.

First, the criterion of publishing *rigorous* research means to be the most respected source on sustainable tourism science. *JoST* has been at the forefront of addressing global issues, such as calling for research that links to the United Nations' Sustainable Development Goals (Bramwell et al., 2017). The journal aims to publish papers that contribute to making the tourism industry more sustainable, and to understand how the tourism industry can contribute to society in meeting its sustainability needs. Despite clear articulation of this aim in our editorial guidelines, we still receive papers that shoehorn the word sustainability into the title or the abstract, but do not address any aspect of sustainability in the research content. This is a common reason for submissions being rejected and points to the importance for authors of reading the editorial guidelines of their target journals before submitting their papers. Many of the submitted papers that are within *JoST*'s scope are cross-sectional surveys of tourists', employees' and residents' attitudes and behavioural intentions towards sustainability; we increasingly find that the peer-review process rejects them. Instead, *JoST* would like to receive papers that measure real behaviours, experimental studies or evaluations of interventions.

We interpret the need for *novel* and *significant* research as publishing bold, solution-oriented research, as *JoST* considers itself to be the journal FOR sustainable tourism. While novelty and significance cannot be at the expense of rigour, we will always favour those trailblazing manuscripts that are timely and current, that speak to the realities of today's society. We are working hard to be more plural in the topics we publish, and to broaden the scope of what is understood as sustainability. A disproportionate number of papers focus on just a few environmental impacts, and we are keen to receive papers that broaden our understanding of what sustainability is. From a significance point of view, we are keen to receive papers that go beyond measuring current behaviour to report on efforts to create behaviour change.

As an extension of supporting significant research, we work with authors to make their research more *accessible*, by helping disseminate knowledge beyond academia. For example, we have created a list of sustainable tourism journalists whom we approach with our own press releases about articles we publish that we think can have some traction with the media. While potential media attention is not a criterion that we use to determine which papers are accepted for publication, it certainly informs the level of effort we are willing to exert in promoting the papers. We hope our focus on media and dissemination encourages researchers who want to be proactive in creating change to select us as their journal of choice. This point leads on nicely to our aim to publish research that is *impactful*, by which we mean research with the potential to influence policy and practice. Papers that show potential to change practices are of particular interest to *JoST*. We dedicate additional editorial time to help authors to draw out the impact opportunities from their research, and, in some cases, to disseminate their work amongst government and industry bodies if we believe the latter can benefit from the paper's findings.

Finally, we aim to be *diverse* and *inclusive*. We are acutely aware that most research published in the top ranked journals concentrates on well-established topics and comes from researchers based in a few, typically well-developed, countries. The editorial team provides additional support to authors from countries that are currently underrepresented who submit papers with publication potential, by providing pre-peer-review advice on how to improve the paper, to improve their chances of a positive outcome. We also aim to be an *empowering* journal, which nurtures a sense of community and has a culture that supports academics.

Each journal has a scope, an aim and a set of rules that are more or less explicit. We explained the *JoST* aims and what they mean from the journal's perspective, so that potential authors understand that they need to collect this type of information about each of the journals they are considering, and apply this information to their research objectives. If they've already conducted their research before considering their target journal, they should instead use this kind of information to inform and guide how they write their paper.

References

Bramwell, B., & Lane, B. (1993). Sustainable tourism: An evolving global approach. *Journal of Sustainable Tourism, 1*(1), 1–5.
Bramwell, B., Higham, J., Lane, B. & Miller, G. (2017). Editorial: Twenty-five years of sustainable tourism and the *Journal of Sustainable Tourism*: Looking back and moving forward. *Journal of Sustainable Tourism, 25*(1), 1–9.
Font, X., Montano, L., Wu, J., Coghlan, A., Woosnam, K. & Li, S. (2023). The purpose of a sustainable tourism journal. *Journal of Sustainable Tourism, 31*(1), 1–13.

JOURNAL OF TOURISM FUTURES, EDITORS: DR STEFAN HARTMAN, DR IAN YEOMAN AND DR ALBERT POSTMA

The *Journal of Tourism Futures* (*JTF*) was established in 2015 by the European Tourism Futures Institute (ETFI) at NHL Stenden University of Applied Sciences, the Netherlands. We felt the need for a forward-looking journal, as the tourism industry is continually facing new challenges, e.g., related to changes related to consumer demand, technology, politics, governance and climate, to over-tourism and the need for more community-centred and generative approaches, and many more. We felt the need to have a journal that addresses such topics, contributes to theory building but also provides better information to the tourism industry about implications of changes that are upcoming – a key part of the work we do at ETFI.

The journal is published by Emerald Publishing, as a Platinum Open Access journal, and can be found at: https:// www .emeraldgroup publishing .com/ journal/jtf. Platinum Open Access means the publishing costs are covered by the ETFI and authors do not pay any fees. The journal puts out three issues per annum. Over time, we were able to add a book review editor, expanded the team of associate editors, broadened the editorial team (taking into account diversity in terms of geography, gender, career stage, etc.) and have invited key individuals from tourism practice to join our advisory board.

The Evolution of the *Journal of Tourism Futures*

The reason to start the journal related strongly to the launch of the ETFI itself. The ETFI was established as a co-production between NHL Stenden University and public and private sector stakeholders in 2010, primarily to study tourism futures along the lines of strategic foresight and scenario planning. The Institute's activities help those stakeholders to make sense of complex situations and uncertain futures so as to enhance their capacity to adapt and build resilience. In 2015, the *Journal of Tourism Futures* was initiated to further strengthen the body of knowledge that is relevant to understanding and coping with dynamic tourism futures, aiming to attract contributions on methodologies (e.g., scenario planning, strategic foresight, forecasting), theories (e.g., sustainable tourism, resilience), and key trends and development.

Considering that the *JTF* only started in 2015 and looking at its performance now, it can be considered a rising star. We started without any name (no reputation) and fame (no impact factor) and decided to go for a niche topic in tourism literature. Nevertheless, the journal was able to quickly attract a good inflow of papers – being heavily promoted by the ETFI and being a Platinum Open Access journal – including contributions by renowned academics on timely topics such as the "Transformation and the regenerative future of tourism" (2022), " Tourism in crisis: Global threats to sustainable tourism futures" (2021) and "The future of experiential travel" (2019). Added to that, the choice to do regular special issues with guest editors proved to be a success, bringing in their quality network and resulting in quality contributions. Accepted papers are published quickly and become accessible via EarlyCite. Rather rapidly, the journal grew in name and fame. In line, the inflow of manuscripts to review has grown massively. *JTF*'s evolution allowed us to regularly update and expand our editorial advisory board and install a team of associate editors. In doing so, we carefully considered diversity in terms of academic background, geographical spread, gender and career stage.

Tips for Authors on How to Increase Your Chances of Getting Published

The team of editors is happy to see a growth in quantity and quality of manuscripts. However, there is also a huge number of manuscripts that are rejected, even before going into review. Key issues are often strikingly simple, e.g., papers that do not fit the goals and aims of the journal, underdeveloped or missing sections (often the methodology section!), papers without proper structure or papers that do not meet the technical requirements (e.g., word count). Once papers make it into the review process, some authors feel it is a run race. Review reports are not given the fullest attention, remarks are conveniently skipped over, minor revisions are made whilst major revisions are needed. Editors will notice and will deal accordingly, potentially resulting in new rounds of reviews or, in the worst case, a reject after all.

Based on the experience of the editors, here are some tips to get published in *JTF*:

- First, critically examine the aims and scope of the journal carefully before writing the manuscript, not when it is (nearly) finished. Write your paper with a strategy to get published in mind. We only consider papers in the area of the future of tourism. If a paper does not align with the aims and scope, it will be rejected.

- Second, the *JTF* offers multiple possibilities to publish: research articles, viewpoint papers, trends papers, book reviews and conference reports. Viewpoint and trends papers are shorter papers and could help really timely, new, experimental and controversial ideas to get published.
- Third, carefully check *JTF*'s previously published volumes and issues to understand the types and styles of papers. Use these papers as inspiration so as not to reinvent the wheel and avoid submitting articles with missing or underdeveloped sections.
- Fourth, give review reports your fullest attention. Reviewer reports can be confrontational. Nevertheless, they are written by your peers who are the experts on the topic. Provide a detailed response to the reviewer comments. The more structured, the better. Show you are comprehensive and do not leave out a single comment. In your response, be confident about your manuscript and dare to disagree with the findings of reviewers. If you decide to do so, obviously, only include good, convincing arguments.

The Future of the *Journal of Tourism Futures*

Given the greater focus on the future, *JTF* is expected to further grow in importance and impact, and we are considering several changes. First is adding more issues annually, if our resources will allow for it. Second, we will consider an even stronger focus on tourism futures, potentially adjusting the aims and scope accordingly. Third, we will consider more emphasis on special issues and related calls for papers on key futures topics that are co-identified by our advisory board members. Fourth, we will consider closer alignment with another journal that is published by our university (NHL Stenden University of Applied Sciences) opening a possibility of a "sister journal" in the future.

JOURNAL OF TRAVEL RESEARCH, EDITORS: JAMES PETRICK AND NANCY MCGEHEE

The *Journal of Travel Research*'s (*JTR*) mission "is to be the premier, peer-reviewed research journal focused on the business of travel and tourism development, management, marketing, economics and behavior" (Sagepub, 2023a, p. 1). *JTR* prefers publishing papers which are cutting edge or are breaking new and important ground that will become the foundation for interest in tourism research in the future. Additionally, the editors of *JTR* are seeking global diversity of authors, subject matter and methodologies that embrace the complexity of the travel and tourism phenomenon. All research published is expected to provide substantive theoretical, practical and methodological contributions to the travel and tourism literature. *JTR* does not have a preference towards any particular methodologies. What matters is whether the research is appropriately designed for the research question, well executed and of significant interest to its readership. It is important that authors explain and justify why the selected theoretical foundation and methodological approach is the most appropriate, given the research aims and objectives. Hence, the journal prefers that submissions be grounded in theory, provide relevant approaches to current issues and utilise innovative methodologies that are globally useful and replicable. Many studies are appropriately undertaken with a focus on addressing a particular local situation or context. To be appropriate for *JTR*, there should be a clear argument for why the larger tourism research audience finds it relevant, useful or a contribution to the overall body of knowledge.

As outlined in *JTR*'s submission guidelines (Sagepub, 2023b), the journal accepts three different types of submissions, all requiring full review. The first and most commonly submitted are empirical research articles. These are standard, research-based submissions and should focus on practical solutions to problems related to tourism development, sustainability, management, marketing or economics.

The second type of submission is "Foundations of Tourism Research and Conceptual Articles". These manuscripts are expected to come from international leaders in the field. They should be more conceptual than other submissions and assist in building theory in a substantive and important area of inquiry. These articles should culminate in distinct propositions to the field, expand the current theoretical understanding of the area of study, and propose new opportunities and ideas. These submissions must either be invited or commissioned by the co-editors and require a detailed proposal prior to being reviewed. The submitted proposal should outline the goals of the research and highlight why the author(s) have the expertise to write the manuscript.

The last type of submission is "Letters to the Editor". The primary goal for these submissions is to encourage discourse related to past or current research. Other goals include reviewing gaps not covered by past studies, commentary on current events, the state of our field and its research, reviewing research endeavours, and brief discussions about methodologies, research problems or assumptions. These submissions are shorter, more conversational and less formal than other submissions.

All submitted manuscripts are subject to a complete review process. This process starts with a desk review by one or both co-editors. At this stage, the co-editors decide if the manuscript is rejected, unsubmitted or accepted for review. Manuscripts which are rejected are not permitted to be resubmitted. These typically suffer from fatal flaws including very poor grammatical structure typically related to a lack of attending to the submission guidelines, a lack of theoretical foundation or a subject matter that does not fall within the vision of *JTR*. Unsubmitted manuscripts typically have highly relevant subject matter and show potential for publication, but need more clarification or are lacking important information which is needed before they can be reviewed.

Manuscripts that pass desk review are sent out for full review. Unlike most journals, *JTR* uses an editorial board (full-time reviewers) instead of associate editors (persons who recruit others to review). *JTR*'s current editorial board consists of 166 international leaders in travel research, from every continent, who represent the full diversity of research, methodological and statistical expertise. When a manuscript goes under review, one or both of the co-editors match three editorial board members to review each manuscript. Reviewers are selected based on their research interest areas and methodological expertise. This is slightly different from journals with associate editors who assign their manuscripts to one associate editor, who then has the responsibility of recruiting reviewers. Due to the typical difficulty in seeking external reviews by associate editors, it is believed that *JTR*'s process enables a richer review process. The primary objective of this review process is not to accept or deny manuscripts, but to make submitted research better.

Editorial board members are tasked to determine whether the submitted research is relevant, significant, original, rigorous and articulate. Their subsequent reviews are expected to give feedback in each of these areas and to give authors specific directions on how to improve their manuscript. Their reviews are sent to the co-editors who take into consideration the totality of the reviews in their decision related to the fate of each manuscript.

Manuscripts are rejected for many reasons, but most have shortcomings related to their conceptual grounding, innovativeness, practical implications or methodological contributions. Due to the sheer volume of submissions, not all "good" submissions are able to be published simply because there are more deserving manuscripts.

In summary, to be publishable in the *Journal of Travel Research,* manu scripts must simultaneously:

- Be on important, contemporary travel and tourism research issues;
- Have a significant impact on theory and methodology;
- Be of widespread interest and relevance to the journal's audience;
- Report research which fits the aim and scope of the journal;
- Be expressed and presented in English to a very high standard.

References

Sagepub (2023a). https:// us .sagepub .com/ en -us/ nam/ journal -of -travel -research/ journal200788#aims-and-scope.
Sagepub (2023b). https://journals.sagepub.com/author-instructions/JTR.

TOURISM MANAGEMENT, EDITOR: CATHY H.C. HSU

Tourism Management (*TM*) is a scholarly journal which focuses on the management of travel and tourism. The remit of the journal, similar to the tourism phenomenon, is quite broad by nature. Tourism is interpreted as an umbrella term that encompasses various players, including tourists, residents, travel-related businesses, accommodation sectors and other relevant hospitality service providers. In addition to such a broad scope, the journal welcomes research based on an interdisciplinary approach. Thus, the authorship and readership are quite diverse, including scholars affiliated with tourism programs and those from other disciplines such as general management, computer science and communication studies.

As a scholarly journal, articles are expected to contribute to theoretical and/or methodological advancement, beyond having a solid theoretical foundation and applying an existing theory to the phenomenon under investigation. The intention is to encourage authors to identify theoretical shortcomings and use the tourism context to advance theoretical development and push the knowledge boundary forward. To accomplish this, multi-methods and multi-sources of data are often required to triangulate findings and enhance the rigour and external validity of empirical findings. Cross-sectional surveys are known for various biases, thus are insufficient if used as the sole source of evidence.

Due to its management focus, articles published are expected to have evidence-based practical implications derived from the study. The journal requires authors to include a 150-word impact statement that informs the readers what contribution or beneficial effects the study brings to the wider society and community beyond academia. Therefore, *TM* generally does not publish conceptual papers, which tend to have scholarly merit but limited practical implications. For innovative ideas and scholarly debates, short communications can be submitted under the "Current Issues" category for consideration. *TM* also does not publish bibliometric or pure systematic literature review articles. However, authors can take a step further by evaluating prior work to offer more insightful, less descriptive synthesis to signpost a particular topic outlining where the subject has developed from with a strong theoretical focus, where the literature is now and where it might develop theoretically/methodologically in the future. Such a creative piece offering a holistic view of the progress made can be submitted under the "Progress in Tourism Research" category.

There appear to be "hot topics" attracting researchers' attention from time to time. In the past couple of years, *TM* has received a large number of submissions about the COVID-19 pandemic, on scale development, based on big data and using experimental designs, to name a few. Scholars, particularly young scholars, are advised to stay true to their own interest and not indiscriminately follow such hot (and soon to be cold) topics or methods.

Another recent phenomenon often seen is the inclusion of several rounds of data collection or studies in one manuscript, probably due to the encouragement of multi-method, multi-source data. However, if the multiple studies do not have a common thread or are simply different phases of a larger project, such an act of "packaging" serves no substantive purpose and does not enhance the rigour or quality of the work. In addition, to make substantial contributions to the literature, manuscripts submitted are expected to report a complete study, rather than a small part of a project. If the project is divided into too many potential articles, each paper's contribution may be marginal which can be easily spotted by reviewers.

Quality work does take time to polish. Editors often see submissions on interesting topics that have the potential for publication, if the paper is properly crafted. As authors did not allow sufficient time to reflect and refine the presentation, the paper's potential is not properly communicated to reviewers. Thus, it is strongly recommended that authors take the time, have someone take an objective look, put the work aside for a while to refresh one's perspective, and go through iterations before submission. Because journals now do not allow resubmission of rejected manuscripts without significant changes, including the title, abstract and a large portion of the text, it is important to make sure that the best possible work is submitted for review.

As part of the crafting of a good article, authors are strongly encouraged to develop their storytelling and writing skills. Manuscripts seem to become longer, partly due to the use of multiple methods and data sources. Regardless, if the storyline is clear, the authors can streamline the writing and communicate the message succinctly. Repetitive, descriptive, overly decorated statements could distract readers' understanding of the main points and con tributions. Academic writing is an acquired skill, and native English speakers may not have the absolute advantage. Thus, scholars whose native language is not English should not necessarily feel they are at a disadvantage.

The peer review, submission, resubmission process does take time. Reviewers often observe issues related to factors that have been taken for granted by authors and not articulated clearly in the manuscript. Reviewers could also provide expert views and additional insights to help authors enhance their work. In cases when the reviewers' comments are inaccurate or disagreed on by authors, a professionally stated rebuttal with sound reasons is perfectly acceptable. Thus, reviewer comments are meant to be taken constructively, rather than defensively.

Considering the low acceptance rate of various journals (e.g., approximately 8% for *TM*), when authors are given a chance to revise the manuscript, the opportunity should be treasured. Putting personal emotions aside, digesting reviewer comments and refining the manuscript reflect the professionalism and maturity of the researchers, as revamping a submission could be more challenging, time-consuming and exhausting than preparing the initial submission. The good news is: persistence does pay off!

TOURISM RECREATION RESEARCH, EDITOR: TZUNG-CHENG HUAN

Introduction

Tourism Recreation Research (*TRR*) is a multidisciplinary international journal originally from India and established in 1976. As one of the pioneer tourism journals, *TRR* encourages scholars to submit innovative and impactful papers that focus on tourism and/or recreation. Tourism and recreation manuscripts that additionally implicate related fields, such as hospitality, leisure, events and sport, are also welcome to the extent that they engage with knowledge integration and the holistic pursuit of contemporary social issues (Singh, 2021; Singh & Naqvi, 2019; Vishwakarma & Mukherjee, 2019). The journal places a strong emphasis on original research and readability. The followings are some key recommendations for having work published in *TRR*.

Key Recommendations for Successful Publication

Compact but sophisticated introduction
As the opening statement, the introduction is a critical part of a research paper. The introduction is a lens for viewing the research paper. The introduction should be compact yet contain all the essentials such as research background, problems, objectives and theoretical/managerial issues. Authors must help a reader see what is unique and valuable about the article.

Literature review
A successful literature review should cover theories, hypotheses and models. Presenting a theory should involve a theory that is clearly relevant to developing research hypotheses and models of the research. The presence of references that are or that seem peripheral to the research is negative. A guide to the relevance of literature is literature leading to hypotheses and to solving the research problems and achieving research objectives. For example, the literature review could identify research models and show their relation to delivering theoretical improvements or new theories.

Rigorous research methodology

Sound methodology is required to produce useful and meaningful research, to make sure data collection is designed and executed so the data collected or used can detect effects that matter. Deriving results correctly and showing that has been done is necessary. Detecting statistically significant effects is of no value if the effects are too small to matter or if why they matter is not explained. Whether quantitative, qualitative or mixed-methods research, communication about data collection, processing and explanation of results must be appropriate to the audience of the journal.

Consistent results

The results should include findings and discussions that show how the paper addresses research objectives and hypotheses. The discussion of findings should use references for putting findings in the context of research that has been done and showing unique achievements of the research. In other words, how the results of the study being submitted differ from, are partially confirmed by, or are the same as results of previous studies must be addressed. This discussion must be done recognising that focusing on things that are unique but not important detracts from the value of research.

Solid conclusion

With the closing statement is the author/s' opportunity to highlight why the paper is important. A problem is highlighting without simply repeating what has been said. A good test is to see if the conclusion covers theoretical contributions, managerial implications, research limitations and the need for future study, presenting important matters in the text that are not just repetitions of what is found elsewhere in the paper.

Potential journal contributors are encouraged to use a journal's website to see that the material in a paper conforms to what the journal wants. This involves content as well as formatting of content. It is more than meeting the technicalities of using and recording references as expected.

Letter to editor-in-chief

A cover letter or an equivalent submission document is important in order to get consideration for publication. The following should be covered, depending on what is appropriate for the journal:

- The uniqueness and value of your article and why it will be cited;
- Acknowledgement of grant support to show the research approval by grant reviewers;
- Use the services of colleagues, and, if appropriate, of a professional copy-editor to avoid issues with the article in the review process;

- Try to cite articles appearing within five years to increase two-year and five-year impact factors
- Briefly explain the manuscript's fit in terms of other articles published in the *TRR* (e.g., describe how the manuscript relates to one to three articles published in the *TRR*).
- When possible, recommend reviewers who published on similar topics, ideally having cited them.

Tips for Ensuring Success in Publication

Here are some key matters contributors need to consider for success in publication in top journals. First, collaboration with experienced contributors is a good way to write a manuscript that solves many problems before submission. Ensure that when students are your co-authors that the work meets high professional standards. Early career cooperation with a well-published and respected mentor who is prepared to guide you to improve and publish your research is desirable. Good mentors can not only work as your co-authors but also as endorsers for your publications.

Arguing with reviewers can create unfavourable outcomes. The goal is to use reviewers' comments to revise/improve your article. Reviewers are the anonymous heroes behind many articles and their review comments and suggestions should, unless problematic, be used in revision. The response notes to reviewers should address issues raised clearly by showing action taken. If a review says something is wrong and it is not, cite an authority. If a reviewer wants a change you feel is inconsistent with authorities you follow, cite the authorities whilst being careful that you understand the reviewer's view. If you feel you do not have sufficient time to revise and resubmit your paper, request a specific extension to your deadline.

If the topic will allow you to do a good review, then accept review invitations from your target journals. A review that raises issues about your competence is not something you should get involved in. Also, as needed, look for information on writing a good review. You can learn from other reviewers by looking at review comments when reviews involve the return of a paper for revision (Huan, 2020). To get into reviewing, you can send your CV to the editors-in-chief for the chance of becoming a volunteer reviewer. Through reviews, you can build your career by getting a review award or being invited to be an editorial board member, which can involve being asked to review six papers in a year in a timely and professional manner.

Never Give Up!

Receiving a rejection letter, even a desk rejection letter, is the most typical outcome of submissions. A rejection letter with helpful comments can be a stepping stone for improving a paper or research to have a later successful submission. Never give up! However, learn that some papers can be improved and published while some research ideas need improvement to the extent of the preparation of a new paper.

References

Huan, T.C. (2020). Keys for authors to be enriched as excellent reviewers: The launch of *TRR* annual outstanding reviewer award. *Tourism Recreation Research*, *45*(2), 143, DOI:10.1080/02508281.2020.1755508.

Singh, S. (2021). Shradhanjali: Remembering TEJ VIR SINGH (June 1929–April 2021). *Tourism Recreation Research*, *46*(2), 143, DOI:10.1080/02508281.2021.19 26094.

Singh, S., & Naqvi, M.A. (2019). Tej Vir Singh: A passionate Indian in pursuit of tourism knowledge, *Anatolia*, *30*(3), 454–465, DOI:10.1080/13032917.2019.1624379.

Vishwakarma, P., & Mukherjee, S. (2019). Forty-three years journey of *Tourism Recreation Research*: A bibliometric analysis, *Tourism Recreation Research*, *44*(4), 403–418, DOI:10.1080/02508281.2019.1608066.

TOURISM REVIEW, EDITOR: DIMITRIOS BUHALIS

Tourism Review (*TR*) has been publishing innovative research on tourism topics since 1947 and is the oldest journal dedicated to this field. Two Swiss scholars named Walter Hunziker and Kurt Krapf recognised the need for scientific research in the field of tourism. To support this development, they created *The Tourism Review*, which was published in English, French and German, and aimed to promote public debate between policy makers and scientific discovery. The journal was designed to complement professional bodies in the tourism industry and to support researchers and professionals by sharing knowledge and expertise in multiple languages. Hunziker and Krapf were concerned about the role of tourism in post-war economic development and global understanding, and they saw the journal as a living organism that would support knowledge and debate in the wider political and economic environment. The launch of the journal was followed by the establishment of the Association Internationale d'Experts Scientifiques du Tourisme (AIEST) in 1950, which has since become a worldwide network of tourism experts.

The primary objective of *TR* is to promote a greater understanding of tourism and to increase the influence and importance of tourism research on a global scale. *Tourism Review* is a research platform that strives to be inclusive by incorporating multidisciplinary research, theory and best practices to improve the understanding of tourism and make it accessible to everyone. The journal aims to explore the tourism phenomenon and industry holistically, considering it as an ecosystem that affects consumers, the industry, policy and destinations with a global perspective.

TR publishes a range of article types. All papers go through the usual double-blind review process. We accept articles in four categories, namely:

- Research papers (6,000-word articles on cutting-edge research);
- Cutting-edge conceptual research (6,000-word articles synthesis of research);
- Perspective papers (short 1,500-word articles focusing on future perspectives); and
- Research innovations (short 1,500-word articles on PhD research or innovative research methodologies).

As a generalist journal *Tourism Review* provides original, creative, multi- and interdisciplinary contributions on a very wide range of issues including:

- Understanding needs of all stakeholders in the tourism ecosystem;
- Tourism business environment and ecosystem;
- Tourism management, stakeholders and strategies;
- Tourism demand, markets, consumer behaviour, segmentation;
- Tourism policy, governance, community and economic integration;
- Tourism planning and development, regional planning;
- Managing and marketing tourism products and services;
- Destination networks and ecosystems;
- Destination competitiveness and sources of competitive advantage;
- Tourism marketing, branding, positioning, promotion, pricing;
- Information communication technology, social media and reputation management;
- Distribution of tourism and intermediation strategies;
- Impacts of tourism: economic, socio-cultural and environmental;
- Sustainability, ecotourism, climate change;
- Triple bottom line and corporate social responsibility;
- Tourism geography, mobilities, migration, place, coastal, rural, mountain, urban;
- Industry: transportation, hospitality, attractions, festivals, leisure;
- Events and sports tourism, legacy and impacts;
- Crisis management, risk and disaster management, business continuity;
- Cultural heritage, festivals, art and creative industries;
- Human resources and talent management, global employability;
- Accessibility, inclusive design and tourism for all.

Tourism Review, like most leading academic journals, is facing several challenges. Most challenges gravitate around research ethics leading to serious ethical violations. Research misconduct involves questionable research practices that fall short of the standards of ethics, research and scholarship required to ensure that the integrity of research is upheld, damaging the credibility of the journal. These may lead to reputation damages for both the journal and offending authors. Other challenges include:

- *The peer-review process*: Attracting dedicated peer reviewers who contribute constructive and honest feedback has become more challenging as there are many work-related pressures. Many academics enjoy reviews of their own papers but are reluctant to offer their reviewing services for others.
- *Authorship and credit*: Attributing proper credit to those who have contributed to the research is becoming more challenging and disputes and unethical practices have been observed. Authorship and the order in which the authors are listed on the paper should be agreed prior to submission. *Tourism Review* has a right first-time policy on this and no changes can be made to the list once submitted.
- *Plagiarism*: Plagiarism is a significant issue in research publishing, and it can be challenging to detect and prevent especially with the development of generative artificial intelligence which can produce text instantly.
- *Fabrication and falsification*: Similarly, fabrication and falsification refer to the act of creating or manipulating data to support a particular conclusion.
- *Dominant cultural and geographical focus*: Several regions dominate the production of research papers and this is reflected in authors and also research context.
- *Language barriers*: Researchers from non-English speaking countries may struggle to have their work published in international journals creating language barriers.

To address these challenges we follow the COPE's (Committee on Publication Ethics) integrity and ethics guidance. COPE provides guidance on all aspects of publication ethics and guidelines for addressing these issues.

Since 2017, *Tourism Review* has developed as a truly global cutting-edge journal. More papers have been submitted and accepted, and in 2020 it published a 75-year anniversary paper. It was admitted to SSCI and its Impact Factor on Clarivate grew from 1.06 (2018), to 2.908 (2019), 5.947 (2020) and 7.689 (2021) to become a Top 10 and a Q1 journal. Its Scopus CiteScore grew too from 2.1 in 2019 to 4.5 in 2020 and 8.2 in 2021. Its Scopus CiteScore Tracker score in March 2023 was 12.5 (see Figure 3.3).

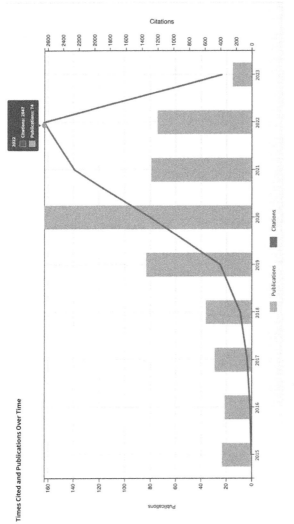

Figure 3.3   Tourism review: journal statistics

Following the vision of the founders back in 1947, the *Tourism Review* promotes the exchange of ideas across different regions, cultures and disciplines. Its inclusive strategy encourages the publication of innovative and diverse tourism research from all over the world. The journal is committed to enhancing the impact and relevance of outstanding tourism research for the betterment of global society, and it continues to grow in strength.

FURTHER INFORMATION

Tourism Review: https://www.emeraldgrouppublishing.com/journal/tr.

Call for papers: http:// www .em eraldgroup publishing .com/ products/ journals/author_guidelines.htm?id=tr.

PART II

THE PAPER

4. Crafting a refereed journal paper
Chris Cooper

INTRODUCTION

Tourism academics advance knowledge of the field primarily by publishing their research in refereed journals (Wright, Ketchen and Clark, 2020a, 2020b). These publications are the currency of academic life determining an academic's reputation, promotion and career prospects and thus their pay. Whilst publishing research and sharing ideas is both satisfying and rewarding, it is also a challenging and highly competitive business. Publishing in top journals demands high-quality research with powerful theory, good research design and compelling findings (Hitt, 2020), and increasingly research with a high degree of real-world impact. Yet publishing in refereed journals is shrouded in mystery, often seeming to be a black box process where the mechanics are little understood by those submitting papers. This chapter aims to demystify the question of what makes a good paper, how to approach it and how to play the game. It explains what editors and reviewers are looking for and hints at some of the success factors for good papers. Of course, there are no guarantees in terms of having a paper accepted – top journals desk reject anywhere from 50% or more of submissions and tend to have a 5–10% acceptance rate. The chapter is structured as follows. First, it provides some insights in how to choose the best journal for your work, and then goes on to look at the role of contribution and positioning of papers. The chapter then provides detailed guidelines about each section of an academic paper and closes with some of the practicalities around submission protocols.

WHICH TOURISM JOURNAL?

The choice of tourism journal to submit your research to is critical and will partly determine your success in having the paper taken to review. It is important to consider the target journal before you begin the final stages of writing as the paper will need to be directed to that particular journal. So, what are the considerations?

First, the type of paper will influence the choice and fit of the journal. Is it a conceptual or empirical paper? Is it qualitative or quantitative in approach? Is it interdisciplinary? Is it a review paper? For example, in disciplines outside tourism there are journals that specialise in short papers such as 'letters' (such as physics), whilst others only take literature reviews (see Baruch, 2020).

Second, journal cultures vary, but there are ways to demystify them. Always look at the aims and scope of the journal as these are written by the editors, whilst the journal website is generally composed by the publisher and therefore not as helpful. Look too at past issues of the journal – in hard copy ideally – to get a feel for how the issues are assembled and the range and type of papers. Special issues also give a strong hint as to the interests of the editors and the editorial board. Similarly, check the impact factor of the journal using Scopus or Web of Science and also the thematic classification using Ulrichsweb (http://ulrichsweb.serialsolutions.com). It is wise to look at papers on similar topics to your own, the references they use and their approach. You can then ensure that the paper looks like and reflects other papers in the journal. Always aim as high as is realistic in your journal choice but also have a reserve journal in mind. Finally, talk to colleagues about their experience of publishing in the journal – there is no substitute for first-hand experience.

CONTRIBUTION AND POSITIONING

Closely linked to the choice of journal is the contribution of how the paper is positioned in the tourism field. One of the main reasons for a paper's rejection is lack of contribution (Palmatier, 2016). In other words, the paper has failed to make it clear how it develops and contributes to the intellectual and research agenda of the tourism field. Contribution can be in terms of (Bergh, 2020):

1. Advancing theory and the tourism field;
2. Approaching new and complex problems in the tourism field; or
3. Applying original, innovative additions or concepts to the tourism field.

It is important to flag the contribution early on in the introduction to the paper and to reaffirm it in the discussion and conclusion. The introduction will be the first part of the paper that is read by editors and reviewers and should be around one and a half manuscript pages. It is the opportunity to sell the contribution and significance of the paper and encourage others to take the time to read it. The introduction should be concise and clear, identifying the field and the paper's objective, summarising theory and the conceptual approach, and presenting the empirical approach (Palmatier, 2016). In terms of contribution to the field, development of a strong narrative literature review summarising the field and locating the contribution of the paper is a useful approach.

Similarly, compelling findings that add a new perspective on tourism will confirm contribution – for example, novel data sets from multiple perspectives or longitudinal data often deliver new and fresh viewpoints on existing knowledge. Finally, it is important to signpost the contribution to the reader and assessors of the paper using headings and subheadings and ensuring that the terminology and hypotheses reflect the spirt of the contribution claimed.

Positioning is really about the content of the paper and should tell the reader about the conversational community (often in terms of theory) that it is joining. It is important to identify similar papers in the chosen journal and reflect their format and structure (Barney, 2020), as well as to ensure that literature from the journal is cited. This should convince the reader that the authors understand the conversation's main findings and conclusions. Barney (2020) goes into detail about how to write a compelling introduction that clearly positions a paper.

STRUCTURE OF THE PAPER

This section of the chapter examines each substantive section of a typical refereed paper and outlines some clear lessons in terms of what to do – and what to avoid. Once your paper is written you will need a title – the shorter, the more concise and the more specific the better. Short titles have impact and are memorable.

The structure of papers does differ but typically a journal paper will have seven sections:

1. Abstract
2. Introduction
3. Theoretical background and literature
4 Methodology
5. Findings/analysis
6. Discussion
7. Conclusion.

This structure can vary as a result of, say, journal requirements which may ask for a breakdown of the abstract into findings, methods and contribution. It may also vary as a result of the subject area and approach of the paper. However, if any of the sections are missing – for example, the literature and theory, the paper is likely to be desk rejected.

The Abstract

Writing the abstract is important and difficult. An abstract should not be written as an afterthought or dashed off quickly to get the paper submitted. The abstract is the first part of the paper that is read by the editor and is used to send to potential referees to elicit their support to review. A good abstract will clearly state the objectives of the paper, its originality and value and what is new. It will go on to outline the research problem/question, the method, results and conclusion. An abstract should not simply repeat the first paragraph of the paper, nor should it misrepresent the paper or make claims that are not justified. Do not include citations in the abstract.

As part of the abstract, journals require keywords. Again, these must be chosen carefully and strategically to truly represent the paper. The keywords will be used by search engines to categorise your paper and thus determine citations. So do not try to be clever and use esoteric or uncommon words, and do not use words that only occur in your paper. Do look at other similar papers as a sense check for your keywords.

Introduction

As noted above, the introduction should be around one and half manuscript pages and is the opportunity to position your paper in relation to the field and clearly state its purpose. It should clearly frame and answer questions about the topic (Chapman and Cahan, 2015). The introduction should state why the paper is of interest to the journal, and in particular for an international audience, and outline the research question, otherwise the paper will risk lacking focus.

Theoretical Background and Literature

The literature review is a central building block of any paper but is difficult to do well. It should build a story around what is known and what is not known in the field to provide a focus for the research and identify the 'gap' that your research question addresses. In other words, the literature review shows that the author has read widely in the field and understands the main issues and debates and can clarify the paper's contribution to the field. It is now common to provide a structured literature review table that identifies the main authors and describes the emergent themes. It is important that the literature cited is current, as well as mapping the key milestones of the development of the field. This allows the author to provide a holistic review of the literature and the assumptions underlying it (Nairn, Berthon and Money, 2007). An increasingly common reason for desk rejection is that the literature is too dated and recent work is omitted. Similarly, stacking lots of references following a sentence suggests a lack of critical assessment of the literature and it is a mistake to self-cite too often. Authors can demonstrate a critical literature review by presenting it in an ordered and legible way rather than simply sequentially listing by saying that author A said this, and author B said the other.

Methodology

A common issue raised by referees is that the method is not described in sufficient detail to assess what was done, when and why. It is not a time to take short cuts and the method should be described fully. The method section explains the approach taken to answer the research question and should provide full insights as to how the research process was designed and managed. It is the author's opportunity to show that the method has been understood and used appropriately. A highly cited paper will often be one that has rigorously used robust and innovative methods and applied intellectual precision. This also ensures that the findings cannot be challenged. No method is perfect, so a limitations section is now expected.

Findings/Analysis

This section should deliver a clear narrative about the findings and how the analysis unfolded to answer the research question. Here, it is important not to rely purely on the numbers in the results but to make sure they are clearly interpreted in a manner that tells a compelling story about the findings. Similarly, do not overdo the number of tables and figures. In other words, what does the analysis show, what was found in the course of the research and how does it link to the literature already cited? There are two approaches to linking the findings to the wider context of the field and the research question. The first is to use the findings section purely to report the results and keep the wider implications for a separate discussion section. The second is to blend the two, showing how the results link to and inform the wider context. The approach that you take will depend upon your own personal writing style and also the nature of the research question and the results.

Discussion

If you decide to have a separate discussion section it is the opportunity to demonstrate that you can see the bigger picture in terms of how the findings link to the broader tourism field and the conversations in your literature review. In doing so, the discussion should incontrovertibly answer the research question and cement the objectives and contribution of the paper. Here too is the opportunity to cover the question reviewers often raise – the so what? question. The discussion section is also where some authors outline the implications of the results. Others leave this for the conclusion. Again, this is personal choice and depends on the type of paper and the narrative flow. Implications are normally divided into two sections – theory and practice. The theoretical implications reinforce the contribution of the paper to the wider tourism field, whilst implications for practice may include practical suggestions for managers and the impact of the research on wider society or policy.

Conclusion

It is a common mistake to think of a conclusion as a summary. A summary simply repeats and provides a precis of the work. A conclusion closes the circle and shows how the research links to the wider literature and the field and addresses the issue of how the findings can be generalised. It should also include a brief section on limitations and a section on pointers for future research in the field as a result of the paper. This is not the place to introduce new material or new ideas, nor to make statements about the findings that cannot be proven – sometimes known as 'mission creep'. A good conclusion is powerful and memorable, clearly signposting the paper's takeaways for the reader. A good conclusion is therefore difficult to write.

FROM CRAFTING TO SUBMISSION

Writing your excellent paper is only the start of the process of submitting a journal paper – albeit the most important one. However, it is easy to be tripped up by not paying complete attention to the mechanics and rules of the submission process itself. These can be grouped into five considerations:

1.   Proofing and Polishing the Paper

No matter how many times you read your paper you will pick up typos, poor expression, a mix of US and UK spelling, and grammatical errors. References may have been missed, dates wrongly inserted and headings formatted that do not match the journal's guidelines. It is important not to be sloppy at this final stage – it leaves a poor impression on editors and reviewers and may lead to desk rejection. We are professional communicators. There is no excuse for poor writing and if a paper is not well crafted it will be rejected. For any doubts in terms of English expression, the gold standard is Strunk and White (1999), however, for a more accessible guide to writing see: http://www.plainenglish .co .uk/ files/ howto .pdf. For my own writing, I have found Stephen King's (2000) memoir *On Writing* to be highly insightful. If you are not a native

English speaker, make sure your paper is proofed and corrected by a professional. Finally, papers should tell a story from beginning to end and should be understood by intelligent individuals who are not in your field. Always do a 'near review' by asking a lay person to read and comment on your paper – a partner, relative or friend – but not another academic! If there are major flaws, they should see them.

2.   Abide by the Style Guide

Every journal has a style guide for papers, and different types of papers. This will include levels of headings, word limits, referencing styles, tables and figures, and sometimes the structure of the abstract. Some journals will also have specific requirements for papers. Ignore this at your peril. To be honest, these guides are easy to abide by – it is a simple mechanical exercise and will get you onto the desk of the editor. Ignoring these guides is professional suicide.

3.   Anticipate the Referees

Before submission it is useful to try to second guess what the referees may say about your paper. Common complaints from referees are:

Focus and contribution:

- Lack of, or limited contribution;
- Lack of clear and focused objectives/research questions;
- The paper is trying to do too many things; and
- Conclusions do not flow from the paper.

Sections:

- The method is inappropriate; and
- Poor literature review, key material omitted.

Type of paper:

- It is a case study and cannot be generalised;
- It only uses students as the sample;
- It is based on a thesis chapter; and
- It is based on a consulting project.

Style:

- Poor language and expression; and

- In-text citations are not included in the references at the end of the paper (referees often do spot checks).

Wherever possible, check whether you are guilty of any of these comments and fix them before submission.

4.   Submission

Preparing the text
Every journal has slightly different requirements for text submission but generally the stages are as follows:

1. A title page with author affiliations, the corresponding author and an abstract;
2. An anonymised version of the paper without author names and any references that would identify the author anonymised;
3. Separate files with pictures, tables and figures. Double check these for typos, numbering consistency and quality. Check that you do not need to seek permission to use them; and
4. A short cover letter explaining why the paper fits the journal and is relevant to the readership and previous papers.

The journal submission platform
All of the major journal publishers use a web-based submission process. For example, Taylor and Francis, John Wiley and Cambridge University Press use the ScholarOne platform. Always use the platform and do not submit directly to editors, as the paper will be returned and you will lose time. Submitting to the journal platform is time-consuming and takes care and needs accuracy. They are unforgiving of mistakes. You will need to register as an author and then follow the submission process carefully. Do not rush this stage. The platform will eventually prepare a PDF version of the various parts of your paper – cover letter, main body, author names and affiliations and so on. This will be the version of record so check it carefully before uploading. It is difficult and time-consuming to correct mistakes or make changes after this stage. The one advantage of these platforms is that they allow you to check the progress of your paper. This allows you to have some influence over the process, so if you feel the paper has been out for review for too long you can send a (polite and humble) note to the editor asking for an update.

5.   And Finally, Playing the Game

To be a professional academic publishing in refereed journals, you need to understand the rules of the game. This chapter has attempted to demystify these rules and provide advice for writing and successfully submitting good papers. The rules are clear:

- Choose the right journal;
- Identify a clear gap and make a contribution;
- Proof, proof and proof again;
- Always submit through the journal platform;
- Always follow author guidelines;
- Rejection is common, major revisions the norm – and a good outcome;
- Do not submit the same paper to different journals at the same time – it will be picked up by editors and reviewers;
- Do not resubmit a rejected paper to a different journal without revising it – you have free advice from the previous referees, use it;
- Do not plagiarise – journals all have software which will pick up similarities to other publications; and
- Do not submit drafts – it is disrespectable to editors and reviewers.

CONCLUSION

This chapter has provided detailed advice about crafting and submitting a refereed journal paper. Refereed papers are the hard currency of academic life and reputation, and careers depend upon success in getting papers published – rightly or wrongly. Books and book chapters do not count to the same degree when assessing an academic's publications in tourism, although this does vary in other subject areas and disciplines. As other chapters in this book will show, the publishing landscape is now very sophisticated, shaped by journal rankings, impact factors and research assessment exercises. However, a good paper is a good paper, and this chapter has tried to provide some underpinning guidelines to help you write a good paper with high impact in a highly ranked journal.

REFERENCES

Barney, J.B. (2020) Positioning Papers for Publication. In: Wright, M., Ketchen, D.J. and Clark, T. (Eds.), *How to Get Published in the Best Management Journals* (second edition) (pp. 142–152). Edward Elgar Publishing, Cheltenham, UK and Northampton, MA, USA.

Baruch, Y. (2020) Hitting Your Preferred Target: Positioning Papers for Different Types of Journals. In: Wright, M., Ketchen, D.J. and Clark, T. (Eds.), *How to Get Published in the Best Management Journals* (second edition) (pp. 220–232). Edward Elgar Publishing, Cheltenham, UK and Northampton, MA, USA.

Bergh, D.D. (2020) It's All About Contribution! Using the Discussion to Define and Develop Your Paper's Contributions. In: Wright, M., Ketchen, D.J. and Clark, T. (Eds.), *How to Get Published in the Best Management Journals* (second edition) (pp. 164–167). Edward Elgar Publishing, Cheltenham, UK and Northampton, MA, USA.

Chapman, C.S. and Cahan, S. (2015) Researching Accounting in Health Care: Considering the Nature of Academic Contribution. *Accounting and Finance*, 55(2), 397–413.

Hitt, M.A. (2020) Publishing in the Top Journals: The Secrets for Success. In: Wright, M., Ketchen, D.J. and Clark, T. (Eds.), *How to Get Published in the Best Management Journals* (second edition) (pp. 215–219). Edward Elgar Publishing, Cheltenham, UK and Northampton, MA, USA.

King, S. (2000) *On Writing: A Memoir of the Craft*. Hodder and Stoughton, London.

Nairn, A., Berthon, P. and Money, A. (2007) Learning from Giants. *International Journal of Market Research*, 49(2), 257–274.

Palmatier, R.W. (2016) Improving Publishing Success at JAMs: Contribution and Publishing. *Journal of the Academy of Marketing Science*, 44, 655–659.

Strunk, E.B. and White, W. (1999) *The Elements of Style*. Pearson, Harlow.

Wright, M., Ketchen, D.J. and Clark, T. (Eds.) (2020a) *How to Get Published in the Best Management Journals* (second edition). Edward Elgar Publishing, Cheltenham, UK and Northampton, MA, USA.

Wright, M., Ketchen, D.J. and Clark, T. (2020b) Publishing in Management: Exhilaration, Bafflement and Frustration. In: Wright, M., Ketchen, D.J. and Clark, T. (Eds.), *How to Get Published in the Best Management Journals* (second edition) (pp. 1–11). Edward Elgar Publishing, Cheltenham, UK and Northampton, MA, USA.

5. The Herculean task of making a contribution to the scholarship of tourism

Freya Higgins-Desbiolles

INTRODUCTION

"In what ways can your research make a contribution to your discipline?" – a guiding question for shaping a research career.

Hercules is one of the most popular characters in Greek mythology. He was the son of the chief deity Zeus and a mortal woman Alcmene, thereby situating him at the uncomfortable threshold between divine and mortal. He was challenged with 12 nearly impossible labours and thus became the symbol of "Herculean" challenges and difficulties. Doctoral students and early career scholars are similarly placed at a threshold, between advanced learners and accomplished scholars. Their Herculean challenges outnumber the mere 12 bestowed upon the legendary Hercules many times over in a demanding and metrics-driven tourism academy.

One of the most daunting challenges for emerging scholars of tourism is the obligation to make a contribution to the scholarship of tourism through one's work. At these early stages of career, one is often focused on gaining tenured employment in what is an increasingly challenging, competitive and precarious environment. It is often the role of academic mentors to guide one along the path to understanding the field, identifying gaps in knowledge and working collaboratively to accomplish this goal until such time that one is skilled and confident in one's own place in the tourism academy. Newer developments witness an emphasis on working in teams, collaborative approaches and forming "labs" as one pathway to ensure scholarly impact and contribution (Ren, Jóhannesson & van der Duim, 2017).

In the PhD process and in academic research, a key requirement for degree award and also for publication is making an original contribution to knowledge. For instance, one of the preeminent academic journals of tourism, the *Annals of Tourism Research*, advises in its "Guide to Authors": "Purely descriptive research, which does not contribute to the development of knowledge is not considered suitable" (*Annals of Tourism Research*, n.d.). It is not difficult to imagine how challenging this is when one may be new to tourism studies and also when there have been decades of research-producing volumes of publications preceding one's entry into the field.

General advice for doctoral candidates suggests starting with an extensive review of the literature which then assists in identifying gaps in knowledge. This is followed by articulating research questions, identifying suitable research methods and then embarking on data collection, all directed to filling this identified gap. Ladik and Stewart simplify this into a triangular model suggesting one can identify one's unique contribution to knowledge sitting at the intersection where the interwoven domains of concept, context and method come together (2008, pp. 161–163). However, while making logical sense, such advice has proven insufficient for driving solutions to this perennial issue in academia of how one makes a unique contribution in such an oversaturated knowledge space. Tesch et al. (2015) reinforce this insight as their work suggested that the requirement to make an original contribution to knowledge remains ill-defined; from their study, they found that originality, creativity and innovation provide a surer (though not entirely risk-free) pathway to success.

There are a number of helpful articles that have provided invaluable advice on making a contribution to knowledge in scholarship in many fields (e.g., Boer et al., 2015; Corley & Geoia, 2011; Ladik & Stewart, 2008). These stand as recommended reading in conjunction with this chapter as they are specifically focused on making a contribution to tourism studies knowledge. This chapter will begin by analysing how the nature of tourism studies is conducive to making a contribution to scholarship. It will then examine the well-known strategies and framings that scholars have employed to enact and claim contributions to knowledge. The discussion then moves to emerging opportunities presented by critical tourism approaches, new "turns" in tourism and the recent entry of diverse knowledges in the tourism studies domain. Finally, we engage with the recently posed question considering if there are too many tourism publications and what impacts this might have in diminishing tourism scholarship. This chapter offers some recommendations, suggested readings and challenging questions in an effort to help guide emerging scholars on their learning journeys in tourism.

TOURISM STUDIES: THE OPPORTUNITIES OF ILL-DEFINITION AND POROUS BOUNDARIES

The existential question in tourism studies is "what is tourism"? At a superficial level, it is easy to note the popular tendency to slip in terminology from "tourism" to "travel"; often a signal that the speaker wants to distance themselves from "mass" tourism. But this question holds much deeper meaning to our scholarship of tourism, signifying fundamental debates and discourses in tourism studies.

In order to make a contribution to a discipline, one should ideally understand the nature of one's discipline very well. However, tourism can be problematic in a number of ways for such well-intentioned efforts. The first issue is whether tourism can even be considered a "discipline" (and hence why this chapter frequently opts for the term "tourism studies"). Writing in 1997, Echtner and Jamal referred to Kuhn's analysis of paradigms and proposed tourism was then in a "prescience" phase (p. 875). Their assessment of the situation was that tourism studies thereby suffered from a lack of legitimacy and stood theoretically fragmented as a result of drawing from its parent disciplines. Their solution was to call for interdisciplinarity and a generation of a tourism body of knowledge. In contrast, Tribe argued for accepting the "indiscipline" of tourism in order to embrace all of its diversity (including its sociological aspects and its business aspects) (1997). This foundational issue continues to arise periodically (Barca, 2011; Fennell, 2023).

Over the course of time, many "state-of-the-field" articles have been published (Tribe, 2006). It remains true that tourism is a relatively new field of studies, is tainted with a vocational association and struggles to be taken seriously (Fidgeon, 2010, p. 706; Hall, 2005). Franklin and Crang (2001) noted the poverty of tourism theory and failure to strongly engage social and cultural theory in the face of business and policy dominance of the field. Tribe and Liburd (2016) offered an attempted comprehensive analysis of the tourism knowledge system which arguably represents one of the more complex and thorough analyses of tourism studies. Most recently, Fennell presented his own terminology of "tourisation" and argued post-COVID-19 we might best characterise tourism as "… a 'pandiscipline' which synthesizes concepts and theories from other disciplines to better describe and explain tourism-related phenomena" (2023, p. 259).

Consequently, making a contribution to the scholarship of tourism is simultaneously made more complex and also made easier by the fact that tourism is a complex phenomenon that overlaps with many other forces. For instance, tourism is strongly associated with hospitality, leisure, recreation and business, but it is in fact distinct from these important phenomena. Tourism has been explained through notable binaries, including: "impacts-externalities" versus "business-development" (Echtner & Jamal, 1997, p. 878); tourism management versus tourism studies (Robinson, 2012, p. xxvii); and tourism as an industry versus tourism as a social force (Higgins-Desbiolles, 2006). Additionally, approaches to the study of tourism may originate from many disciplines, including anthropology, sociology, business, economics, ecology, geography, politics, psychology, peace and conflict studies.

These understandings of tourism studies have material implications to setting out strategies for making a contribution to the field. For instance, if tourism studies is accepted as focused on business concerns or a vocational field of study, is it enough to make a contribution to better industry practice through one's scholarship? The knowledge binaries of tourism as an "industry" versus tourism as a focus of social science study might present different responses to this question, with the latter perhaps requiring theoretical contributions in order to be published. With increasing emphasis on industry engagement, practical contributions are gaining in appreciation in the tourism academy (as well as encouraging more diverse research dissemination strategies beyond just academic publications).

FIRST TAKE: A FIVE STRATEGY TYPOLOGY FOR ASSERTING KNOWLEDGE CONTRIBUTIONS IN TOURISM

Doran, Pomfret and Adu-Ampong provided a helpful example of making an upfront claim of one's contribution (in an article presenting research analysis of how other researchers have asserted such claims): "in this paper, we make a rare contribution to the tourism literature by examining the language used by authors to make claims of academic originality and contribution in the field of adventure tourism" (2022, p. 238). Employing the Preferred Reporting Items for Systematic Reviews and Meta-Analyses (PRISMA) protocol, they identified five knowledge contribution strategies or framings – incremental, differentiated-context, revelatory, replicatory and consolidatory (Doran et al., 2022). This corresponded to Nicholson et al.'s (2018) earlier typology developed from their study of industrial marketing.

The incremental framing seeks to fill small gaps in the literature, identify neglected aspects of a topic, or address topics where there is disagreement or confusion. Differentiated-context strategies carve out their novel contributions to knowledge by examining different contexts (e.g., geographies, niches, etc.) for tourism phenomena already studied. Revelatory approaches seek novel, surprising insights which can be accomplished by challenging disciplinary dogma or by drawing on external theories and frameworks to devise novel insights into tourism. Replicatory strategies entail repeating earlier studies to substantiate findings and further investigate their value; in the case of such studies, however, it may be more difficult to argue their value in terms of original contributions to the field (Doran et al., 2022, pp. 240–241). Finally, there are consolidatory strategies based on reviews of the existing literature, systematic reviews and meta-analyses, which may illuminate important new insights and connections. Of course, to be successful in publishing any of these types of work, one's framing of the contribution should be backed up by actually fulfilling the claim.

Not all strategies for securing knowledge contribution are necessarily valued equally, however. In Sandberg and Alvesson's (2011) review of 52 articles on organisational studies, they explored the possibilities of "gap-spotting" and "problematisation" as pathways to making a contribution. They found that gap-spotting dominated despite the fact that, in their assessment, work that "challenges assumptions that underlie existing literature" is more interesting and influential (Sandberg & Alvesson, 2011, p. 23).

Doran et al.'s (2022) analysis highlights some of the drawbacks that arise from this dictate for scholars to make an original contribution to tourism studies' knowledge through their scholarly publications. The lack of respect for replicatory studies may work against consolidation of tourism studies' knowledge. Additionally, it may result in fragmentation of tourism theory as "scholars jump from one topic to the next in search of originality" (Doran et al., 2022, p. 241). Finally, it may also lead to stagnation if classic theories are not revisited, revised and possibly replaced through repeated re-examination.

OPPORTUNITIES IN CRITIQUE AND DISSENT: CRITICAL TOURISM

In the effort to establish tourism studies as a discipline and ensure it is taken seriously in academia, there has been some attempt to develop a consensus on an agreed body of tourism theories. However, we must not overlook the purpose and value of divergence, critique and dissent as a "feature in knowledge production" (Fuller, 2014, p. 10). Critical tourism scholarship in particular offers opportunities for critique and dissent in tourism studies that provides fertile ground for new contributions.

Critical tourism scholarship has ushered in new ways of thinking about tourism and promising new lines of enquiry. Bianchi explained that critical tourism seeks to "... find ways of integrating the study of discourse with ongoing, as well as material forms of power (and, as such) ... constitutes a radical departure from the status quo in Tourism Studies" (2009, p. 498). Veijola et al. (2014) have presented their thoughts on "disruptive tourism" which Tribe and Liburd described as embarking on a "... mission to break the rules of conventional knowledge and disrupt the habitual in tourism and its scholarship" (2017, p. 227). Such approaches are arguably models of the revelatory framings that Doran et al. outlined (2022).

Critical tourism scholarship has advanced considerably in the last decade and has found some acceptance in certain tourism academic journals (see, for example, Bramwell & Lane, 2014). However, tourism studies is still dominated by those with a conservative, pro-positivistic predilection and this may present subtle limits for freedom of enquiry in tourism studies. This was signalled by Tribe when he stated: "A key issue that emerges is whether there are factors at work defining the do-able in research, legitimizing certain views and obscuring others" (2006, p. 361). This underscores the imperative to engage with the journal that one wants to publish in by not only reading its aims and scope, but also reading its editorials (such as Bramwell & Lane's referred to above) and additionally assessing the manuscripts recently accepted for publication to gain better insights into what work is welcomed in that journal.

The roles of "turns" in tourism is significant for novel and revelatory approaches. The term "turn" describes analytical shifts in disciplinary thinking. There have been a number of turns in tourism, including the critical turn (Ateljevic, Morgan & Pritchard, 2007), the moral turn (Caton, 2012), the decolonial turn (Chambers & Buzinde, 2015), the story turn (Moscardo, 2021), the local turn (Higgins-Desbiolles & Bigby, 2022) and the newest, the relational turn (Pernecky, 2023). Turns, by their very nature, are conducive to opportunities for novel contributions because they mark a new perspective on disciplinary knowledges and values.

DIVERSE AND PLURIVERSAL KNOWLEDGES IN TOURISM

Until very recently, tourism studies has suffered limitations resulting from the dominance of Western-centric knowledges and the hegemony of the English language (Chambers & Buzinde, 2015). The imperative to better engage with non-Anglo-Western perspectives and worldviews has increased as non-Western students and scholars grow in numbers in the tourism academy, as well as the increasing number of non-Western tourists that tourism scholars study (see Winter, 2009). Transformations are underway heralding change that presents promising opportunities for emerging scholars to explore valuable and new original contributions to knowledge. This includes Indigenous (Smith, 1999), decolonial (Grosfoguel, 2007) and Global South epistemologies (De Sousa Santos & Meneses, 2020).

There is a critical question concerning who can appropriately offer contributions from decolonial, Indigenous and Global South epistemologies: Should only Global South scholars work in this emerging scholarly space in tourism studies? An affirmative answer is justified on multiple grounds: to rectify the historical imbalance favouring Western hegemony; to surrender space in the academy for marginalised and oppressed voices to explore, build and share their knowledges; and also, to better ensure integrity to the worldview. It was in such a spirit that it was announced on TriNet that a new section of the *World*

Leisure Journal would allow for short commentaries from scholars based in the Global South. Its focus:

> …will aim to evidence the diversity related to leisure practices and concepts beyond the Eurocentric, Anglophonic and Global North world. We know that colonial narratives in leisure studies have been privileged, and we want to open spaces to decentralise and decolonise academic thinking.
> Decentralising academic thinking is to consider different realities and points of view. It is to seek a balance of stories and narratives to minimise stereotypes. Decolonising academic thinking is how we rethink and reframe research, curriculum, and educational practices that have traditionally upheld Eurocentric, Anglophonic, and pro-colonial views. (Chief Editor Sandro Carnicelli, 3 April 2023, email announcement on TriNet)

Knowledges drawn from a space of pluriversality may offer a different response to the question of who can justly conduct decolonial forms of research and analysis. Drawing inspiration from a multitude of influences, including post-development studies and grounded community epistemologies, pluriversality also offers new vistas for tourism studies. Mignolo claims he first heard the term "pluriverse" during the early stages of the Zapatista movement in Mexico, where the term was used to describe a "… decolonial political vision of a world in which many worlds could coexist …" (2018, p. ix).

Pluriversal approaches have already shown promise in opening up new possibilities for tourism studies by allowing space for many forms of knowledge and novel possibilities for tourism's value (e.g., Bellato, Frantzeskaki & Nygaard, 2023; Everingham, Peters & Higgins-Desbiolles, 2021). It offers a counter to the limitations of the universalising, modernist Western knowledge framings which work to narrow tourism to its instrumental, developmentalist uses.

The wealth of these diverse knowledges in transforming tourism research and teaching practices is only just beginning to be explored. One glimpse into the alternative ways of being, knowing and doing was revealed by a recent interview with Max Liboiron published in *Nature* (Ramen, 2023). Here they discuss their anti-colonial feminist research practices as values-based science. One insight offered is the practice of community peer review, through which the collaborating communities shape the research questions and ground the work of the research in their knowledges, their concerns and their needs. Not only is this value-full, responsive research (not customary in science disciplines particularly), it is also in its essence original and impactful. An example from within tourism studies is the work based on Māori cosmologies by Mika and Scheyvens which offered a unique framework for Indigenous tourism (2022).

A COUNTER-INTUITIVE: PUBLISH LESS TO STRENGTHEN THE TOURISM DISCIPLINE

Today, there is a pressure to publish frequently and to make rather grandiose claims to amplify one's work in the competitive game of winning opportunities that are the necessary steps to tenure and promotion. This leads to a pressure to game the system through massive outputs (through, for example, "salami slicing"; see Jackson et al., 2014) and sometimes dubious practices of collaborating with outputting teams (see Pruschak & Hopp, 2022). Slips in ethics are encouraged when doctoral supervisors, recognising the value of doctoral students' work sitting at the cutting edge, place their name on their students' publications even when it contravenes ethical codes for co-authorship (see Scott, 2022). Clearly, the metrics-driven, managerial university system is placing pressures to publish that have deleterious impacts on the quality of work being produced and the ethics of the academy.

With little sense of irony, tourism journal editors McKercher and Dolnicar (2022) asked in their article if we are overwhelmed with too much tourism scholarship (which they numbered at publication of 10,752 articles per year):

> Are we publishing too many articles? Assuming each journal article makes a significant contribution, how many significant contributions could one expect would be generated in a year? How many of the 10,752 articles present a new idea, advance knowledge, or fill a genuine research gap? How many inspire us? (p. 1)

With these critical questions, they raised concerns that tourism scholars Lee and Benjamin responded to: "With 10,752 articles published alone in 2021 and the pace of academic publishing accelerating at an unyielding pace, what we and our students face today is the deflation of academic knowledge" (2023, p. 2). As we contemplate making a contribution to scholarly tourism knowledge, these insights challenge us to think more critically on the tasks before us in building our research careers.

In fact, according to Collini, original contributions might be best secured by publishing less and writing more:

> …the truth is that one of the main obstacles to genuine intellectual productivity in contemporary academia is that most scholars publish too much. I do not say that they *write* too much: "write more and publish less" is a valuable injunction, encouraging us to explore our thinking more, and only to publish when we are sure we have something worth saying. (2016, p. v)

SOME OTHER RECOMMENDATIONS

Dedication to the Work of Scholarship

While there has been a small backlash about the excessive demands of current academic workload (see Lee & Benjamin, 2023) and a championing of slow scholarship (Berg & Seeber, 2016), one must do some dedicated work to make a contribution. This is best underpinned by curiosity and reading widely. New insights into tourism studies can arise from many inspirations, including the news, the arts, film, other disciplines, and one's own hobbies and personal interests. A successful and balanced approach might be best secured through a commitment to "life-long learning" (see Cuffy, Tribe & Airey, 2012) – something that is often included in our teaching and learning matrices. Nevertheless, those that are in precarious employment in tourism academia may not have the luxury of pursuing a slow scholarship strategy (and precarity is growing in academia in these challenging times).

Risk Taking Through Creative and Disruptive Work

Tesch et al. (2015) explained that creativity and taking unique pathways may be a solid approach to making a contribution. Tribe and Liburd similarly argued that there is greater opportunity for tourism research "… to be much more creative, experimental and imaginative. Very little tourism research is represented using poetry, drama, painting, sculpture, opera, dance, installations, video, photography, performance or story-telling …" (2016, p. 57). A recent example is accessible in the work of Erwin and Sturm (2022, p. 515) who employed interactive performance to create an "… *in situ*, liminal, emotive peace tourism experience …" to demonstrate that intercultural encounters can change conflict situations.

Another strategy, following Sandberg and Alvesson's advice (2011, p. 23) is to undertake work that seeks originality through challenging the knowledge base of the field. This is also in line with the "disruptive" approach advocated by Veijola et al. (2014). One example is found in the work of Higgins-Desbiolles et al. (2019) who proposed rethinking the tourism system by defining tourism through a focus on the local "host" community, rather than the traditional focus on the tourism industry and the tourists.

There are also opportunities to look at a given topic from multiple angles and identify novel insights that might arise from this approach. An example can be found in the application of moral theory to efforts to develop a framework for quantifying and attributing reparations to major carbon fuel producers to address climate change (see Grasso & Heede, 2023). The grounding in moral theory worked to "reframe the debate on international climate funding by focusing on the financial responsibility of fossil fuel companies for climate harm …" (Lakhani, 2023, n.p.).

Finding the Right Journal Outlet

The number of academic journals focused on tourism and affiliated studies has proliferated in recent times. Researching and finding the best journal for one's research is another of the tasks that is essential to success. Most scholars will have a tendency to gravitate to a focused set of journals that resonate with their portfolio of research work and interests (perhaps characterised by topic focus, or by qualitative/quantitative methods, for example). Following those journals' editorials and communications of changing focus would be a wise practice (for the *Journal of Tourism and Hospitality Management*, see Sigala et al., 2021).

It is interesting to note that a newer journal, the *Annals of Tourism Research Empirical Insights*, has emerged as a "companion title to the highly-regarded *Annals of Tourism Research* and publishes empirically-based full research articles and research notes where findings have implications beyond the study context, and are relevant to a broader audience of academy, policy and/or industry practitioners" (*Annals of Tourism Research Empirical Insights*, n.d.). One of the editors-in-chief of this journal noted in a TriNet discussion that this journal intentionally "… neither requires nor expects a novel theoretical contribution and welcomes replication studies" (Editor-in-Chief Ksenia Kirillova, email communication, 26 May 2023). Such insights reinforce the wisdom of continually working to stay informed of journal aims and scopes.

CONCLUSION

It takes dedicated hard work to build knowledge and insights into the multifaceted and ever-changing phenomenon of tourism. However, equally true is that the diversity of the tourism phenomena offers many opportunities of interest and one is only limited by one's passion and creativity to carve out a space for making valuable contributions to knowledge.

As this chapter comes to its conclusion, we might also reflexively consider what values motivate our work, as per Tribe and Liburd:

> We are all part of a knowledge production machine, the elements of which are often hidden or taken for granted (black boxed). If we wish to claim greater agency and participate in research for a better world we need to have a sophisticated understanding of how this machine works so that we might mobilise our forces for greater agency and more mindful research and impact in the world (of tourism). (2016, p. 59)

Tourism is an important force for building positive futures for people and places around the world. In asking critical questions of ourselves as we work to make scholarly contributions, we can build a research career with impact and value. Additionally, if we bring our whole selves, our values-filled, creative, playful, artistic, curious selves, to our endeavours our horizons expand further than we can imagine. This, coincidentally, shrinks the "daunting challenge" posed by the necessity to make a contribution to tourism scholarship.

ACKNOWLEDGEMENTS

The requirement to make an original contribution to knowledge can unfortunately also induce a competitive and boastful attitude. To soften this tendency, we might all acknowledge that our brilliant and "original" insights arise from the influences of those who come before us, those who have walked with us as mentors and also those we have inducted into these pathways, our students and research collaborators. I acknowledge and say thanks for the inspirational work of my colleagues, the many generous TriNet conversations and the editors who have shepherded this valuable project (with the usual caveats that all faults, omissions and deficiencies remain with the author).

REFERENCES

Annals of Tourism Research (n.d.). Guide to authors. Retrieved 13 May 2023, from: https://www.elsevier.com/journals/annals-of-tourism-research/0160-7383/guide-for-authors.

Annals of Tourism Research Empirical Insights (n.d.). Retrieved 12 June 2023, from: https://www.sciencedirect.com/journal/annals-of-tourism-research-empirical-insights.

Ateljevic, I., Morgan, N. & Pritchard, A. (2007). *The Critical Turn in Tourism Studies* Oxford: Elsevier.

Barca, M. (2011). Third Academic Tourism Education Conference: The scientific state of tourism as a discipline. *Anatolia*, 22(3), 428–430, DOI:10.1080/13032917.2011.640883.

Bellato, L., Frantzeskaki, N. & Nygaard, C.A. (2023). Regenerative tourism: A conceptual framework leveraging theory and practice. *Tourism Geographies*, 25(4), 1026–1046, DOI:10.1080/14616688.2022.2044376.

Berg, M. & Seeber, B.K. (2016). *The Slow Professor: Challenging the Culture of Speed in the Academy*. Toronto: University of Toronto Press.

Bianchi, R.V. (2009). The "critical turn" in tourism studies: A radical critique. *Tourism Geographies*, 11(4), 484–504, DOI:10.1080/14616680903262653.

Boer, H., Holweg, M., Kilduf, M., Pagell, M., Schmenner, R. & Voss, C. (2015). Making a meaningful contribution to theory. *International Journal of Operations and Production Management*, 35(9), 1231–1252.

Bramwell, B. & Lane, B. (2014). The "critical turn" and its implications for sustainable tourism research. *Journal of Sustainable Tourism*, 22(1), 1–8, DOI:10.1080/09669582.2013.855223.

Caton, K. (2012). Taking the moral turn in tourism studies. *Annals of Tourism Research*, 39(4), 1906–1928, DOI:10.1016/j.annals.2012.05.021.

Chambers, D. & Buzinde, C. (2015). Tourism and decolonisation: Locating research and self. *Annals of Tourism Research*, 51, 1–16, DOI:10.1016/j.annals.2014.12.002.

Collini, S. (2016). Foreword. In M. Berg & B.K. Seeber (Eds.), *The Slow Professor: Challenging the Culture of Speed in the Academy* (pp. iv–vi). Toronto: University of Toronto Press.

Corley, K.G. & Geoia, D.A. (2011). Building theory about theory building: What constitutes a theoretical contribution? *Academy of Management Review*, 36(1), 12–32.

Cuffy, V., Tribe, J. & Airey, D. (2012). Lifelong learning for tourism. *Annals of Tourism Research*, 39(3), 1402–1424, DOI:10.1016/j.annals.2012.02.007.

De Sousa Santos, B. & Meneses, M. (Eds.) (2020). *Knowledges Born in the Struggle: Constructing the Epistemologies of the Global South*. Abingdon: Routledge.

Doran, A., Pomfret, G. & Adu-Ampong, E.A. (2022). Mind the gap: A systematic review of the knowledge contribution claims in adventure tourism research. *Journal of Hospitality and Tourism Management*, 51, 238–251, DOI:10.1016/j.jhtm.2022.03.015.

Echtner, C.M. & Jamal, T.D. (1997). The disciplinary dilemma of tourism studies. *Annals of Tourism Research*, 24(4), 868–883.

Erwin, J. & Sturm, T. (2022). Living in the wake of rural Irish Troubles: Building an institution for sustainable peace through emotive out-of-place tourism. *Journal of Sustainable Tourism*, 30(2–3), 515–532, DOI:10.1080/09669582.2021.1912055.

Everingham, P., Peters, A. & Higgins-Desbiolles, F. (2021). The (im)possibilities of doing tourism otherwise: The case of settler colonial Australia and the closure of the climb at Uluru. *Annals of Tourism Research*, 88, 103178, DOI:10.1016/j.annals.2021.103178.

Fennell, D. (2023). Tourisation theory and the pandiscipline of tourism. *Journal of Travel Research*, 62(1), 259–262, DOI:10.1177/00472875221095217.

Fidgeon, P.R. (2010). Tourism education and curriculum design: A time for consolidation and review? *Tourism Management*, 31(6), 699–723, DOI:10.1016/j.tourman.2010.05.019.

Franklin, A. & Crang, M. (2001). The trouble with tourism and travel theory? *Tourist Studies*, 1(1), 5–22.

Fuller, S. (2014). *The Knowledge Book: Key Concepts in Philosophy, Science and Culture*. Abingdon: Routledge.

Grasso, M. & Heede, R. (2023). Time to pay the piper: Fossil fuel companies' reparations for climate damages. *One Earth*, 6(5), 459–463, DOI:10.1016/j.oneear.2023.04.012.

Grosfoguel, R. (2007). The epistemic decolonial turn. *Cultural Studies*, 21(2–3), 211–223, DOI:10.1080/09502380601162514.

Hall, C.M. (2005). *Tourism: Rethinking the Social Science of Mobility*. Harlow: Prentice Hall.

Higgins-Desbiolles, F. (2006). More than an "industry": The forgotten power of tourism as a social force. *Tourism Management*, 27(6), 1192–1208, DOI:10.1016/j.tourman.2005.05.020.

Higgins-Desbiolles, F. & Bigby, B.C. (Eds.) (2022). *The Local Turn in Tourism: Empowering Communities*. Bristol: Channel View.

Higgins-Desbiolles, F., Carnicelli, S., Krolikowski, C., Wijesinghe, G. & Boluk, K. (2019). Degrowing tourism: Rethinking tourism. *Journal of Sustainable Tourism*, 27(12), 1926–1944, DOI:10.1080/09669582.2019.1601732.

Jackson, D., Walter, G., Daly, J. & Cleary, M. (2014). Editorial. Multiple outputs from single studies: Acceptable division of findings vs. "salami" slicing. *Journal Of Clinical Nursing*, 23(1), 1–2, DOI:doi.org/doi:10.1111/jocn.12439.

Ladik, D.M. & Stewart, D.W. (2008). The contribution continuum. *Journal of the Academy of Marketing Science*, 36, 157–165, DOI:10.1007/s11747-008-0087-z.

Lakhani, N. (2023). Fossil fuel firms owe climate reparations of $209bn a year, says study. *The Guardian* (Online). Retrieved 22 May 2023, from: https:// www .theguardian .com/ environment/ 2023/ may/ 19/ fossil -fuel -firms -owe -climate -reparations-of-209bn-a-year-says-study.

Lee, K.-S. & Benjamin, S. (2023). The death of tourism scholarship ... unless ... . *Annals of Tourism Research*, 98, 103520, DOI:10.1016/j.annals.2022.103520.

McKercher, B. & Dolnicar, S. (2022). Are 10,752 journal articles per year too many? *Annals of Tourism Research*, 94, 103398.

Mignolo, W.D. (2018). Foreword. On pluriversality and multipolarity. In B. Reiter (Ed.), *Constructing the Pluriverse: The Geopolitics of Knowledge* (pp. ix–xvi). New York: Duke University Press.

Mika, J.P. & Scheyvens, R.A. (2022). Te Awa Tupua: Peace, justice and sustainability through Indigenous tourism. *Journal of Sustainable Tourism*, 30(2–3), 637–657, DOI:10.1080/09669582.2021.1912056.

Moscardo, G. (2021). The story turn in tourism: Forces and futures. *Journal of Tourism Futures*, 7(2), 168–173, DOI:10.1108/JTF-11-2019-0131.

Nicholson, J.D., LaPlaca, P., Al-Abdin, P., Breese, R. & Khan, Z. (2018). What do introduction sections tell us about the intent of scholarly work: A contribution on contributions. *Industrial Marketing Management*, 73, 206–219, DOI:10.1016/j. indmarman.2018.02.014.

Pernecky, T. (2023). Advancing critico-relational inquiry: Is tourism studies ready for a relational turn? *Journal of Sustainable Tourism*, DOI:10.1080/09669582.2023.22 11248.

Pruschak, G. & Hopp, C. (2022). And the credit goes to ... – Ghost and honorary authorship among social scientists. *PLoS ONE*, 17(5), e0267312, DOI:10.1371/ journal.pone.0267312.

Ramen, S. (2023). What it means to practise values-based research. *Nature*, Career Q & A. Retrieved 10 June 2023, from: https://www.nature.com/articles/d41586-023 -01878-1.

Ren, C., Jóhannesson, G.T. & van der Duim, R. (2017). *Co-creating Tourism Research: Towards Collaborative Ways of Knowing*. New York: Routledge.

Robinson, P. (Ed.) (2012). *Tourism: The Key Concepts*. London: Routledge.

Sandberg, J. & Alvesson, M. (2011). Ways of constructing research questions: Gap-spotting or problematization? *Organization*, 18(1), 23–44.

Scott, R.H. III (2022). Ensuring ethics and integrity in co-authorship. *AACSB*. Retrieved 10 June 2023, from: https://www.aacsb.edu/ insights/ articles/ 2022/ 11/ ensuring-ethics-and-integrity-in-co-authorship.

Sigala, M., Kumar, S., Donthu, N., Sureka, R. & Joshi, Y. (2021). A bibliometric over-view of the *Journal of Hospitality and Tourism Management*: Research contributions and influence. *Journal of Hospitality and Tourism Management*, 47, 273–288, DOI:10.1016/j.jhtm.2021.04.005.

Smith, L.T. (1999). *Decolonising Methodologies: Research and Indigenous Peoples*. London: Zed Books.

Tesch, J., Baptists, A.V., Frick, L., Holley, K. & Rimmick, M. (2015). The doctorate as an original contribution to knowledge: Considering relationships between original-ity, creativity, and innovation. *Frontline Learning Research*, 3(3), 51–63.

Tribe, J. (1997). The indiscipline of tourism. *Annals of Tourism Research*, 24(3), 638–657, DOI:10.1016/S0160-7383(97)00020-0.

Tribe, J. (2006). The truth about tourism. *Annals of Tourism Research*, 33(2), 360–381, DOI:10.1016/j.annals.2005.11.001.

Tribe, J. & Liburd, J.J. (2016). The tourism knowledge system. *Annals of Tourism Research*, 57, 44–61, DOI:10.1016/j.annals.2015.11.011.

Tribe, J. & Liburd, J.J. (2017). Tourism knowledge: A robust, adaptable system (reply to Isaac and Platenkamp). *Annals of Tourism Research*, 63, 226–227, DOI:10.1016/j. annals.2017.01.015.

Veijola, S., Molz, J.G., Pyyhtinen, O., Höckert, E. & Grit, A. (2014). *Disruptive Tourism and Its Untidy Guests: Alternative Ontologies for Future Hospitalities.* Basingstoke: Palgrave Macmillan.

Winter, T. (2009). Asian tourism and the retreat of Anglo-Western centrism in tourism theory. *Current Issues in Tourism*, 12(1), 21–31.

6. Getting the methods right

Rodolfo Baggio

INTRODUCTION

Since the very beginning of what we identify as modern science, the communication of ideas, theories, insights and findings has been considered the essence of knowledge dissemination and intellectual progress for the advancement of all disciplines. However, the simple act of sharing information has not been reputed sufficient to ensure the credibility and impact of a scholar's work. The way results are obtained, observations and experiments conducted, and interpretations or extensions formulated has been seen as a crucial element. The methodological approach is, after all, the main factor that marks the distinction between sparse studies of phenomena and systems and what today we recognize as "science" (Hansson, 2021).

The modern communication of science was born in the second half of the 17th century, when the members of the newly born scientific societies started to hold regular meetings to discuss their discoveries and disseminate their research findings in journals. Since the foundation of these societies, rules or guidelines were established for presenting and discussing ideas, theories, experiments and results with the aim of persuading the audience of the relevance and reliability of the work done (Lareo Martín & Montoya Reyes, 2007). This passed through two important elements: first, the clarity of the methods and techniques used, with an emphasis on the possibility to replicate the studies; and second, the opinions and comments of other scientists who were asked to review what was done. It must be noted however, that only very recently has the peer review become a standard step in the procedure followed for accepting and publishing a paper in a scientific journal. A well-known incident is the famous refusal by Albert Einstein, in 1936, to reply to the comments of an anonymous reviewer and his decision to withdraw the paper from the journal he had sent it to (Kennefick, 2005).

WHAT REVIEWERS VALUE: A LITTLE BACKGROUND

Now the question is: how do reviewers value the different aspects of the section of a paper that describes the methods used and how relevant is this evaluation for the acceptance of the paper?

As said above, the way in which a study has been conducted is of great importance for the validity of its results and for the possibility of replicating it, and is one of the cornerstones of what is called "scientific method". This is reflected in the main criteria by which reviewers judge a manuscript. The literature on this topic is relatively scarce, but no matter what the discipline is, there are clear indications on the importance of the methods section.

Ryan (1979, p. 1) explicitly writes that referees require: "a detailed description of the research method, including its appropriateness for the particular research and the precise ways in which the variables were measured and analyzed". Similar comments can be found in other papers that deal with the matter; in all of them the methods used are considered to be one of the top areas that are scrutinized and issues in the methodological approach taken are one of the major causes of rejection (see, e.g., Siler & Strang, 2017; Yuksel, 2003).

In particular for the tourism and hospitality domain, McKercher et al. (2007) analyse a significant number of reviews and demonstrate that the most common area where reviewers find flaws is methodology (74% of papers). Other studies also explicitly describe what these issues are and attribute the problems to the use of inappropriate statistical tests (or a lack of statistics altogether), unsuitable techniques used for answering the hypotheses, or using old techniques that have been surpassed by more recent or powerful approaches that provide more robust outcomes (Menon et al., 2022; Sanchez, Makkonen & Williams, 2019). Often then, as McKercher et al. (2007) state, communication problems are more common than technical flaws. Therefore, great care should be taken in writing this section.

One more consideration is in order here. Originality is a fundamental requirement in scholarly papers. If one of the objectives of scholarly research is to contribute new insights, theories and findings to the existing body of knowledge, then originality is the key aspect that distinguishes impactful research from mere repetition or replication. By presenting new ideas, theories or perspectives, researchers push the boundaries of understanding and stimulate intellectual discourse. At the same time, original research opens up opportunities for further investigation, allowing later researchers to build upon existing knowledge and explore new directions. Moreover, when presenting novel matters, they demonstrate their expertise, creativity and ability to think critically, thus enhancing the reputation and the impact of the work done.

Clearly, originality does not imply the complete absence of any influence of prior knowledge since new research is typically built upon existing theories, concepts and methods. Originality lies rather in the ability to combine existing know-how in new, innovative and meaningful ways (Buckley, 2023; Rodriguez Sanchez et al., 2022).

In this respect, methodology can be an ideal candidate for ensuring novel contributions to the field of study. Novelty and creativity in methodology can involve several elements. They can concern the development of entirely new techniques, not previously explored, to address research questions or phenomena. Or they can present innovative combinations of known and established methods, tailoring the components in order to solve the problem at hand. All of this can be expressed by presenting new frameworks, models or approaches, or by incorporating in original and ingenious components from existing methodologies, from the tourism and hospitality domain or from other disciplines (Kara, 2015).

METHODOLOGY AND METHODS: A SHORT DIGRESSION

Methodology and methods are terms often used interchangeably, but a difference exists. The original meaning of *methodology* referred to the exploration of how knowledge and inquiry were framed within academic disciplines or schools of thought. Therefore, rather than providing solutions, a methodology offers a theoretical perspective for identifying proper practices to address the research question. Over time, the meaning has expanded to encompass the design of a particular study and the set of procedures, tools and instruments used to conduct research. This includes the techniques for data gathering, management and analysis, as well as the implications of the study's outcomes. More precisely the term *method*, instead denotes the specific procedure and technique employed in the research process. Several different methods can be chosen for a particular study, and they are linked and justified within a methodology.

The effectiveness and significance of a research work depend greatly on the methodology employed. Therefore, providing a careful and rigorous description is essential when evaluating the quality and relevance of a scientific publication.

Research methodologies are commonly categorized into two classes reflecting, usually, quantitative and qualitative approaches. The choice between these approaches is commonly considered to depend on the researcher's perspectives and positions, the problem under examination, and the availability of suitable data. Quantitative investigations mainly utilize structured, numerical data, while qualitative approaches involve non-structured elements such as texts, images, video or audio recordings (for a summary see Pandey & Pandey, 2021).

Throughout the history of research in tourism and hospitality, various methodologies have been employed. From a historical perspective, the dominant research approach was quantitative in the mid-20th century, with a growing sophistication in the use of statistical techniques. However, since the early 1990s, there has been an increase in mixed-methods research. In fact, it has been recognized that both qualitative and quantitative methods possess almost equally strengths and weaknesses (Choy, 2014) and the boundaries between the two are not always rigid so that some phenomena can be better understood through a combination of both methodologies (Davies, 2003; Kelle, 2006).

For example, a study on tourist behaviour might employ quantitative surveys to gather data on travel patterns and preferences, while also conducting qualitative interviews to explore the underlying motivations and emotions driving those behaviours (see Gao et al., 2022). Complex networked systems like tourism destinations often require mixed-methods techniques that integrate both quantitative and qualitative methods to provide more comprehensive and meaningful analyses (Mariani & Baggio, 2020).

By using mixed-methods approaches, researchers can provide a more nuanced and multifaceted analysis of the subject matter. Mixed-methods can provide investigators with better ways to explore the complex interactions between tourists, host communities and the environment, and the dynamic characteristics of these interconnections ultimately provide results in explaining complex social issues that are more accurate than those that rely on either qualitative or quantitative methods alone (Creswell, 2003; Khoo-Lattimore, Mura & Yung, 2019).

The recent advances in artificial intelligence, machine learning and data digitization have further blurred the lines between qualitative and quantitative methodologies. These technological developments now allow researchers to work with any combination of structured and non-structured data (qualitative and quantitative), leading to more creative and impactful research perspectives in the field of tourism and hospitality (Mariani, 2020; Schweinfest & Jansen, 2021; Tiguint & Hossari, 2020).

Overall, the integration of different methodologies in tourism and hospitality research can pave the way for new and innovative lines of inquiry, contributing to the development of methodologies uniquely tailored to the tourism domain.

WRITING THE METHODS SECTION

The methodology section serves to describe the actions taken and the approach adopted for answering the research question. The main objective is to allow readers to evaluate the credibility and the validity of the research findings and to let them, at least in principle, replicate the study. In this section, it is therefore important to cover all the key aspects of the research process.

In essence, this section supplies a detailed account of the research design. This can be considered as the strategic agenda of the project, providing insight into how the study is conducted. It shows how various components of the research, such as samples, measures, treatments or programs, are combined and used to address the research questions. The research design works in the same way as an architectural outline, translating logical concepts into a series of procedures that optimize the actions taken for validating and exploiting the data for a specific problem. The research design aims to "plan, structure, and execute" the research in order to maximize the "validity of the findings" (Mouton & Marais, 1996, p. 175). It comprises everything from the philosophical and epistemological assumptions to the design of the research and the collection of the data. It can be informally described as an action plan that guides the journey from the initial set of questions to a set of answers (Yin, 2003, p. 19).

Obviously, the nature of the research conducted needs to be clear, so it might be worth repeating at the beginning of the methodology section what the specific problem or research questions are. Then the basic elements described here are the data required and the methods used, together with other tools or materials that might have been employed in the work presented. The section is typically written in the past tense because by the time of writing the study is completed.

Although the order of the elements is not crucial, it might be advisable to put first those more relevant for the research described and those that more contribute to the originality so much sought after by journal editors and reviewers.

A possible outline is the following:

Introduction

The section starts with a brief account of the methodological approach used to investigate the problem at hand. The selection of the methodology plays a crucial role in ensuring the appropriateness and effectiveness of the research design. An appropriate choice enables researchers to address the question effectively and achieve the desired objectives. Here the author will delve into the different aspects of the methodological approach, including its connection to the overall research design, the research instruments employed, the data analysis techniques, the provision of background information, the sampling process and the consideration of research limitations. If needed, some ontological and epistemological considerations are also illustrated.

Ontology refers to our beliefs about the nature of reality and the social world, focusing on what exists and what can be known. It involves assumptions about the objective or subjective nature of social entities (Smith, 2012). Epistemology, on the other hand, relates to our understanding of knowledge and how it is acquired (Steup & Ram, 2020). These philosophical positions form the foundation for the *modus operandi* chosen by the researcher and for the accumulation of the findings (Ayikoru, 2009). What a researcher chooses, in fact, cannot be completely value-free since their values always influence the whole process. Therefore, occupying a chosen position helps authors define their views and understandings in the creation of knowledge, and having a clear philosophical research position enriches the methodologies and the designs applied in a particular domain.

Methodological Approach

The methodological approach adopted in the study is stated and discussed here. Quantitative, qualitative or mixed-methods will inform the next parts dealing with the details of the data, procedures and other materials used for the study. Here, as for the literature review section, it is useful to provide a brief account of the sources examined while researching a particular methodological topic, citing those reputed more relevant for the choice and application of what is used. It is important, however, not to limit such a review to a description of the different sources but to complement it with an explanation of the selection operated and of the use made, and to show how the information coming from these sources has been organized and interpreted.

Relevance to Research Design

The chosen methodological approach must be closely aligned with the research problem to ensure the achievement of the research objectives. It is crucial to establish a clear connection between the methods employed and the research problem being investigated. In this part the authors will also make clear what the novelty or the contributions to the knowledge domain are if this is the main point supporting the originality of what is presented as discussed above.

Research Instruments and Data Collection

Research instruments are the tools employed to collect data for analysis, together with the criteria used for selecting them or the sampling technique used. These instruments can vary depending on the chosen methodology. In quantitative research, common research instruments include surveys, question-naires and psychometric scales. These tools enable researchers to efficiently gather numerical data from a large number of elements or participants. In qual-itative research, instruments may include interview guides, observation protocols and document analysis frameworks. These instruments aid in capturing rich and detailed information regarding individuals' perspectives, behaviours and social contexts. On the other hand, when using archival research or analysing existing data, providing background information about the documents and their origins is crucial to ensure transparency and credibility.

In this part, the assessment of the quality of what is collected is also presented (Pipino, Lee & Wang, 2002). The main point here concerns the following aspects (all or the most important for the study):

- Timeliness: the degree to which the data are available at the time needed;
- Completeness: the degree to which all necessary data are available;
- Accuracy: the degree to which data represent the situation examined;
- Uniqueness: the degree to which data are unique and cannot be confused with other entities;
- Validity: the degree to which the data comply with requirements such as formats, types and ranges; and
- Consistency: the degree to which data, if collected in different places, match or not.

This assessment is especially important when the sources for the data used are digital online platforms or environments (Cai & Zhu, 2015).

Finally, since it is quite common to face problems when collecting or generating data, the author should not ignore them or pretend they did not occur. Detailing how the obstacles met were overcome can be a noteworthy part of this section as it provides the reader with a sound justification for the decisions made to minimize the impact of any problems encountered.

Data Analysis

The data analysis process is determined by the methodology chosen and the nature of the data collected. In quantitative research, statistical analysis techniques such as descriptive statistics, inferential statistics and regression analysis are commonly employed to examine relationships, test hypotheses and derive meaningful inferences from numerical data. In qualitative research, data analysis involves thematic analysis, content analysis or discourse analysis, which focus on identifying patterns, themes and meanings within textual or observational data. Mixed-methods research integrates both quantitative and qualitative data analysis approaches for identifying recurrent themes and patterns within the data, provides insights into the subjective experiences and perspectives of participants and, in essence, gain a comprehensive understanding of the research problem. Theoretical perspectives can also be employed to interpret and explain the observed behaviours and patterns. Existing theories and frameworks relevant to the research problem are surveyed to provide a comprehensive understanding of the phenomenon under investigation.

The reporting of the process followed is of high importance and should concisely include all of the major aspects including the actions taken for cleaning and preprocessing the data, the samples used and their validity, and the software tools used. A practice of growing diffusion in other disciplines is that of asking (often requiring) the attachment (as separate additional materials) of the data used and the software scripts with which the analyses were conducted if no common applications were employed. In the tourism and hospitality domain, this is not yet a widespread habit but some journals have started to suggest this routine.

There are many possible ways of correctly and thoroughly reporting the methods and techniques used. Given the wealth of possible methods, in case of doubts it is suggested to consult one of the guidelines available, such as the one published by the American Psychological Association (APA, 2010), the OECD *Frascati Manual* (OECD, 2015), or books such as the one by Baggio and Klobas (2017) for quantitative methods and Denzin and Lincoln (2023) for qualitative approaches.

It is also important to provide some background information when using methods (or combinations of methods) that may be unfamiliar to the readers. This ensures that they (and mainly the reviewers) have a clear understanding of the methodology and its relevance to the research context. Explaining the meaning in a concise and comprehensive manner establishes a solid foundation to comprehend the design and interpret the findings accurately. When such explanations might require large spaces the author can summarize the main concepts and provide a list of relevant literature.

Ethical Considerations

There are several ethical considerations that researchers need to take into account during the data gathering and presentation process, mainly if the study involves human participation. This, in many countries, is ensured through the approval of an ethical committee, a fact that needs to be reported. When this is not strictly required it would be appropriate to briefly state what has been done for:

• Ensuring voluntary participation;
• Collecting consent to be involved;
• Safeguarding privacy;
• Ensuring confidentiality and anonymity;
• Evaluating possible impacts of the study on participants; and
• Ensuring objectivity throughout the research process.

By adhering to these ethical considerations, researchers demonstrate their commitment to conducting research with integrity and respect for the participants.

Addressing Methodological Limitations

Finally, it is worth acknowledging and addressing potential limitations that may have arisen during the study process. Practical limitations, such as time constraints or limited resources, can impact the data gathering process and potentially affect the generalizability of findings. By acknowledging these limitations, authors demonstrate their awareness of the potential challenges and their commitment to mitigating their impact on the research outcomes. It is crucial to provide a rationale for choosing a specific methodology despite the potential risks or limitations, emphasizing its strengths and alignment with the research problem.

Above is a full list of possible contents for the methodology section. Usually, a paper does not contain all of these elements but a careful choice must be made depending on the specific study in order to include the most relevant pieces. Since practically all journals have limitations on the length of the manuscript, it might be advisable to include detailed information in an appendix or in a document of supplementary materials, so as to keep the section concise, easily readable and comprehensible – otherwise the reading of the methodology section could be rather daunting and tedious and distract the reader (or the reviewer) from the comprehension and the appreciation of what was done.

Several possible mistakes seem to be quite common and are worth mentioning next.

Details

As said, it is essential to offer a well-defined and comprehensive account of the research design, sampling techniques, data collection methods and data analysis procedures. Moreover, it is important not to overlook any challenges encountered during the data handling process. but to describe how these issues were addressed. On the other hand, unnecessary information should be avoided. This includes, for example, superfluous explanations of basic or very common procedures, unless some relevant modifications have been made. The methodology section is not a step-by-step guide for a particular method, and any element that does not contribute to the understanding of why a specific method was chosen, or how the data were processed, should be discarded. The focus should be on how the author applied a method, rather than illustrating the mechanics of execution. It is normally assumed that readers already possess a fundamental understanding and at least an elementary awareness of basic or common methods and of how to investigate the research problem on their own. If some details of a basic technique is seen as critical, as said above, the researcher can refer to appropriate literature.

Lack of clarity

The methodology section should be written using clear and concise language, avoiding technical jargon or unnecessary complexity that may lead to confusion among readers because of unclear explanations such as, for example, using ambiguous terms to designate parameters or conditions. Also, the overuse or misuse of the passive voice may result in bad writing or grammar mistakes that can confuse readers.

Inconsistencies

Another error to avoid is inconsistencies in the section, where the research design, sampling techniques, data collection methods and data analysis procedures do not align or lack coherence. The same can be said about the terminology used. It is crucial to ensure that all elements of the section are consistent and aligned with the research objectives.

Lack of justification

The methodology section should include a justification for the chosen research methods and procedures. Often, this justification is absent, and authors fail to explain why a particular method was chosen over other options. It is essential, as already said above, to provide a justification for selecting the research methods and justify their suitability for the research objectives.

CLOSING REMARKS

The methodology section plays a crucial role in a scholarly paper, acting as its core foundation. By providing a detailed account of the study's design and execution, readers and reviewers are provided with all the information needed to understand the work done. Moreover, it shows authors' awareness of the philosophical and theoretical bases that guide their investigations and gives credibility and validity to the research outcomes. A well-designed and executed methodology ensures reliable and faithful results, while a flawed approach can endanger the integrity of the study. Furthermore, its significance lies in its potential to facilitate replication of the study. Replicability is a crucial aspect of academic research, as it allows others to validate and build upon previous findings. Additionally, a well-presented methodology can highlight the originality and novelty of the researchers' contributions.

The methodology section demands careful attention to its essential characteristics: clarity, conciseness, completeness and relevance. By observing these principles, researchers can ensure that their methodology not only enhances the quality of their work but also strengthens the credibility of their findings.

In this chapter, we have provided a brief exploration of the key meanings and aspects of a methodological approach. Moreover, we have offered a guideline for effectively compiling this vital section. By following these guidelines, researchers can improve the rigour and impact of their academic efforts and contribute meaningfully to their fields. Ultimately, a well-executed methodology section reinforces the scholarly foundation of the paper and enhances the broader understanding and knowledge of the scientific community.

REFERENCES

APA. (2010). *Publication Manual of the American Psychological Association* (6th ed.). American Psychological Association.

Ayikoru, M. (2009). Epistemology, ontology and tourism. In J. Tribe (Ed.), *Philosophical Issues in Tourism* (pp. 62–79). Channel View.

Baggio, R., & Klobas, J. (2017). *Quantitative Methods in Tourism: A Handbook* (2nd ed.). Channel View.

Buckley, R. (2023). Originality in research publication: Measure, concept, or skill? *Journal of Travel Research*, *62*(5), 1159–1163.

Cai, L., & Zhu, Y. (2015). The challenges of data quality and data quality assessment in the big data era. *Data Science Journal*, *14*, article 2.

Choy, L.T. (2014). The strengths and weaknesses of research methodology: Comparison and complimentary between qualitative and quantitative approaches. *IOSR Journal of Humanities and Social Science*, *19*(4), 99–104.

Creswell, J.W. (2003). *Research Design: Qualitative, Quantitative, and Mixed Methods Approaches* (2nd ed.). Sage.

Davies, B. (2003). The role of quantitative and qualitative research in industrial studies of tourism. *International Journal of Tourism Research*, *5*, 97–111.

Denzin, N.K., & Lincoln, Y.S. (Eds.) (2023). *Handbook of Qualitative Research* (6th ed.). Sage.

Gao, J., Zhang, Y., Chang, P.J. & Xiao, X. (2022). A mixed-methods study of the ways in which vacation factors Impact tourists' use of emotion regulation strategies. *Tourism Review International*, *26*(3), 289–306.

Hansson, S.O. (2021). Science and pseudo-science. In E.N. Zalta (Ed.), *The Stanford Encyclopedia of Philosophy* (Fall 2021 Edition). https://plato.stanford.edu/archives/fall2021/entries/pseudo-science/.

Kara, H. (2015). *Creative Research Methods in the Social Sciences: A Practical Guide*. Policy Press.

Kelle, U. (2006). Combining qualitative and quantitative methods in research practice: Purposes and advantages. *Qualitative Research in Psychology*, *3*(4), 293–311.

Kennefick, D. (2005). Einstein versus the *Physical Review*. *Physics Today*, *58*(9), 43–48.

Khoo-Lattimore, C., Mura, P. & Yung, R. (2019). The time has come: A systematic literature review of mixed methods research in tourism. *Current Issues in Tourism*, *22*(13), 1531–1550.

Lareo Martín, I., & Montoya Reyes, A. (2007). Scientific writing: Following Robert Boyle's principles in experimental essays – 1704 and 1998. *Revista alicantina de estudios ingleses, 20,* 119–137.

Mariani, M. (2020). Big data and analytics in tourism and hospitality: A perspective article. *Tourism Review, 75*(1), 299–303.

Mariani, M., & Baggio, R. (2020). The relevance of mixed methods for network analysis in tourism and hospitality research. *International Journal of Contemporary Hospitality Management, 32*(4), 1643–1673.

McKercher, B., Law, R., Weber, K., Song, H. & Hsu, C. (2007). Why referees reject manuscripts. *Journal of Hospitality & Tourism Research, 31*(4), 455–470.

Menon, V., Varadharajan, N., Praharaj, S.K. & Ameen, S. (2022). Why do manuscripts get rejected? A content analysis of rejection reports from the *Indian Journal of Psychological Medicine*. *Indian Journal of Psychological Medicine, 44*(1), 59–65.

Mouton, J., & Marais, H.C. (1996). *Basic Concepts in the Methodology of the Social Sciences.* HSRC Publishers.

OECD. (2015). *Frascati Manual 2015: Guidelines for Collecting and Reporting Data on Research and Experimental Development.* OECD Publishing.

Pandey, P., & Pandey, M.M. (2021). *Research Methodology Tools and Techniques.* Bridge Center.

Pipino, L.L., Lee, Y.W. & Wang, R.Y. (2002). Data quality assessment. *Communications of the ACM, 45*(4), 211–218.

Rodriguez Sanchez, I., Mantecón, A., Williams, A.M., Makkonen, T. & Kim, Y.R. (2022). Originality: The holy grail of tourism research. *Journal of Travel Research, 61*(6), 1219–1232.

Ryan, M. (1979). What some journal referees look for in evaluating manuscripts. *62nd Annual Meeting of the Association for Education in Journalism* (5–8 August), Houston, Texas.

Sanchez, I.R., Makkonen, T. & Williams, A.M. (2019). Peer review assessment of originality in tourism journals: Critical perspective of key gatekeepers. *Annals of Tourism Research, 77,* 1–11.

Schweinfest, S., & Jansen, R. (2021). Data science and official statistics: Toward a new data culture. *Harvard Data Science Review, 3*(4).

Siler, K., & Strang, D. (2017). Peer review and scholarly originality: Let 1,000 flowers bloom, but don't step on any. *Science, Technology, & Human Values, 42,* 29–61.

Smith, B. (2012). Ontology. In G. Hurtado & O. Nudler (Eds.), *The Furniture of the World – Essays in Ontology and Metaphysics* (pp. 47–68). Brill.

Steup, M., & Ram, N. (2020). Epistemology. In E.N. Zalta (Ed.), *The Stanford Encyclopedia of Philosophy* (Fall 2020 Edition). https://plato.stanford.edu/archives/fall2020/entries/epistemology/.

Tiguint, B., & Hossari, H. (2020). Big data analytics and artificial intelligence: A meta-dynamic capability perspective. *International Conference on Business Management, Innovation & Sustainability (ICBMIS)* (15–16 June), Dubai (AE).

Yin, R.K. (2003). *Case Study Research, Design and Methods* (3rd ed.). Sage.

Yuksel, A. (2003). Writing publishable papers. *Tourism Management, 24*(4), 437–446.

7. Writing a literature review

Noel Scott, Hafidh Al Riyami and Mohammad Soliman

INTRODUCTION

If you wish to write a good literature review, it is first important to understand how knowledge is created and distributed. The creation of new knowledge about a topic proceeds through a process of accumulation. The amount of accumulated knowledge about any topic is more than one person can easily read. Therefore, when a researcher decides to investigate a problem for the first time, they face a dilemma. Do they try and solve the problem themselves or do they spend time investigating if it has been solved before? It is argued here that a sensible person will ask themselves "Has this problem occurred before and, if so, was a satisfactory solution found?" (Baker, 2000, p. 219). If they don't examine the prior literature on a topic, then they run the risk of wasting their time by trying to solve a problem that has already been solved many times before.

This raises another problem as it is likely that the exact problem, which is being studied, has not been studied before. Every problem that can be studied must be different in some way from previous ones, even if it is only due to its location or timing. Therefore, if the researchers are looking for information about a problem, they should not expect that that exact problem has been solved. Instead, they must look for previous information that is "like" it to some extent. It may be that the researchers can find information about a similar problem that was studied in another country. Perhaps they find that a similar problem was studied not in tourism but in information technology or psychology or other disciplines. Perhaps they find that previous researchers have studied it using theory x and method y. Others have studied it using theory z and method a. This chapter discusses the process of reviewing, analysing and synthesizing this previous literature to determine if it is worthwhile to solve the problem using a new approach or using existing theory and methods. Here it is argued that there is always some relevant previous literature that can help study a problem.

When reviewing the relevant previous literature about a problem, it is also important to consider how an academic will view this task compared to a consultant or a layperson. For a consultant or layperson, finding out information about how a problem has been solved in the past is an end in itself. A consultant or layperson may view finding information on a problem and how it has been solved in the past as a place to stop a literature review. However, an academic has another purpose. Their aim is to critique the previous literature and see how some outstanding theoretical or methodological problems can be addressed. The purpose of an academic is to increase the usefulness of the previous literature by identifying its theoretical problems and trying to solve those. An academic tries to improve how problems are solved by identifying inconsistencies or limitations of the previous literature on a topic. Note that they also should try and provide a practical answer to the problem, but their priority is to identify and contribute to solving abnormalities found in the theory or method used to study a problem. The differences between the two approaches, using the literature versus improving the literature, are shown in Figure 7.1.

This chapter provides some guidance for academics in writing a literature review. Given that the purpose of an academic is to improve the literature, then the purpose of the literature review is to critically examine prior knowledge, identify problems not previously noted or addressed, and then suggest ways forward.

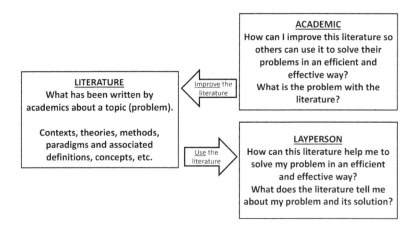

Figure 7.1   Differences in the purpose of an academic and a layperson in reviewing the literature

The skill and ability to conduct a thorough, critical analysis and synthesis of the literature on a topic that identifies problems and anomalies is therefore central to being an academic. It is what an academic does. The resulting literature review is the "foundation and inspiration for substantial, useful research to solve some problems in the literature" (Boote & Beile, 2005, p. 3).

Another reason why a literature review is important for an academic is as a way to establish their authority and expertise in a topic area. A review of the literature on a topic for an aspiring academic is important because without it you will not demonstrate that you have acquired an understanding of the topic, of what has already been done on it, how it has been researched and what the key problems are. A doctoral thesis literature review allows the candidate to demonstrate they understand the previous research on their topic and also that they can identify a problem or anomaly that is worth exploring. This amounts to showing that you have understood the main theories in the subject area and how they have been applied and developed, as well as identifying some anomaly. Note that some academics call this anomaly a "gap". However, a gap may imply that there is no previous research on a topic. Instead, an anomaly means that there has been previous research, but some problem exists with it.

Demonstrating the ability to write a review is therefore a part of an academic's development – of becoming an expert in the field (Hart, 1998). Scholarly activity is about knowing how to: do competent research; read, interpret and analyse arguments; synthesize ideas and make connections across disciplines; write and present ideas clearly and systematically; and identify and address anomalies. For a professor, a literature review is an opportunity to demonstrate expert knowledge of a topic and through an evaluation of the literature, provide direction for others researching in the same area. A literature review is a means to cement a person's reputation as an international expert in a topic area. The characteristics of literatures at different levels of academic development are shown in Figure 7.2.

SKILLS NEEDED FOR COMPLETING A LITERATURE REVIEW

To complete any complex academic task, it is necessary to have the prerequisite skills, and a literature review is no different. These skills include time management; ability to organize and access the resources required; use of computers and programs, especially bibliographic software; finding source material by searching online databases; reading source material and abstracting information from it; and writing and referencing in an appropriate academic style. These skills develop over time and with practice. It is highly recommended to take any opportunity for training in these skills. It is also important to learn about and use bibliographic software such as Endnote™, Mendeley™

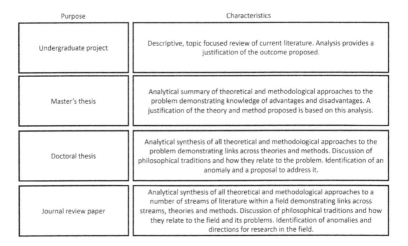

Figure 7.2   Types of literature reviews and their characteristics

or Zotero™. These software tools facilitate the recording of bibliographic information and for making notes about the papers read, as well as organizing copies of each paper for easy retrieval (often in PDF format), insertion of citations in a manuscript and formatting of the reference list.

NATURE OF THE TOURISM LITERATURE

Before beginning a literature review, it is important to consider the general field of literature of interest, in this case tourism. There is an active debate on the status of tourism as either a discipline or a field of study (Hall, Williams & Lew, 2014; McKercher & Prideaux, 2014). For example, Tribe (1997) argues that tourism consists of two different fields of study, an interdisciplinary business-related field and a non-business-related field. Alternatively, Coles, Hall and Duval (2006) recommend viewing tourism from a beyond-disciplinary or a post-disciplinary perspective. The focus should be on learning rather than on disciplines (Hall, Williams & Lew, 2014). McKercher and Prideaux (2014) assert that tourism is not a discipline, but a field of study.

In this chapter, tourism is considered a field of study. This means that the tourism literature does not contain its own theories but obtains them from other disciplines. It is an applied field without consensus theories which "guide researchers towards particular problems" (Coles, Hall and Duval, 2006, p. 302). It does not have "a core of interrelated common concepts and questions that guide problem choice together with a corresponding social organisation" (Hellström, Jacob & Wenneberg, 2003, pp. 251–252). This has important implications for what body of knowledge to review.

Because tourism is an applied field and applies theories and concepts from other disciplines, a review of the literature that is published in tourism journals only cannot be exhaustive. This is especially true since there is a time lag between the publication of a theoretical innovation in the original discipline (e.g., psychology) and its application in tourism. For this reason, it is considered best practice to compare the theory and methodological literature in tourism with that in the original discipline where those theories originated. This issue therefore is important in defining the scope of the review.

SCOPE OF THE REVIEW

As mentioned above, it is important to specify the scope of the literature to be reviewed. Knowledge about the topic being reviewed is not only contained in the individual journal articles that have been written on it. Academic knowledge proceeds by a process of accumulation and thus any recent paper is built upon a set of assumptions, definitions, theories, world views (paradigms) and methods. An academic who is conducting a review needs to understand this (often implicit) contextual assumed knowledge. Thus, when beginning a review, it may be useful to provide some boundaries on the paradigmatic assumptions that are within scope, the breadth of the review in terms of whether to include tourism literature only or to include original disciplinary literature and so on. This scope will also determine the number of in-scope papers to be reviewed.

Too large a scope may mean that the reviewer is overwhelmed by the number of theories and concepts and their historical developments, streams and branches of literature, off-shoots and factions. On the other hand, a scope that is too narrow means that there may be too few papers to make a substantive literature review. This issue needs to be monitored and the scope narrowed or widened depending on the review results. It is important to remember, however, that the purpose of a journal review paper is to identify anomalies and areas for improvement in the literature. Therefore, the scope of the review should be wide enough to identify such an anomaly. There is little significance to a review that finds all the papers in a topic area use the same theory and have not identified any problems with it. Alternatively, it takes expertise to review a whole field of study and make any meaningful recommendations on its status, problems and directions for further research.

THE LITERATURE REVIEW

After this introduction, it should be noted that there are different traditions between disciplines in terms of the purpose of an academic paper and even within disciplines or fields of study or journals. As mentioned above, the generic purpose of any academic journal paper is to contribute to improving the "literature". This is why the academic literature has its own journals separate from other channels of communication such as newspapers. Chapman (2015, pp. 397–398) writes that academics should "make contributions through our core activity of framing and answering clear and precise questions about our chosen topics of interest".

A number of journal editors have written to clarify the purpose of a review paper (Bem, 1995; LePine & Wilcox-King, 2010). However, the value of making a contribution is difficult to agree on. Indeed, questions of purpose and value are ultimately personal. The issue of value of a journal paper is ultimately decided by a journal editor based on their own and usually two reviewers' opinions (Gilmore et al., 2006).

Most academics may agree, however, that a literature review is a central building block for any piece of research but can be the most difficult to write (Nairn, Berthon & Money, 2007). Nairn et al. (2007, p. 259) write that "Insightful literature reviews go beyond classification and criticism to provide a holistic overview of a body of literature and the assumptions that underpin it, from which hiatuses, paradoxes and trends can be discerned. Producing such a synthesis may present a major challenge to a new researcher, particularly if the literature comprises heterogeneous methods of enquiry …"

CONTRIBUTION

The literature in any academic field advances with each paper published. Indeed, to be publishable, a journal article must contribute to knowledge. Because it is important, the contribution of each paper should be clearly identified in the abstract and justified as a contribution in the discussion.

Phillips and Pugh (1994) in their study of doctoral research, identified nine ways to try and make a contribution. These are:

1. Doing empirically based work that has not been done before;
2. Using already known ideas, practices or approaches but with a new interpretation;
3. Bringing new evidence to bear on an old issue or problem;
4. Creating a new synthesis that has not been done before;
5. Applying something done in another country to one's own country;
6. Applying a technique usually associated with one area to another;

7. Being cross-disciplinary by using different methodologies;
8. Looking at areas that people in the discipline have not looked at before;
9. Adding to knowledge in a way that has not previously been done before.

However, the above are possible ways to produce a contribution and do not necessarily mean that the attempt to contribute to knowledge is successful. Instead, it is necessary to justify why the new knowledge is a contribution.

STRUCTURE OF THE TOURISM LITERATURE – PARADIGM FUNNEL

When reading the literature on a topic, it is useful to quickly identify what type of contribution each paper makes. This is why, when you are writing a paper, it is important that your abstract clearly identifies it, as this is often the only part of a paper that is read. While each journal article should make a contribution, most published articles apply existing theory and methods to collect empirical data in a particular context. The paradigm funnel model indicates that out of every 100 papers published, most (around 90) are empirical studies applying past knowledge (Lee & Scott, 2015). In addition, of the remainder, only a few will make a methodological contribution, fewer still will make a theoretical contribution and perhaps only one in a 1,000 will question the paradigmatic assumptions of a field.

The implications of this model are that most of the papers reviewed can be grouped into a category that simply applies existing theory and methods and confirm that they apply in various contexts. Therefore, these papers can be quickly read and categorized, unless they identify some problem or anomaly. Other papers may seek to add additional variables not previously tested but again these papers may not challenge the theory or methods used. The more interesting papers that should be identified in a review are those that test the theory or methods commonly used. And of course, if a paper challenges an existing paradigm, then it is especially important.

DISCIPLINES BEFORE THEORY AND BEFORE METHODOLOGY

Another useful tip when reviewing the literature on a topic – it is better to begin with identification of the discipline that a paper fits into, and then the relevant theory(s) that have been used to study a topic. Each discipline (sociology, psychology) has associated paradigms, assumptions, theories and methods, etc. For example, sociology assumes that a person's behaviour is determined by the social environment. Psychology assumes that a person's actions are determined by their own thinking. Since these assumptions may not be compatible, it is important to separate them. Similarly, there is generally an association between a theory and its associated methodology. Therefore, separating out papers into disciplinary groups first and then examining the theories and associated methods can save time, effort and avoid confusion.

CONDUCTING A LITERATURE REVIEW

Identifying the Research Question

An important issue to note is that the purpose of a literature review for a PhD, an empirical paper or for an academic review paper are different. The purpose of a PhD or empirical paper literature review is to identify a research question and justify why it is important to answer it. Essentially this means describing the contribution expected. On the other hand, a literature review as a standalone journal paper usually analyses and synthesizes all the papers on a topic to identify anomalies and problems and seek to reconcile them. Therefore, a journal review paper is more extensive in scope than a doctoral thesis literature review. A doctoral thesis review narrows down to a specific question, while a journal review explores more streams and branches of knowledge about a topic.

Whatever type of review, a literature review must begin with a question to answer. This question should usually concern some problem or anomaly. A question such as "How many papers have been published in tourism journals on topic X?" is therefore not a suitable question for a review.

Reading the Literature – Familiarization

The "literature" or body of knowledge that you can read on any topic is enormous. If you are new to a topic, as you may be if you are a doctoral candidate, then it is important to avoid being overwhelmed. Many doctoral candidates begin their examination of a topic by reading the most recent published papers in relevant journals. This can rapidly become confusing because each one of these most recent articles is part of an ongoing stream of research on a topic. This stream of research will have associated with it a few key authors, a certain theory and its related paradigmatic assumptions. Understanding and positioning an article within the wider literature on a topic requires identifying the stream of literature to which it belongs and contrasting and comparing that stream's use of theory with those used by other streams. In this way, a particular published article can be grouped together with others of the same type. However, identification of the paradigms, theories and topics of interest that distinguish a particular stream of literature can be difficult if a researcher is new to a field of study or topic area. Becoming familiar with the stream of literature on a topic and how it is similar or different to another stream is easier if the researcher is aware of how the literature on a topic is organized.

There are different ways that knowledge is organized such as encyclo-paedias, handbooks, monographs, journal articles and conference papers. An encyclopaedia provides the broadest view on a topic. The purpose of an encyclopaedia is to introduce a topic and orientate the reader by identifying a history of its development, commonly accepted definitions, concepts and theories. This allows a researcher to classify a current article into previously accepted theoretical groupings. However, when reading an encyclopaedia, one must be aware that an entry may have been written five to twenty years before. Therefore, an encyclopaedia is best used for gaining an orientation to the historical development and approaches to a topic. Examples include the *Encyclopædia Britannica*, and then the more specialist ones such as *Encyclopedia of Tourism* (Jafari, 2000; Jafari & Xi, 2016) and *Encyclopedia of Tourism Management and Marketing* (Buhalis, 2022).

Encyclopaedias provide a broad discussion of a topic while handbooks discuss aspects of a particular subject or topic in greater detail. They are usually edited by a subject specialist and provide a greater depth on subtopics and streams of literature. Examples include tourism management (Cooper et al., 2018), tourism experiences (Dixit, 2020), halal tourism (Hall & Prayag, 2019) and dark tourism (Stone et al., 2018).

Next, previous journal review articles on a topic can be invaluable as they provide an expert's view of how a topic is organized and identify various streams of literature. A published literature review normally discusses histori-cal development, definitions of key concepts, theoretical approaches, method-ology used and problems or issues in the existing literature. Examples include political science and tourism (Matthews & Richter, 1991), psychology of tourist behaviour (Pearce, 1996), family holidays (Schänzel, Smith & Weaver, 2005), human resources (Baum, 2015) sports tourism research (Weed, 2006a), tourism experiences (Brent Ritchie, Tung & Ritchie, 2011), wine tourism research (Bonn, Cho & Um, 2018), and so on. Most recently, the use of the systematic quantitative literature review (SQLR) method has become popular. These SQLR reviews (really scoping reviews) are useful to get a handle on the breadth of the literature and its bibliographic structure (main themes, theories and methods used, key authors and articles), but often are not critical and do not synthesize the literature as recommended below. During the familiarization stage, the analyst listens to and reads through the material, listing key ideas and recurrent themes; and at this stage the analyst is not only gaining an overview of the richness, depth and diversity of the previous research, but also beginning the process of abstraction and conceptualization (Ritchie & Spencer, 1994).

Finally, after reading and familiarizing yourself with relevant encyclopaedia entries, handbooks and review articles, you are better able to read and categorize more recent journal articles. However, before reading recent articles, it is useful to develop a code framework that can be used to classify each one as you read it.

Analysis and Coding of Recent Journal Articles

Once the selected material has been reviewed, the researcher attempts to identify the key issues, concepts and themes by which the paper can be examined and referenced. "Coding" refers to the process whereby a thematic framework or code list is systematically applied to the data in its textual form. Coding involves making numerous judgements as to the meaning and significance of the paper.

As you have read through the encyclopaedia entries, handbooks and review articles, you can begin to develop a code frame to use when reading recent papers. A code frame is a list of alphanumeric codes that are applied to an article or section of an article, paragraph or sentence. When applied this means that the information coded is part of that code group. For example, you may be examining the topic of tourism emotion. In your reading, you may have noted that there are three psychological paradigms that have been used to study emotion: A1. Introspectionism; B1. Behaviourism, and C1. Cognitivism. If you read an article and identified it as using a cognitive paradigm, then you would apply a code of C1 to that article. This may be the beginning of a series of codes with other codes developed for the particular type of cognitive theory used in each paper you read. As the code frame develops, you can have codes for different methodologies, and other aspects of the articles as well. Often these codes are used as headings in a table or Excel spreadsheet with each row being a paper you have read (give each paper a number). Then you will be able to identify similar articles by their common codes.

This method is a type of content analysis (Harwood & Garry, 2003; Krippendorf, 2004) and the tables are sometimes called data display matrices (Whittemore & Knafl, 2005). Ritchie and Spencer (1994) describe a similar technique for synthesizing and interpreting qualitative data by sifting, charting and sorting material according to key issues and themes.

Final Analysis and Synthesis

Analysis can be demonstrated in a paper by developing themes and contrasting and comparing different papers. Webster and Watson (2002) discuss using a table to develop themes and contrast and compare papers. Others discuss reassembling notes based on results of reading and using organizational aids such as post-its, flags, etc. A concept diagram can be a useful organizing framework. There are a variety of papers that discuss theory (Sutton & Staw,

1995) and theory development (Langley, 1999; Shepherd & Suddaby, 2016) that may be useful.

Synthesis is one of the least defined parts of a literature review. However, it is more easily understood if we remember that the purpose of a literature review is to answer a well-defined question. Therefore, the final synthesis presented in a paper is just the answer to that question. A literature review is just an "argument" or claim provided as an answer to that question along with the evidence on which the argument is based.

WRITING A REVIEW

There are a number of books and papers that discuss and provide advice on "writing a review" (Baker, 2000; Boote & Beile, 2005; Bowman, 2007; Briner & Denyer, 2012; Cooper, 1989; Furunes, 2019; Hart, 1998; Jesson, Matherson & Lacey, 2011; Kucan, 2011; Nairn, Berthon & Money, 2007; Randolph, 2009; Rocco & Plakhotnik, 2009; Snyder, 2019; Torraco, 2005; Weed, 2006b). However, before beginning writing, the author needs to know what type of literature review is being written. Three types of review are most common: a scoping review (of which a systematic literature review is the usual type found), a bibliographic review and a narrative review.

Scoping Reviews

Definitions of scoping studies are few and far between. At a general level, scoping studies "aim to map rapidly the key concepts underpinning a research area" (Arksey & O'Malley, 2005, p. 21). A scoping study does not seek to "synthesize" evidence or to aggregate findings from different studies. Recently the systematic literature review (SLR) method has increased in popularity beginning in the medical literature (Starr et al., 2009). In this context, the SLR method was seen as a means of providing evidence about treatments for a specific illness or drug response. Here, the literature review can be seen as collecting, analysing and synthesizing information relevant to a particular and quite narrow research question.

The systematic review has been proposed for use in management and social science research, although some significant differences were noted between medical and management applications (Tranfield, Denyer & Smart, 2003). Tranfield et al. (2003, p. 220) argue that a systematic review can be applied in management to provide an evidence base for "practitioners" and "collective insights through theoretical synthesis into fields and sub-fields for academics". Tranfield et al. (2003, p. 220) propose that a systematic literature review is useful for developing academic research questions. However, these authors also note that medicine and management differ in the homogeneity of the research culture. Medicine research is subjected to rigorous scientific evaluation while management is split between positivist and phenomenological perspectives with low consensus on research questions. Thus, implicit in a systematic literature review is that it is based on a positivist paradigm and its purpose is to provide an evidence base that is based on a theoretical synthesis.

In practice, most systematic literature reviews in tourism do not provide a theoretical synthesis but instead merely count the number of papers of various types (i.e., in each journal, from each country, by author, etc.). Next, they may conduct some bibliographic analysis of keywords or co-authorship, etc. to determine themes that may be used to group papers together. Finally, they may identify gaps in the literature and areas for further research. However, these do not meet the criteria for a publishable review paper as they do not have a specific research question and do not usually identify anomalies in the previous literature. These systematic literature reviews instead appear to be aimed at identifying research questions and thus they are classified as scoping studies. In theory, a systematic literature review may provide a theoretical synthesis but in practice most do not.

Recent authors have chosen to focus on the methodological advantages of a systematic literature review, highlighting that they are useful in addressing potential problems of scope and bias evident in a narrative review (Pickering & Byrne, 2014). However, these writers are silent about other criteria of a publishable paper such as a need for synthesis, and so on. This appears to have led some authors to ignore the need for identification of theoretical anomalies. A number of recent papers that cite Pickering and Byrne (2014) do not appear to provide synthesis and merely summarize public knowledge (Khoo-Lattimore, Mura & Yung, 2019; López-Bonilla & López-Bonilla, 2020; Marais, du Plessis & Saayman, 2017; Ritchie & Jiang, 2021).

Bibliographic Studies

Some authors may argue that a SLR can contribute to the literature (Koseoglu et al., 2016). A bibliographic study contributes to the theoretical area of sociometrics – for example, Glänzel and Thijs (2003, p. 5, cited in Koseoglu et al., 2016) write:

> It is a common misbelief that bibliometrics is nothing else but publication and citation-based gauging of scientific performance or compiling of cleaned-up bibliographies on research domains extended by citation data. In fact, scientometrics is a multifaceted endeavor encompassing subareas such as structural, dynamic, evaluative, and predictive scientometrics.

Koseoglu et al. (2016) go on to indicate that the purpose of a bibliographic study is to: "highlight the unknown patterns in fields or disciplines, these studies help researchers develop theories or test hypothesis" (p. 191).

They suggest that tourism should value bibliographic studies although they imply but do not state that this should be on the proviso that the study advances knowledge of "patterns in the discipline". Further, they state that: "[bibliographic] methods are applicable for the tourism field to develop theories and testing". And they go on to write: "Hence, since the impacts of bibliometric studies may not be clearly understood to develop theories or testable predictions in the field, these methods may not be used enough for theory development and testing" (Koseoglu et al., 2016, p. 191).

In summary, bibliographic studies can advance theory or method in a new field of tourism bibliographics. The point is that the usefulness of a bibliographic study from this perspective would be to advance bibliographic theory or methods applied to the tourism literature. This would be the same as advancing sociological theory by applying it in the tourism context. If this is the purpose of a SLR then it should be discussed and justified in terms of theoretical contribution. There remains a need to explain the contribution of a bibliographic paper to tourism. Otherwise, the paper should be published in a bibliographic journal.

Narrative Review

A number of authors have discussed how to write a narrative literature review (Baker, 2000) that provides analysis and synthesis. For example, Torraco (2005) considers that an integrative literature review is a form of research that reviews, critiques and synthesizes representative literature on a topic in an integrated way such that new frameworks and perspectives on the topic are generated. In the tourism literature, Weed (2006b) supports the need for synthesis and considers that a literature review should provide undiscovered public knowledge rather than merely a summary of public knowledge and that some theoretical synthesis is necessary to achieve this purpose. The characteristics of a narrative review are that it tells a story, leading the reader to the conclusions through a narrative pathway.

CONCLUSIONS

This chapter has discussed writing a literature review. A literature review is considered central to the role of an academic. A review forms the basis for contributing to the academic literature by identifying anomalies in the prior literature. Each literature review should have a well-formulated and specific question. To be publishable, a literature review, like all journal articles, must contribute to knowledge. Most papers published in a field do not identify anomalies.

The chapter indicates that the nature of tourism as a field of study means that a review should include papers from outside the field. A generic method is proposed that involves identifying the origin of the theoretical concepts being examined and then going on to examine how those concepts have developed in the original discipline.

The steps in writing a literature review are discussed. The systematic literature review is discussed, and a number of problems are identified. A narrative review format is recommended.

It is important to note that a literature review is not a summary of the literature and instead is an opportunity for an author to identify an academic problem (anomaly), analyse and synthesize the literature about it and make a recommendation about how to resolve that problem.

REFERENCES

Arksey, H., & O'Malley, L. (2005). Scoping studies: Towards a methodological framework. *International Journal of Social Research Methodology*, *8*(1), 19–32.

Baker, M. (2000). Writing a literature review. *The Marketing Review*, *1*, 219–247.

Baum, T. (2015). Human resources in tourism: Still waiting for change? – A 2015 reprise. *Tourism Management*, *50*, 204–212.

Bem, D.J. (1995). Writing a review article for *Psychological Bulletin*. *Psychological Bulletin*, *118*(2), 172–177.

Bonn, M.A., Cho, M. & Um, H. (2018). The evolution of wine research. *International Journal of Contemporary Hospitality Management*, *30*(1), 286–312.

Boote, D.N., & Beile, P. (2005). Scholars before researchers: On the centrality of the dissertation literature review in research preparation. *Educational Researcher*, *34*(6), 3–15.

Bowman, K. (2007). A research synthesis overview. *Nursing Science Quarterly*, *20*(2), 171–176.

Brent Ritchie, J.R., Tung, V.W.S. & Ritchie, R. (2011). Tourism experience management research: Emergence, evolution and future directions. *International Journal of Contemporary Hospitality Management*, *23*(4), 419–438.

Briner, R.B., & Denyer, D. (2012). Systematic review and evidence synthesis as a practice and scholarship tool. In Rousseau, D.M. (Ed.), *Handbook of Evidence-Based Management: Companies, Classrooms and Research*. Oxford University Press (pp. 112–129).

Buhalis, D. (2022). *Encyclopedia of Tourism Management and Marketing*. Edward Elgar Publishing.

Chapman, C.S. (2015). Researching accounting in health care: Considering the nature of academic contribution. *Accounting & Finance*, *55*(2), 397–413.

Coles, T., Hall, C.M. & Duval, D. (2006). Tourism and post-disciplinary enquiry. *Current Issues in Tourism*, *9*(4–5), 293–319.

Cooper, C., Volo, S., Gartner, W.C. & Scott, N. (2018). *The SAGE Handbook of Tourism Management: Theories, Concepts and Disciplinary Approaches to Tourism*. Sage.

Cooper, H.M. (1989). *Integrating Research: A Guide for Literature Reviews* (2nd ed.). Sage.

Dixit, S.K. (2020). *The Routledge Handbook of Tourism Experience Management and Marketing.* Routledge.

Furunes, T. (2019). Reflections on systematic reviews: Moving golden standards? *Scandinavian Journal of Hospitality and Tourism*, 1–5.

Gilmore, A., Svensson, G., Carson, D. & Perry, C. (2006). Academic publishing. *European Business Review, 18*(6), 468–478.

Glänzel, W., & Thijs, B. (2003). Bibliometric as a research field: A course on theory and application of bibliometric indicators, Course Handouts, http://nsdl.niscair.res.in/jspui/bitstream/123456789/968/1/Bib_Module_KUL.pdf (1.20.2016).

Hall, C.M., & Prayag, G. (2019). *The Routledge Handbook of Halal Hospitality and Islamic Tourism.* Routledge.

Hall, C.M., Williams, A.M. & Lew, A.A. (2014). Tourism: Conceptualisations, disciplinarity, institutions and issues. In Lew, A., Hall, C.M. & Williams, A.M. (Eds.), *The Wiley Blackwell Companion to Tourism.* John Wiley, 3–24.

Hart, C. (1998). *Doing a Literature Review: Releasing the Social Science Research Imagination.* Sage.

Harwood, T., & Garry, T. (2003). An overview of content analysis. *The Marketing Review, 3*(4), 479–498.

Hellström, T., Jacob, M. & Wenneberg, S. (2003). The "discipline" of post-academic science: Reconstructing paradigmatic foundations of a virtual research institute. *Science and Public Policy, 30*(4), 251–260.

Jafari, J. (Ed.) (2000). *Encyclopedia of Tourism.* Routledge.

Jafari, J., & Xi, H. (Eds.) (2016). *Encyclopedia of Tourism.* Springer.

Jesson, J., Matherson, L. & Lacey, F. (2011). *Doing Your Literature Review: Traditional and Systematic Techniques.* Sage.

Khoo-Lattimore, C., Mura, P. & Yung, R. (2019). The time has come: A systematic literature review of mixed methods research in tourism. *Current Issues in Tourism, 22*(13), 1531–1550.

Koseoglu, M.A., Rahimi, R., Okumus, F. & Liu, J. (2016). Bibliometric studies in tourism. *Annals of Tourism Research, 61*, 180–198.

Krippendorf, K. (2004). *Content Analysis: An Introduction to its Methodology* (2nd ed.). Sage.

Kucan, L. (2011). Approximating the practice of writing the dissertation literature review. *Literacy Research and Instruction, 50*(3), 229–240.

Langley, A. (1999). Strategies for theorizing from process data. *The Academy of Management Review, 24*(4), 691–710.

Lee, K.-H., & Scott, N. (2015). Food tourism reviewed using the paradigm funnel approach. *Journal of Culinary Science & Technology, 13*, 95–115.

LePine, J.A., & Wilcox-King, A. (2010). Editors' comments: Developing novel theoretical insight from reviews of existing theory and research. *Academy of Management Review, 35*(4), 506–509.

López-Bonilla, J.M., & López-Bonilla, L.M. (2020). Leading disciplines in tourism and hospitality research: A bibliometric analysis in Spain. *Current Issues in Tourism*, 1–17.

Marais, M., du Plessis, E. & Saayman, M. (2017). A review on critical success factors in tourism. *Journal of Hospitality and Tourism Management, 31*(Supplement C), 1–12.

Matthews, H.G., & Richter, L.K. (1991). Political science and tourism. *Annals of Tourism Research, 18*(1), 120–135.

McKercher, B., & Prideaux, B. (2014). Academic myths of tourism. *Annals of Tourism Research, 46*, 16–28.

Nairn, A., Berthon, P. & Money, A. (2007). Learning from giants. *International Journal of Market Research, 49*(2), 257–274.

Pearce, P.L. (1996). Recent research in tourist behaviour. *Asia Pacific Journal of Tourism Research, 1*(1), 7–17.

Phillips, E.M., & Pugh, D. (1994). *How To Get a PhD*. Open University Press.

Pickering, C., & Byrne, J. (2014). The benefits of publishing systematic quantitative literature reviews for PhD candidates and other early-career researchers. *Higher Education Research & Development, 33*(3), 534–548.

Randolph, J. (2009). A guide to writing the dissertation literature review. *Practical Assessment, Research & Evaluation, 14*(13).

Ritchie, B.W., & Jiang, Y. (2021). Risk, crisis and disaster management in hospitality and tourism: A comparative review. *International Journal of Contemporary Hospitality Management, 33*(10), 3465–3493.

Ritchie, J., & Spencer, L. (1994). Qualitative data analysis for applied policy research. In Bryman, A. & Burgess, B. (Eds.), *Analysing Qualitative Data.* Routledge (pp. 171–195).

Rocco, T.S., & Plakhotnik, M.S. (2009). Literature reviews, conceptual frameworks, and theoretical frameworks: Terms, functions, and distinctions. *Human Resource Development Review, 8*(1), 120–130.

Schänzel, H.A., Smith, K.A. & Weaver, A. (2005). Family holidays: A research review and application to New Zealand. *Annals of Leisure Research, 8*(2–3), 105–123.

Shepherd, D.A., & Suddaby, R. (2016). Theory building: A review and integration. *Journal of Management, 43*(1), 59–86.

Snyder, H. (2019). Literature review as a research methodology: An overview and guidelines. *Journal of Business Research, 104*, 333–339.

Starr, M., Chalmers, I., Clarke, M. & Oxman, A.D. (2009). The origins, evolution, and future of The Cochrane Database of Systematic Reviews. *International Journal of Technology Assessment in Health Care, 25*(Suppl 1), 182–195.

Stone, P.R., Hartmann, R., Seaton, A., Sharpley, R. & White, L. (2018). *The Palgrave Handbook of Dark Tourism Studies*. Palgrave Macmillan.

Sutton, R.I., & Staw, B.M. (1995). What theory is not. *Administrative Science Quarterly, 40*(3), 371–384.

Torraco, R.J. (2005). Writing integrative literature reviews: Guidelines and examples. *Human Resource Development Review, 4*(3), 356–367.

Tranfield, D., Denyer, D. & Smart, P. (2003). Towards a methodology for developing evidence-informed management knowledge by means of systematic review. *British Journal of Management, 14*(3), 207–222.

Tribe, J. (1997). The indiscipline of tourism. *Annals of Tourism Research, 24*(3), 638–657.

Webster, J., & Watson, R. (2002). Analyzing the past to prepare for the future: Writing a literature review. *MIS Quarterly, 26*(2), xiii–xxiii.

Weed, M. (2006a). Sports tourism research 2000–2004: A systematic review of knowledge and a meta-evaluation of methods. *Journal of Sport & Tourism, 11*(1), 5–30.

Weed, M. (2006b). Undiscovered public knowledge: The potential of research synthesis approaches in tourism research. *Current Issues in Tourism, 9*(3), 256–568.

Whittemore, R., & Knafl, K. (2005). The integrative review: Updated methodology. *Journal of Advanced Nursing, 52*(5), 546–553.

8. Positioning the paper for publication
Girish Prayag

INTRODUCTION

Journals speak to different audiences and within each journal, a discourse can usually exist around a research topic and/or area. Often papers have to be positioned to extend and/or challenge this discourse. Positioning a paper has been described as an intangible, difficult and elusive task, often leaving researchers without ideas on how to tackle the task successfully (Černe, 2021). As an example, service quality discourses have over the years transitioned to those of service excellence and now customer experience management. However, from the outset it must be recognized that business people can have a perception that academics are publishing for each other (Geuens, 2011). Thus, in positioning a paper, managerial as well as theoretical relevance are critical. To achieve impact, both academic and industry related, positioning a paper requires trade-offs between theory advancement and managerial significance. In this chapter, I will use storytelling as a communication method to illustrate how to position papers in the tourism/hospitality field irrespective of the journal where they are published. From a traditional marketing perspective, positioning is about how you present yourself, or more commonly refers to how a brand, a product/service or even an idea/concept is presented to an audience. An academic paper follows a similar thought process where you have to "sell" that paper to an audience, which includes editors, reviewers and publishers. Thus, the story you tell is critical to allow the audience to get a sense of what your paper is all about and how the research question(s) or objective(s) has been answered. Using storytelling as a communication method entails generally four processes: (1) dramatization, (2) emotionalization, (3) personalization and (4) fictionalization (Glaser, Garsoffky & Schwan, 2009). However, these processes are often very Western-centric with Indigenous communities often having a different perspective of how stories are constituted and told (Rosile et al., 2013). Nevertheless, these processes are useful to illustrate different facets that can contribute to the overall positioning of a manuscript for a particular journal and/or audience.

Writing a manuscript is both an art and a science. Often grounded in different paradigms, successful execution requires an iterative process for different parts of the manuscript. For example, when two or more authors are involved, writing style and coherence of different sections and arguments could be at odds and, thus, an iterative process is required to position the paper correctly through alignment of different elements. Also, the ontological and epistemological assumptions must match the methods to position a paper properly. While qualitative studies tend to often explicitly state ontological and epistemological assumptions, positivist and mixed-methods research do not always do that. The audience generally has to infer these from the types of data collected and analysed. Nonetheless, the paper has to be clear in its reflection of reality or in portraying what constitutes reality (Rosile et al., 2013).

Next, the chapter introduces storytelling as a communication method then outlines the process of using storytelling to position an academic paper. The four processes are weaved into the general sub-sections of a manuscript, high-lighting important aspects that are critical for a paper to resonate with editors and reviewers. Then the chapter examines ways to position a paper using the AC/DC grid. Finally, the chapter concludes with some key reflections about positioning a paper for different audiences.

THE ACADEMIC PAPER AS STORYTELLING

Stories are vital in making sense of our lives and research (Krauss et al., 2022) but also provide a way to reflect on the entire research process as we embark on writing the first draft of the manuscript. "At its heart, research is storytell-ing" (Christensen, 2012, p. 232), given that it prompts us to do some level of cognitive thinking around the structure and storyline in the manuscript. As an artefact, stories have a particular structure, which makes them recognizable to non-specialists and actionable (Antunes et al., 2020). Research as storytelling generally refers to the narrative traditions of using ethnographic methods to analyse in a chronological context and present findings in a story-like timeline (Walker & Boyer, 2018). In writing an academic paper, this could be thought of as the reflection of the author(s) on the best way(s) to tell the research story and to chronologically explain the entire research process in the manuscript. Storytelling can be a means for researchers to document and present their find-ings (Walker & Boyer, 2018). Over time, this becomes central to a collection of papers that an individual or group can publish on a related topic. These papers should collectively make sense in the mind of the audience, as they need to have an "overall story" to tell. As an example, the collection of papers on tourist emotions published by myself and my co-authors (e.g., Hosany & Gilbert, 2010; Hosany & Prayag, 2013; Hosany et al., 2015; Prayag, Hosany & Odeh, 2013; Prayag et al., 2017) tells a story about the destination emotion scale (Hosany & Gilbert, 2010). The storyline is the initial scale develop-ment paper by Hosany and Gilbert (2010). In subsequent papers, the scale is validated in other contexts (Hosany et al., 2015), and the antecedents and outcomes that are related to the concepts embedded in the scale are also tested (Prayag, Hosany & Odeh, 2013; Prayag et al., 2017). In this way, the collection of papers represents the overall story which is useful not only for publication purposes but also for career development and progression, including promo-tion applications.

Stories have the ability to integrate, coordinate and contextualize knowl-edge. People tell stories in certain ways to communicate practices, to be persuasive, to institutionalize important facets of a phenomenon, to foster acceptance and conformity, and to integrate newcomers in a group (Antunes et al., 2020). While these tend to be central ideas that imbue how academia and industry utilize stories to make a difference, often researchers have to tell their research story in a few lines to various audiences, including stakeholders for various grant applications or accreditation bodies (e.g., EQUIS and AACSB). The storytelling way, thus, provides the framework to do just that. A story has a plot, dramatic tension, character development and pacing (Marzec, 2007). These elements have a strong connection to actors, activities, events and flows that are embedded in the process paradigm (Antunes et al., 2020). For example, the plot tells us the entire research process and in qualitative research the participants' voices allow for character development. Likewise, the dramatic tension could be the results, which is often the case in quantitative research where the results prove or disprove the hypotheses. By implication this means that manuscripts are positioned to tell a process, i.e., the research process. The story illustrates a collection of narrative elements tied together by a narrative arc (Cohn, 2013), which gives coherence and structure to the man-uscript. A narrative arc has a set of scenes (e.g., introduction, literature review, method, findings and implications), which discretize the narrative. In these the actors, for example, which could be residents' and hotel developers' voices, are integrated using a mixed-methods design to highlight tensions between community and tourism development.

I am arguably using storytelling as a communication method rather than a research method per se in this chapter. In particular, the advantage of this approach is that it can explain abstract concepts embedded in the manuscript in a clearer and fun way, providing a sounding board for research dissemination (Christensen, 2012; Krauss et al., 2022), with positive consequences on the so-called academic and/or industry impact. For example, the concept of resil-ience is vague to many audiences but certainly a buzz word for both industry and academia (Prayag, 2023). Through storytelling, this abstract concept can be turned into meaningful practices that can help individuals, communities and organizations to recover and thrive from adversity. Yet, without engagement with non-academic audiences, benefits to community and broader society may not emerge. Thus, non-academic audiences may benefit from papers written using storytelling as a communication method as this distils complex ideas into simple concepts and presents them in a fun way (Cerrato et al., 2018). Researchers should bear in mind that complex, lengthy articles and a variety of journal style guidelines might make an article inaccessible to the very subjects that are part of the research process and the non-academic audience that may benefit from the results. Journal articles are becoming increasingly more irrelevant to business, industry and public sector practitioners (Geuens, 2011). Thus, accessibility can be improved through writing style and dissemination of the findings in a way that encourages stakeholders other than academics to use the article. This is once again a matter of positioning the article for different audiences. The results of the research should mean something in real life (Geuens, 2011).

THE PROCESS OF POSITIONING ACADEMIC PAPERS USING STORYTELLING

In writing and positioning the manuscript for an audience, four storytelling processes can be used: (1) dramatization, (2) emotionalization, (3) personalization and (4) fictionalization (Glaser, Garsoffky & Schwan, 2009). *Dramatization* focuses on organizing information into a beginning, middle and end, which is also the classic layout of a journal manuscript. Yet, this approach is considered to be linear and storytelling by Indigenous scholars often resists such linearity (Rosile et al., 2013). To some, this is called the narrative arc (Joubert, Davis & Metcalfe, 2019), where the beginning captures the audience in a way that they want to read and know more. However, there is no one-size-fits-all in storytelling, and different journals may require different things illustrated in the introduction. However, one particular facet of a manuscript that almost all journals in the tourism/hospitality discipline will require is the abstract. For me, the abstract and the keywords defining the paper are the first part of the story that have to be clear to the audience and really are the beginnings to the story.

"Murky" stories already create confusion in the mind of the audience that may create a barrier for a paper to move to the reviewing process, leading to that much dreaded "desk rejection". To qualify what "murky" potentially means in the abstract of an academic paper, I can think of several things: (1) there are far too many concepts and constructs intertwined in the abstract that cause confusion; (2) the theoretical framework of the study is not clear; (3) there are far too many research questions and objectives; (4) the abstract is unclear as to how the paper relates to the specific discipline or journal; (5) the methods and/or findings are not succinctly described; and (6) most importantly, how the paper advances both theory and practice are not clear. Of course, not all papers would have all of these elements described previously but some of them are expected. For example, conceptual papers might not have a method or funding component while systematic reviews might not have managerial implications per se. Irrespective of the research topic and the journal where an author is considering to publish, the abstract can be described as the "window" to the actual research and therefore should depict the highest clarity of thought.

The introduction then follows, where the research goals should be clear as to whether the research replicates, complements or challenges the existing body of knowledge. Tourism and hospitality journals in particular reward original and novel research and often discard replication or repetition with extension studies by rejecting or desk rejecting them. Though replication studies are shunned by tourism and hospitality scholars, they have a long tradition in other fields such as economics and psychology. Replication studies are not novel and do not necessarily contain breakthrough ideas, but are crucially important for a discipline (Geuens, 2011). They can corroborate earlier findings and consequently lead to new valid theories and frameworks, or otherwise dismiss findings from previous studies as coincidental and contextual (Geuens, 2011). Whether research should complement, extend or radically challenge existing discourses on a topic very much depends on the quality and ranking of journals. The highest ranked journals in tourism and hospitality expect that the manuscript extends substantially the literature. However, some manuscripts may both extend and complement existing studies, and thus, these facets of contribution to theory and practice are not mutually exclusive. In the introduction, it is expected that the manuscript sets the scene for the research problem and its significance to theory and practice, outlines clearly the research question(s), and provides justifications for the method that underpins the study. The introduction can be structured using *emotionalization*, which refers to enhancing the emotional dimension of the content (Glaser, Garsoffky & Schwan, 2009). This means that researchers can create an emotional connection with the reviewers through the content by enhancing clarity and consistency of arguments and linking different ideas in a way that the storyline becomes clearer.

More importantly, the literature review is usually a story that positions the theoretical framing of the study in relation to previous studies and highlights the agreements and tensions around the topic. Far too often researchers fail to create a story through reviewing previous studies, and the sections and sub-sections can be disjointed creating confusion for the reader. This is particularly true in quantitative studies where, for example, a model underpinned by several hypotheses is tested. However, the model itself does not have strong theoretical grounding and therefore the authors are unable to convince readers that the hypotheses are indeed derived from the literature. There are many studies that outline how to write a literature review generally and for a specific discipline (e.g., Cooper, 1988; Randolph, 2009; Green, Johnson & Adams, 2006; Wee & Banister, 2016). At its base, the literature review should allow researchers to delimit the research problem, gain methodological insights, identify contradictory issues in the line of inquiry and highlight areas where further research can be done (Gall, Borg, & Gall, 1996). Cooper's (1988) taxonomy of literature reviews suggests that literature reviews can be classified into six categories: focus, goal, perspective, coverage, organization and audience. For example, focus could be anything from identifying research outcomes, methods and theories to industry applications. The goal should be to integrate and synthesize the existing views and potentially highlight conflicts and criticisms (Cooper, 1988).

Others may decide to write literature reviews as the main manuscript and these need to be positioned differently from a "normal" manuscript. The three basic types of literature reviews are: narrative reviews, qualitative systematic reviews and quantitative systematic reviews (meta-analyses) (Green, Johnson & Adams, 2006). All three types are popular in tourism and hospitality studies but the systematic review remains by far the most common in recent years (Binder, 2019; de Larrea et al., 2021; Prayag & Ozanne, 2018; Russen, Dawson & Madera, 2021). The rigour of such articles rests on applying the PRISMA method of systematic reviews and clearly delimiting the criteria for inclusion and exclusion of articles (Kim et al., 2018). Typically, cross-tabulation analysis between publication year and other criteria (e.g., research subjects, research methods and citations) provided insights into the development and trends of review studies in the tourism and hospitality literature. Kim et al. (2018) also analyse citation counts and other criteria (e.g., research methods, research subjects and journals), which can provide insights into the effects of different types of review studies based on the applied criteria. Narrative reviews are also used to shape the tourism and hospitality discipline (e.g., Cohen, Prayag & Moital, 2014; Mair, Ritchie & Walters, 2016; Yang, Khoo-Lattimore & Arcodia, 2017), with some studies combining both narrative and systematic reviews in the same paper (e.g., Jin & Wang, 2016). More recently, meta-analyses (e.g., Crouch, 1995; Gursoy et al., 2019; Li, 2014; Zhang, 2022) in tourism and hospitality studies have become the way to ascertain that effects and relationships between a set of variables are not due to contextual differences. This is particularly important to move forward the quantitative facet of tourism scholarship. Irrespective of the type of literature review undertaken, the story in the paper needs to communicate rigour and comply with guidelines that inform such reviews.

Storytelling cannot uncover the whole breadth of knowledge and experiences but certainly can uncover thoughts, desires, feelings, emotions and experiences (Koll, Von Wallpach & Kreuzer, 2010). Thus, the chosen method becomes critical in justifying how the knowledge was generated, including the type of analysis conducted to uncover that knowledge. There is also novelty of the method that can be weaved into the storytelling. The ability to combine methods (e.g., mixed methods with observational data) does not only give something to add to the story but also the opportunity for researchers to optimize procedural aspects throughout the research process. For example, digital and analogue methods of coding videos can create a storyline around methods, while in qualitative studies free association techniques and collage creation can create novelty in the method. Increasingly, top-ranked journals expect some form of methodological contribution. For example, segmentation remains a key facet of marketing practice and the classic cluster analysis using Ward's method is not at all novel and in fact is highly disputed (see Ernst & Dolnicar, 2018). There are relatively more recent methods such as bi-clustering (Dolnicar et al., 2012) and bagged clustering (Dolnicar & Leisch, 2004; Prayag et al., 2015). However, a combination of different clustering methods may provide a stronger methodological contribution than one method alone (D'Urso et al., 2015; Bruwer, Prayag & Disegna, 2018).

The method section of the manuscript nonetheless has to outline the *how*, *who*, *when*, *what* and *where* of *why* a research approach was chosen. The "how" is about clearly outlining the data collection procedures, while the "who" outlines the screening criteria employed for sampling, i.e., the targeted participant or respondent. Far too often manuscripts fail to account properly for these facets in describing the methods. The "when" and "where" give the exact timing and location of the interviews or surveys. Details are critical to give credibility to the research method employed and without those, the paper fails to position the research as being trustworthy and credible. The "what" is often related to questions asked in an interview or survey and whether these are appropriate for answering the research question(s). However, of all these questions, the "why" remains critical as the answer to this question positions the paper within a specific paradigm. In qualitative research, this paradigm is explicit while in mixed-methods and quantitative research, the paradigm informing the research can be implicit.

Nonetheless, employing *personalization* as a storytelling process, which concerns heightening the personal aspects (Glaser, Garsoffky & Schwan, 2009), can be very effective for qualitative and mixed-methods research. This aspect can improve reception and recall in qualitative studies, while also sharing evocative descriptive details from participants. *Fictionalization* is related to mixing fictional with factual information (Glaser, Garsoffky & Schwan, 2009). However, in academic research this is frowned upon as research is based on evidence (Krauss et al., 2022). It is essential to remain true to accurate descriptions of methods and data but also these need to be appropriate in relation to the data and avoid misrepresentation. Thus, critical is the data analysis method, which provides the evidence. In qualitative studies, the characters in your story must be given voice but the researcher is interpreting the voice, and should be mindful about the voices that are silenced. How much extrapolation is also allowed from interviews? At the design stage of the research, the methods should capture the breadth of knowledge, diagnostic potential (do results inform the research questions?), resource intensity (how demanding is the data collection – cost, time and expertise), comparability (how easy and meaningful is it to compare results to other studies and over time?) and actionable (how actionable are the results?) (Koll, Von Wallpach & Kreuzer, 2010). The method section should also focus on readability and comply with any journal guidelines on this section. For example, reporting means and standard deviations of measured items is common practice in quantitative studies, alongside the correlations between items. In qualitative studies, reporting of the coding process from open coding to axial coding, followed by theme generation can be expected.

The results/findings should be structured in a way that shows a clear alignment with previous sections of the manuscript. This implies that the introduction sets the scene and knowledge gaps, the literature review frames the existing knowledge and the theoretical tensions, the method outlines how the knowledge is uncovered, and the results present this knowledge in a comprehensive way. There is no standard format to present findings as long as they make sense in relation to the research question(s) and method(s) employed. In quantitative studies, sometimes reviewers are reluctant to accept a paper where results run counter to previously published papers in that journal or those published in high-ranked journals (Geuens, 2011). A classic barrier is that reviewers will not generally accept quantitative studies based on non-significant results, when these are as important as the significant ones. Only recently has there been a call in tourism studies for more open research models (Liburd, 2012), which is different from the open-access model that has been progressing rapidly in this field, alongside predatory journals (Alrawadieh, 2020). In open research models, both the research design and the final manuscript are peer reviewed. At the stage of research design, reviewers are involved in assessing the quality and rigour of the design to answer the research question(s). In the research process, irrespective of whether the results are significant or not, the paper gets published if it has met all the publishing requirements.

The final section of the manuscript, discussion/implications, is often considered as the most important. This is because it brings together the literature review and the findings, which then inform the theoretical and managerial implication. As such, researchers have to engage in clearly showing how the results answer the research question(s) and also why they matter in the bigger picture in relation to the discipline and, if necessary, the relevance for other disciplines. Increasingly, the findings must allow for theory replication and extension. The managerial findings should go beyond stating that managers should do this or that and rather focus on what practices should be changed based on the study's results. Likewise, changes to process, system and procedures must be suggested to allow managers to benefit from the results. The "so-what question" is omnipresent in the review process often acting as a gatekeeper to eventual publication in a particular journal, and in this section of the paper, reviewers would often explicitly examine whether authors have done justice to this question. Nonetheless, without a clear theoretical and/or managerial contribution, a paper is unlikely to make it to publication. Hence, the next section attempts to illustrate how to shape the contribution using Černe's (2021) AC/DC grid but adapted for the purposes of positioning a paper.

AC/DC POSITIONING GRID FOR BETTER RESEARCH IMPACT

The AC/DC positioning grid provides a framework for positioning the theoretical stance of your paper (Černe, 2021). While it is not always necessary to have an over-arching theory for a paper, the theoretical stance must be clear. This implies that the study can be grounded in several theories as long as they make sense together or the paper can draw on the main principles of a theory but then apply it in different ways. For example, resilience theory and social capital theory (SCT) are what can be called "grand" theories (Ozanne et al., 2022). However, when articulated and applied in papers, one could adopt SCT as applied to organizations where there are three well-accepted dimensions (cognitive, structural and relational aspects) (e.g., Chowdhury et al., 2019; Ozanne et al., 2022) or others could apply it to evaluate community aspects such as bridging, bonding and linking (Aldrich & Meyer, 2015; Kyne & Aldrich, 2020). Nonetheless, these grand theories can provide the basis for theoretical contribution to tourism/hospitality scholarship.

In Table 8.1, authors may seek to advance or progress a particular domain in hospitality or tourism and therefore the manuscript can be expected to shift the existing discourse radically or marginally. Such a contribution is expected to steer the scholarly conversation in a new direction based on the findings (Černe, 2021). The paper needs to sharply define concepts or constructs in developing a coherent set of explanations and offering a compelling point of critique that counters past thinking on the topic. For example, this is what Vargo and Lusch's (2004) seminal paper on service dominant logic achieved and subsequent debates are rife in the marketing literature on this proposed concept (Ballantyne & Varey, 2008). The tourism literature has adopted the concept and showed its applicability to the tourism experience (Font et al., 2021; Shaw, Bailey & Williams, 2011). Using the advance or progress approach entails presenting theoretical arguments and/or empirical evidence. Literature reviews (systematic, narrative and meta-analysis) may also progress

Table 8.1   AC/DC grid and positioning a paper

Contribution to tourism/ hospitality scholarship	Type of paper	Method	Storytelling process
Advance/progress	Conceptual, Empirical, Systematic Reviews/Narrative Reviews/Meta-Reviews/ Research Notes	Mono/ multi-method/ PRISMA	Dramatization, emotionalization, personalization
Complement/integrate	Empirical/Replication Studies	Mono/ multi-method	Dramatization, emotionalization, personalization
Debunk/contrast	Empirical/Meta-analysis/ Replication Studies	Mono/ multi-method	Dramatization, emotionalization, personalization
Confirm/corroborate	Empirical/Meta-analysis/ Replication Studies	Mono/ multi-method	Dramatization, emotionalization, personalization

Source: Adapted from Černe (2021)

the discipline, highlighting what has been done and what has been ignored and/ or requires further research. Methods employed could be anything from mono to multi-methods but also PRISMA for systematic reviews. In crafting these papers, three of the four storytelling processes may be employed as shown in Table 8.1.

In complementing existing discourse in the tourism or hospitality discipline, authors may seek to add something to the current body of knowledge by, for example, providing additional insights. This tends to be grounded in empirical studies but also replication studies as I have highlighted before. The contribution could be contextual by applying existing theoretical concepts in a new context or using a different theoretical perspective on an issue that has already been evaluated (Černe, 2021). Authors could also integrate different concepts and findings from different disciplines to offer a new perspective (Černe, 2021). For example, the shift from understanding emotions retrospectively by asking respondents what they felt during a tourism experience (Hosany, Martin & Woodside, 2021) to measuring emotions in real time (Kim & Fesenmaier, 2015) using psychological measures (Tuerlan, Li & Scott, 2021). Thus, research in tourism has progressed from measuring emotions superficially to the use of methods (e.g., EEG, EMG and skin conductance) that can uncover deep-rooted emotions. Under such an approach, again authors can use mono- or multi-methods to complement the existing discourse and three of the four storytelling processes can be used.

In debunking or contrasting existing research, authors are attempting to show that the tourism or hospitality discourse on the topic does not hold universally true, or in a specific setting (Černe, 2021). Thus, empirical evidence is required to contrast existing studies that then support further theoretical development. The findings and implications, for example, serve to offer counter views or can highlight the need for new viewpoints or a recombination of existing viewpoints (Černe, 2021). Meta-analyses might be useful here to show that the effects on variables of interest do hold true across contexts and that such relationships are spurious. Once again, mono- or multi-methods are to be considered for debunking existing findings and the three storytelling processes of dramatization, emotionalization and personalization can be employed.

Finally, confirming or corroborating existing studies is firmly grounded in providing empirical evidence and can be considered the lowest level of contribution in contrast to advance or progress. This level is particularly driven by reproducibility and replicability which has been shunned by both tourism and hospitality scholars. It should be viewed as a stepping stone for higher levels of contribution such as those related to advance or complement (Černe, 2021). However, it must be noted that meta-analyses might be useful here too as well as the three storytelling processes.

CONCLUSION

Most editors and reviewers judge a paper on its positioning as it has an enormous impact on the decision to accept or reject a paper (Geuens, 2011). The paper needs to be about an issue that matters, whether conceptually or empirically, or both. The main contribution to theory and practice must be clear from the outset and the research question(s) must be grounded in this contribution. The manuscript must clearly outline the entire research process, including how the knowledge was generated and analysed. The results obtained should show alignment with the research question and the implications should be clear for theory and practice. Throughout, care must be taken in regards to how the story is told and what facets are emphasized, including the actors, plot and character development. The story nonetheless is the packaging and therefore relies on the product itself, and the latter should be the main focus (Geuens, 2011). Underlying the fact that current research needs to provide something new beyond the existing body of knowledge, authors often get lost in how much novelty is required to make the paper acceptable. However, replication studies within tourism are much needed to confirm certain phenomena but that would require educating editors too on their importance and relevance. There is a reproducibility and replicability crisis in the social sciences (Černe, 2021). Likewise, there exists a stream of literature on how to craft a paper and this literature is not devoid of creativity and imagination (Černe, 2021). This chapter provides the AC/DC positioning matrix as a way to think about contribution, methods and story and how these elements need to be aligned to avoid a desk rejection and instead allow for the eventual publication of the paper.

REFERENCES

Aldrich, D.P., & Meyer, M.A. (2015). Social capital and community resilience. *American Behavioral Scientist*, *59*(2), 254–269.

Alrawadieh, Z. (2020). Publishing in predatory tourism and hospitality journals: Mapping the academic market and identifying response strategies. *Tourism and Hospitality Research*, *20*(1), 72–81.

Antunes, P., Pino, J.A., Tate, M. & Barros, A. (2020). Eliciting process knowledge through process stories. *Information Systems Frontiers*, *22*, 1179–1201.

Ballantyne, D., & Varey, R.J. (2008). The service-dominant logic and the future of marketing. *Journal of the Academy of Marketing Science*, *36*, 11–14.

Binder, P. (2019). A network perspective on organizational learning research in tourism and hospitality: A systematic literature review. *International Journal of Contemporary Hospitality Management*, *31*(7), 2602–2625.

Bruwer, J., Prayag, G. & Disegna, M. (2018). Why wine tourists visit cellar doors: Segmenting motivation and destination image. *International Journal of Tourism Research*, *20*(3), 355–366.

Černe, M. (2021). Framing theoretical contributions: The AC/DC positioning grid. *Dynamic Relationships Management Journal*, *10*(2), 1–5.

Cerrato, S., Daelli, V., Pertot, H. & Puccioni, O. (2018). The public-engaged scientists: Motivations, enablers and barriers. *Research for All*, *2*(2), 313–322.

Chowdhury, M., Prayag, G., Orchiston, C. & Spector, S. (2019). Postdisaster social capital, adaptive resilience and business performance of tourism organizations in Christchurch, New Zealand. *Journal of Travel Research*, *58*(7), 1209–1226.

Christensen, J. (2012). Telling stories: Exploring research storytelling as a meaningful approach to knowledge mobilization with Indigenous research collaborators and diverse audiences in community-based participatory research. *The Canadian Geographer/Le Géographe Canadien*, *56*(2), 231–242.

Cohen, S.A., Prayag, G. & Moital, M. (2014). Consumer behaviour in tourism: Concepts, influences and opportunities. *Current Issues in Tourism*, *17*(10), 872–909.

Cohn, N. (2013). Visual narrative structure. *Cognitive Science*, *37*(3), 413–452.

Cooper, H.M. (1988). Organizing knowledge synthesis: A taxonomy of literature reviews. *Knowledge in Society*, *1*, 104–126.

Crouch, G.I. (1995). A meta-analysis of tourism demand. *Annals of Tourism Research*, *22*(1), 103–118.

de Larrea, G.L., Altin, M., Koseoglu, M.A. & Okumus, F. (2021). An integrative systematic review of innovation research in hospitality and tourism. *Tourism Management Perspectives*, *37*, 100789.

Dolnicar, S., Kaiser, S., Lazarevski, K. & Leisch, F. (2012). Biclustering: Overcoming data dimensionality problems in market segmentation. *Journal of Travel Research*, *51*(1), 41–49.

Dolnicar, S., & Leisch, F. (2004). Segmenting markets by bagged clustering. *Australasian Marketing Journal (AMJ)*, *12*(1), 51–65.

D'Urso, P., Disegna, M., Massari, R. & Prayag, G. (2015). Bagged fuzzy clustering for fuzzy data: An application to a tourism market. *Knowledge-Based Systems*, *73*, 335–346.

Ernst, D., & Dolnicar, S. (2018). How to avoid random market segmentation solutions. *Journal of Travel Research*, *57*(1), 69–82.

Font, X., English, R., Gkritzali, A. & Tian, W.S. (2021). Value co-creation in sustainable tourism: A service-dominant logic approach. *Tourism Management*, *82*, 104200.

Gall, M.D., Borg, W.R. & Gall, J.P. (1996). *Education Research: An Introduction* (6th ed.). White Plains, NY: Longman.

Geuens, M. (2011). Where does business research go from here? Food-for-thought on academic papers in business research. *Journal of Business Research*, *64*(10), 1104–1107.

Glaser, M., Garsoffky, B. & Schwan, S. (2009). Narrative-based learning: Possible benefits and problems. *European Journal of Communication Research*, *34*(4), 429–447.

Green, B.N., Johnson, C.D. & Adams, A. (2006). Writing narrative literature reviews for peer-reviewed journals: Secrets of the trade. *Journal of Chiropractic Medicine*, *5*(3), 101–117.

Gursoy, D., Ouyang, Z., Nunkoo, R. & Wei, W. (2019). Residents' impact perceptions of and attitudes towards tourism development: A meta-analysis. *Journal of Hospitality Marketing & Management*, *28*(3), 306–333.

Hosany, S., & Gilbert, D. (2010). Measuring tourists' emotional experiences toward hedonic holiday destinations. *Journal of Travel Research*, *49*(4), 513–526.

Hosany, S., Martin, D. & Woodside, A.G. (2021). Emotions in tourism: Theoretical designs, measurements, analytics, and interpretations. *Journal of Travel Research*, *60*(7), 1391–1407.

Hosany, S., & Prayag, G. (2013). Patterns of tourists' emotional responses, satisfaction, and intention to recommend. *Journal of Business Research*, *66*(6), 730–737.

Hosany, S., Prayag, G., Deesilatham, S., Cauševic, S. & Odeh, K. (2015). Measuring tourists' emotional experiences: Further validation of the destination emotion scale. *Journal of Travel Research*, *54*(4), 482–495.

Jin, X., & Wang, Y. (2016). Chinese outbound tourism research: A review. *Journal of Travel Research*, *55*(4), 440–453.

Joubert, M., Davis, L. & Metcalfe, J. (2019). Storytelling: The soul of science communication. *Journal of Science Communication*, *18*(05), E.

Kim, C.S., Bai, B.H., Kim, P.B. & Chon, K. (2018). Review of reviews: A systematic analysis of review papers in the hospitality and tourism literature. *International Journal of Hospitality Management*, *70*, 49–58.

Kim, J., & Fesenmaier, D.R. (2015). Measuring emotions in real time: Implications for tourism experience design. *Journal of Travel Research*, *54*(4), 419–429.

Koll, O., Von Wallpach, S. & Kreuzer, M. (2010). Multi-method research on consumer–brand associations: Comparing free associations, storytelling, and collages. *Psychology & Marketing*, *27*(6), 584–602.

Krauss, J.E., Mani, S., Cromwell, J., San Roman Pineda, I. & Cleaver, F. (2022). Bringing research alive through stories: Reflecting on research storytelling as a public engagement method. *Research for All*, *6*(1), 1–16.

Kyne, D., & Aldrich, D.P. (2020). Capturing bonding, bridging, and linking social capital through publicly available data. *Risk, Hazards & Crisis in Public Policy*, *11*(1), 61–86.

Li, M. (2014). Cross-cultural tourist research: A meta-analysis. *Journal of Hospitality & Tourism Research*, *38*(1), 40–77.

Liburd, J.J. (2012). Tourism research 2.0. *Annals of Tourism Research*, *39*(2), 883–907.

Mair, J., Ritchie, B.W. & Walters, G. (2016). Towards a research agenda for post-disaster and post-crisis recovery strategies for tourist destinations: A narrative review. *Current Issues in Tourism*, *19*(1), 1–26.

Marzec, M. (2007). Telling the corporate story: Vision into action. *Journal of Business Strategy*, *28*(1), 26–36.

Ozanne, L.K., Chowdhury, M., Prayag, G. & Mollenkopf, D.A. (2022). SMEs navigating COVID-19: The influence of social capital and dynamic capabilities on organizational resilience. *Industrial Marketing Management*, *104*, 116–135.

Prayag, G. (2023). Tourism resilience in the "new normal": Beyond jingle and jangle fallacies? *Journal of Hospitality and Tourism Management*, *54*, 513–520.

Prayag, G., Disegna, M., Cohen, S.A. & Yan, H. (2015). Segmenting markets by bagged clustering: Young Chinese travelers to Western Europe. *Journal of Travel Research*, *54*(2), 234–250.

Prayag, G., Hosany, S., Muskat, B. & Del Chiappa, G. (2017). Understanding the relationships between tourists' emotional experiences, perceived overall image, satisfaction, and intention to recommend. *Journal of Travel Research*, *56*(1), 41–54.

Prayag, G., Hosany, S. & Odeh, K. (2013). The role of tourists' emotional experiences and satisfaction in understanding behavioral intentions. *Journal of Destination Marketing & Management*, *2*(2), 118–127.

Prayag, G., & Ozanne, L.K. (2018). A systematic review of peer-to-peer (P2P) accommodation sharing research from 2010 to 2016: Progress and prospects from the multi-level perspective. *Journal of Hospitality Marketing & Management*, *27*(6), 649–678.

Randolph, J. (2009). A guide to writing the dissertation literature review. *Practical Assessment, Research, and Evaluation*, *14*(1), 13.

Rosile, G.A., Boje, D.M., Carlon, D.M., Downs, A. & Saylors, R. (2013). Storytelling diamond: An antenarrative integration of the six facets of storytelling in organization research design. *Organizational Research Methods*, *16*(4), 557–580.

Russen, M., Dawson, M. & Madera, J.M. (2021). Gender diversity in hospitality and tourism top management teams: A systematic review of the last 10 years. *International Journal of Hospitality Management*, *95*, 102942.

Shaw, G., Bailey, A. & Williams, A. (2011). Aspects of service-dominant logic and its implications for tourism management: Examples from the hotel industry. *Tourism Management*, *32*(2), 207–214.

Tuerlan, T., Li, S. & Scott, N. (2021). Customer emotion research in hospitality and tourism: Conceptualization, measurements, antecedents and consequences. *International Journal of Contemporary Hospitality Management*, *33*(8), 2741–2772.

Vargo, S.L., & Lusch, R.F. (2004). Evolving to a new dominant logic for marketing. *Journal of Marketing*, *68*(1), 1–17.

Walker, E.B., & Boyer, D.M. (2018). Research as storytelling: The use of video for mixed methods research. *Video Journal of Education and Pedagogy*, *3*(1), 1–12.

Wee, B.V., & Banister, D. (2016). How to write a literature review paper? *Transport Reviews*, *36*(2), 278–288.

Yang, E.C.L., Khoo-Lattimore, C. & Arcodia, C. (2017). A narrative review of Asian female travellers: Looking into the future through the past. *Current Issues in Tourism*, *20*(10), 1008–1027.

Zhang, J. (2022). A meta-analysis of econometrics studies of tourism and low-carbon development. *Tourism Management Perspectives*, *43*, 101006.

9.   Publishing in special issues

Dallen J. Timothy

INTRODUCTION

As the contributions in this book have made perfectly clear, publishing papers is not easy, but it is rewarding. One of the most common formats for publishing in refereed journals is the special issue, or themed issue. Themed issues have become particularly widespread during the past quarter century in all fields of science, social science, health care, and business. Special issues (SIs) are collections of papers published together in a specific volume and issue (or more than one issue) of a refereed journal. They focus on a "specific topic of research that usually has broad appeal … [and are] an outstanding way to explore a particular theme, review previously unaddressed issues, and even propose or develop brand new approaches to the topic" (Elsevier, 2023, n.p.). Special issues are typically led by guest editors, who work with the journal editors to compile a critical volume of papers that meet the academic standards of the journal.

This chapter describes special issues of journals and what is entailed in putting them together, as well as their role and value in academic publishing. The chapter also describes the advantages and benefits of SIs for publishers and journals, individual scholars, and guest editors. In addition, it mentions a few controversial elements of SIs but encourages emerging scholars not to let these controversies dissuade them from publishing in SIs because the benefits far outweigh the costs.

JOURNAL SPECIAL ISSUES

Although books, book chapters, conferences, and conference proceedings are increasingly important outlets for researchers in tourism, journals remain the fundamental knowledge source in most of the social sciences and business fields, including tourism (Olk & Griffith, 2004). The majority of academic tourism papers are published as "regular articles" in ordinary issues of refereed journals. However, many tourism journals publish special issues, or collections of papers around a common theme, published together in a single issue (or double-issue) and volume. In the field of tourism and hospitality, there has been a notable growth in SIs from 1995 to 2023 as a percentage of total issues and in absolute numbers (Backman & Munanura, 2015; Steinberg & Boettcher, 2023). Special issues have been instrumental in raising awareness of tourism as a serious area of scholarship and have raised the bar for tourism studies generally.

The main purposes of SIs are to position extant work in the broader landscape of knowledge, feature areas in need of additional research, and provide empirical studies that extend, refute, or confirm established theories, concepts, paradigms, and methodologies. According to Huber (2019), themed issues satisfy a number of needs, depending on the type of SI and its purposes. First, they interrogate established theories and shed light on how these theories can better be utilized in academic research. Second, SIs introduce emerging and novel ideas that have "the potential to generate a new stream of research in the future but is less well known ..." (Huber, 2019, p. 210). Third, themed issues can raise the profile of small subgroups or subtopics (even sometimes esoteric but important subjects) within a field (Delamothe, 2001; Thiessen, 2013) that are "both evocative and academically eugenic" (Singh, 2014, p. 295). Examples in the realm of heritage tourism include arts and crafts, souvenirs, nostalgia, diaspora travel, genealogy tourism, cemetery and battlefield heritage, dark tourism, cultural festivals, culinary heritage, and authenticity, to name only a few (Chhabra, 2019; Earl & Hall, 2023; Isaac, 2021; Timothy & Ron, 2013). Focusing on these types of specialty areas can create a greater awareness of diverse conceptual groundings, theories, and methods. Similarly, SIs can help shed light on challenges in marginal regions of the planet by focusing on critical issues in parts of the world that have not received adequate research attention, such as Backman and Munanura's (2015) SI in the *Journal of Ecotourism* on ecotourism in sub-Saharan Africa. The contributors to that themed issue elucidated urgent issues in African ecotourism, including the tourism implications of neoliberalism; the importance of partnerships, cultural sensitivity, and capacity building; the important roles of tourism NGOs in nature conservation; ecotourism's role in enhancing livelihoods; and the critical need to understand principles of sustainability such as transparency, accountability, biodiversity protection, and participatory governance. This collection of 11 research papers and an editorial represents one of the strongest clusters of research and critical thinking about the implications of ecotourism in Africa, from which other less developed regions of the Global South can learn vital lessons. Huber's (2019) final category of SI value is that themed issues can in fact connect theory and use-inspired academic research to practice. Articles with significant management implications will appeal to practitioners and thereby raise awareness in the industry of the value of academic research.

Some journals encourage conference organizers to propose an SI based on a conference's themes and the papers presented, whereas other journals' policies avoid such practices. Themed issues have also occurred serendipitously, when a handful of articles come through the normal submission process and are then "bundled into a themed virtual issue ... and promoted accordingly" (Hartel, 2022, p. 882). Editors-in-chief may identify a conceptual gap in their journals, or in the field more generally, and invite guest editors to organize a themed issue. For the most part, however, SI themes are identified by potential guest editors (Tomaselli, 2009), often in consultation with editors-in-chief. Guest editors propose the topic to the journal's chief editor and develop a proposal for consideration. Once agreed upon, the guest editors extend a call for contributions, organize the reviews, and decide which papers should be accepted for publication.

Editors-in-chief and individual journal policies will vary in their approaches to guest-edited issues. Some editors give full autonomy to guest editors to handle all elements of the process, including calls for papers, inviting and evaluating manuscript reviews, working with individual authors on revisions and resubmissions, and accepting papers that have met the journal's publication standard. Other editors prefer to have a strong presence in the guest editing process, with the final say on which papers will be accepted for publication.

Three approaches to soliciting contributions to an SI are generally applied. First, the guest editors publish a general call for papers. These are usually disseminated through professional listservs, affiliated social media, and highlighted on the journal's website. The call outlines the rationale and objectives of the themed issue and offers a list of potential topics that align with the theme and would fit together in the collection. This "shotgun" approach often results in many expressions of interest that are unaligned with the theme of the issue and wide gaps in manuscript quality. It also frequently results in the non-delivery of papers by the established deadline. A less frequent, but effective method, is a targeted approach in which leaders in the field are invited to contribute to the SI. Such an invitation does not guarantee a publication, as all manuscripts, whether targeted or submitted based on a general call, should undergo a full peer-review process to maintain the integrity of the journal. The third approach often used is a mix of the previous two – a general call for papers and a few targeted invitations to fill in any conceptual or empirical gaps that might exist in the subject matter.

Some guest editors choose to have potential contributors send expressions of interest and abstracts of their forthcoming papers, so they can gauge the suitability and fit of the paper for the SI. This also enables the guest editors to get a sense of the quality of the potential paper. At this stage, contributions can be declined or approved for full development and submission. Once an author receives approval from the guest editors, individual authors are then able to submit their contribution directly into the journal's editorial platform before a determined due date.

There are several key benefits for a journal and its publisher associated with publishing themed issues. First, SIs can be useful tools for helping newer journals get off the ground. When a new journal is established, it can take years to develop a brand, image, or reputation. Publishers commonly use SIs as a tool to help build awareness of a new journal. For example, one year after its 1993 establishment, the *Journal of Sustainable Tourism* (*JOST*) released an SI on "rural tourism and sustainable rural development", guest edited by Bill Bramwell. Over the next several years, additional theme issues were published; during *JOST*'s first 20 years, 12 SIs were produced, helping establish *JOST* as a signature outlet for papers dealing with sustainable tourism (Bramwell & Lane, 2012).

Another benefit for the journal is the building of a talent pool. According to Leigh and Edwards (2022), guest editing or contributing to an SI may be a way of "fostering talent" for the future success of the journal. Many SI authors and guest editors later become referees, editorial board members, or even co-editors of a journal they have worked with before. Thus, a certain level of familiarity is created and a desire to serve in an editorial capacity can be cultivated.

A third benefit for a journal is the development of a critical mass of thought and scholarship in a specific area or subarea (Chen, 2011). For instance, the *Journal of Heritage Tourism* has published several SIs as a means of drawing scholars together to debate, rethink, and contribute new knowledge to themes such as UNESCO World Heritage Site management, Indigenous cultures, heritage tourism and climate change, dark tourism, and cultural trails and routes. Special issues can bring together the top intellectuals in the field who are open to broad thinking and creative approaches to research. In these ways, a journal gains a reputation as a leader on a given topic. This will result in increased citations, increased submissions, and a healthy backlog of articles in the publication queue.

Fourth, by curating a collection of articles that develop knowledge in a particular field, SIs can provide a "one-stop shop" for academic audiences (Leigh & Edwards, 2022, p. 217) and increase a journal's measurable impact, including metrics such as indexing, impact factors, citation rates, Eigenfactors, and Article Influence Scores (Hartel, 2022; Olk & Griffith, 2004), especially in less prominent journals (Conlon et al., 2006). Such an effect is believed to increase the longevity and relevance of an SI and the papers it includes (Jones & Gatrell, 2014). According to one recent study (Repiso et al., 2021), three-quarters of journals that host SIs had a higher impact factor for SI articles than for non-SI articles. Higher metrics translate into higher numbers of subscriptions, article downloads, and other measures of financial success, not to mention the prestige associated with being the publisher of a high-impact journal.

A final advantage for publishers is increased revenue through the publication of research monographs. Many publishers, including some of the top tourism journal owners re-publish selected themed issues in book form as research monographs. This practice enables non-subscribing consumers to buy a special issue-based book, which increases access to collections of articles and enlarges the revenue stream of the publisher (Steinberg & Boettcher, 2023).

BENEFITS OF PUBLISHING IN A SPECIAL ISSUE

For individual scholars, there are a number of advantages to publishing in a themed issue. Special issues are an effective mechanism for broadening thinking, disseminating research results, and expanding conversations in a particular field (Bramwell & Lane, 2012; Higham & Miller, 2018; Schmidt-Wilk, 2012). SIs have traditionally been outlets for state-of-the-art and emerging research on trending topics (Hartel, 2022; Yuan, 2017), and they can stimulate creativity, innovation, and synchronized scholarly inquiry. Publishing in SIs is a fruitful way for emerging scholars to "rub shoulders" with established scholars, develop networks with editors and other researchers, gain visibility for their work, and become part of a research community with common interests. This can have significant ripple effects when invitations to contribute to other SIs, books, conferences, or consultancy projects come as a direct result of one's contribution to a themed issue.

Increasing one's citation rate may be an intentional reason for publishing in a themed issue, or a natural and organic outcome. According to Elsevier's (2023) author services, SI articles are typically cited more often than those in regular journals. According to Elsevier's data, articles in themed issues are cited upwards of 20% more during the two years post-publication than articles published in standard issues (Elsevier, 2023). Likewise, themed issues are often promoted through social media by the publisher, the editor-in-chief, or the guest editors, thereby receiving more widespread publicity than regular articles.

It has been said that publishing in SIs is easier than publishing in regular journal issues. While this is debatable and varies between guest editors, it might seem to be easier because the guest editors are looking to fill their themed issues and are therefore sometimes more willing to work with contributors to improve their papers to a publishable standard (Bramwell & Lane, 2012), rather than reject them outright as might be the case with regular submissions.

Whether or not it is "easier" to publish in SIs is a debatable point and depends on the journal, its editors, and guest editors, but work is often published faster (Elsevier, 2023; Olk & Griffith, 2004). Generally, SIs are published more quickly than papers in regular publications because SIs are planned well in advance and space might have already been allotted ahead of time in the publication queue. Likewise, given their cutting-edge nature, SIs are often bumped ahead of regularly scheduled issues as a means of hurriedly raising the visibility of the theme of the collection.

BENEFITS OF GUEST EDITING

Editing a themed issue is both a scholarly exercise and a professional service. Relatively few early-career academics guest edit SIs for various reasons, including a lack of name recognition (often needed to convince editors and publishers of their knowledge and their ability to attract known scholars), a lack of reward by their home institutions for this sort of service activity, and a limited network of researchers across the globe. Nonetheless, emerging academics can in fact guest edit SIs if they are resourceful and willing to work hard. Collaborating with more seasoned colleagues is an excellent way of getting started in guest editing themed issues.

There are many benefits of guest editing an SI. It enables the exposure of guest editors' own work to the community of scholars. Their work deepens the association of the guest editors' names with the SI's subject matter and the journal itself. Although most journals have policies against guest editors pressuring or requiring authors to cite the editors' previous work (although it does happen), savvy scholars will typically reference the work of guest editors inasmuch as it is relevant to their own contributions. This, in turn, also enhances the guest editors' visibility and increases their citations and general impact.

Part of the duty of a guest editor is writing an erudite and conceptually sound introduction or editorial piece to the theme issue. This contribution should set the scholarly tone for the entire themed collection, establish the conceptual thread of the SI, and introduce the individual contributions. Unfortunately, many guest editors write very short editorials that cursorily introduce the basic idea of the SI and then mention the main themes of each paper. This could be seen as a wasted opportunity. It would behoove guest editors to write an introductory paper that is a fully reviewed manuscript that provides a solid theoretical treatise on the subject matter at hand. Guest editors should aim to make their editorial frontpiece a fully citable, literature-rich article that takes critical stock of current thinking and postulates new directions for future research.

In addition to the editorial, most journals allow guest editors to submit their own research article to an SI. This enables the guest editors to include their own research paper in the collection, increasing their visibility and contributing to the collection of studies.

Aside from gaining visibility and accruing publications, guest editing a themed issue enables the editors to develop a wider network of collaborators and a deeper understanding of a given subject as they develop calls for papers, work with authors, and assign and make sense of reviews (Leigh & Edwards, 2022). Although they are generally already aware of the theme of the SI, the process of editing a collection of papers on a single subject can deepen their knowledge and provide service and administrative experience that will strengthen these elements of their professional portfolios.

SPECIAL ISSUES: CRITIQUES AND CHALLENGES

There are relatively few drawbacks to publishing in themed issues, compared to the benefits, although SIs have received some criticism over time. As noted previously, SIs sometimes have the reputation of being "easier" to publish in, which may or may not be the case. While it is true that most SIs have a higher acceptance rate compared to other submissions (Leigh & Edwards, 2022), that is more likely a result of the cohesive nature of the topic being investigated and the guest editors' willingness to assist authors in improving their papers to an acceptable level of erudition. Such efforts should be lauded rather than criticized, as it usually enables scholars whose first language is not the language of the journal, or who might be from a developing region with few resources to help them, develop international-standard publications. This lends diversity and provides new ways of thinking, rather than being a drawback.

Leigh and Edwards (2022) suggest that the range and types of contributors to SIs, as previously described, can also be a concern in the scientific community. For example, nepotism may be present, resulting in some editors favoring the work of close colleagues and friends over others. Decisions might be made to accept papers that would not normally muster the support of reviewers during the normal refereeing process. Likewise, other critics suggest that themed issues are often dominated by the "big names" in the field, widening the gap between inexperienced and experienced scholars and creating monopolies on knowledge creation and dissemination in the publication marketplace by the same veteran scholars who almost always appear in relation to a given topic (Das, 2017).

Priem (2006) raises concerns about SIs prioritizing particular themes over others, crowding out other important topics, and quashing innovation and creativity. Nonetheless, other scholars refute such a claim (Hartel, 2022; Yuan, 2017), suggesting that themed issues in fact provide a venue for additional creativity and expansion of knowledge in niche areas that might otherwise find little space in the regular pages of a particular journal. Priem (2006) also argues that SIs displace other articles that might have been waiting longer to be published.

Although some decision makers might contend that SI papers are of a substandard quality, in most cases quite the opposite is true. An empirical study by Olk and Griffith (2004) shows no difference between the quality of papers published in SIs and those published in regular issues. Related to this misperception, one potential challenge might be a scholar's institution valuing themed issues less than papers published through regular means in regular journal issues, owing to perceptions of favoritism, compromised academic practices, or quality. This is rare, but individual institutions have their own cultural biases in what counts as good scholarship and what does not. Despite this potential challenge, common acceptance and empirical research show that the impact of SI papers is no less than the impact of those published outside themed issues, and that biases or "compromised publishing practices" are not endemic or even commonplace in SIs (Steinberg & Boettcher, 2023). Steinberg and Boettcher (2023) recommend that journal SIs should be encouraged, doubts about quality should diminish, and concerns about impact should be alleviated. In fact, their paper provides evidence that tourism and hospitality journal editors, who do not regularly publish themed issues because of concerns over quality and impact, should "reconsider this choice" and acknowledge that SIs "in their publishing practice will not decrease the journal's quality [but rather] contribute to the goals of their publication and increase revenues for the publishers" (Steinberg & Boettcher, 2023, p. 3155).

CONCLUSION

Journals are the main sources of knowledge in the social sciences and business studies, including tourism. Since the 1990s, special issues have become increasingly popular in tourism studies for their ability to concentrate papers about specific themes and topic areas that need additional attention or are emerging as new areas of study. For journals and their publishers, SIs provide unique opportunities and benefits, including a greater association with a particular line of inquiry, a heightened brand awareness, an increased talent pool, an increase in citations, and augmented revenue.

Although many early career scholars do not serve as guest editors for various reasons, it is becoming more common, particularly as they partner with more established colleagues and mentors. Guest editors benefit by widening their network of colleagues, connecting their names to a specific subject, and gaining a deeper understanding of a particular topic. Most importantly, for early career academics, SIs can be a catalyst for developing networks among like-minded scholars, enabling working closely with known editors, elevating their work and name recognition, contributing to progressive thinking, achieving a faster publication time (often), increasing their citation rates and h-index, and overall increasing the visibility of their work in the academy. As Elsevier (2023, n.p.) rightfully notes,

> there's no better way to increase your visibility, and the visibility of your work, than to publish in a special issue of your chosen journal. Not only will you be able to reach a much larger audience, but you will also be collaborating with other experts in your field, and starting important conversations that can advance topic-specific knowledge. Publishing in special issues is unquestionably beneficial to your academic and professional career.

Although there are some negative perceptions about SIs, these are negligible and should not preclude emerging scholars from participating in themed issues as manuscript contributors, guest editors, or reviewers. Such efforts have long-lasting effects and can help affix one's name to a given field of study and produce opportunities for future collaboration.

For decades, journal special issues have functioned as "vanguards of knowledge that create a path into new topics" (Olk & Griffith, 2004, p. 129). Scholars who publish in themed issues contribute to cutting-edge work that can be instrumental in advancing forward thinking, critical analysis, and innovative inquiry. Early career academics should have no inhibitions about choosing SIs as outlets for their work. Any questions about favoritism or quality are superseded by the positive opportunities this sort of involvement provides.

REFERENCES

Backman, K.F., & Munanura, I. (2015). Introduction to the special issues on ecotourism in Africa over the past 30 years. *Journal of Ecotourism*, 14(2–3), 95–98.

Bramwell, B., & Lane, B. (2012). Towards innovation in sustainable tourism research? *Journal of Sustainable Tourism*, 20(1), 1–7.

Chen, X. (2011). Introducing *Theranostics* journal – from the editor-in-chief. *Theranostics*, 1, 1–2.

Chhabra, D. (2019). Authenticity and the authentication of heritage: Dialogical perceptiveness. *Journal of Heritage Tourism*, 14(5/6), 389–395.

Conlon, D.E., Morgeson, F.P., McNamara, G., Wiseman, R.M., & Skilton, P.F. (2006). From the editors: Examining the impact and role of special issue and regular journal articles in the field of management. *The Academy of Management Journal*, 49(5), 857–872.

Das, P. (2017). Aspects of authorship in journal special issues: An experience from DESIDOC Journal of Library and Information Technology. *Journal of Scientometric Research*, 6(3), 159–170.

Delamothe, T. (2001). Forthcoming theme issues and how we chose them. *BMJ: British Medical Journal*, 323, 766–769.

Earl, A., & Hall, C.M. (2023). Nostalgia and tourism. *Journal of Heritage Tourism*, 18(3), 307–317.

Elsevier (2023). Publishing in special issues: Is it good for my career? Online: https:// scientific -publishing .webshop .elsevier .com/ research -process/ publishing -special

-issues -good -my -career/#: ~: text = In %20general %2C %20these %20issues %20are ,often%20than%20regular%20issue%20articles. Accessed 20 August 2023.

Hartel, R. (2022). Special issues. *Journal of Food Science*, 87, 882.

Higham, J., & Miller, G. (2018). Transforming societies and transforming tourism: Sustainable tourism in times of change. *Journal of Sustainable Tourism*, 26(1), 1–8.

Huber, J. (2019). Who benefits from *JACR*? *Journal of the Association for Consumer Research*, 4(3), 210–213.

Isaac, R.K. (2021). Editorial, special issue on dark tourism. *Journal of Heritage Tourism*, 16(4), 363–366.

Jones, O., & Gatrell, C. (2014). The future of writing and reviewing for *IJMR*. *International Journal of Management Reviews*, 16(3), 249–264.

Leigh, J.S., & Edwards, M.S. (2022). What's so special about special issues? A discussion of their benefits and challenges. *Journal of Management Education*, 46(2), 215–225.

Olk, P., & Griffith, T.L. (2004). Creating and disseminating knowledge among organizational scholars: The role of special issues. *Organization Science*, 15(1), 120–129.

Priem, R. (2006). What happens when special issues just aren't "special" anymore. *Journal of Management Inquiry*, 15(4), 383–388.

Repiso, R., Segarra-Saavedra, J., Hidalgo-Marí, T., & Tur-Viñes, V. (2021). The prevalence and impact of special issues in communications journals 2015–2019. *Learned Publishing*, 34(4), 593–601.

Schmidt-Wilk, J. (2012). Teaching-related benefits of editing a pedagogical journal. *Journal of Management Education*, 36(4), 463–467.

Singh, T.V. (2014). The making of a journal: 40 years of tourism recreation research. *Tourism Recreation Research*, 39(3), 293–298.

Steinberg, R., & Boettcher, J.C. (2023). Special issues in hospitality and tourism management journals. *International Journal of Contemporary Hospitality Management*, 35(9), 3154–3171.

Thiessen, D. (2013). Theme issues. *Curriculum Inquiry*, 43(4), 421–425.

Timothy, D.J., & Ron, A.S. (2013). Understanding heritage cuisines and tourism: Identity, image, authenticity and change. *Journal of Heritage Tourism*, 8(2/3), 99–104.

Tomaselli, K.G. (2009). Thirty years of publishing. *Critical Arts: South-North Cultural and Media Studies*, 23(1), 1–5.

Yuan, M. (2017) 30 years of *IJGIS*: The changing landscape of geographical information science and the road ahead. *International Journal of Geographical Information Science*, 31(3), 425–434.

PART III

PUBLISHING ISSUES

10. Research and publishing ethics and integrity

C. Michael Hall and Yael Ram

INTRODUCTION

Research integrity is an increasingly important issue in publishing. Research integrity refers to "a collection of qualities that researchers and research institutions must possess, to ensure that research produces valid and reliable scientific knowledge, in a way that is societally desirable, and with a proper positioning of scientists in society" (Valkenburg et al., 2021, p. 1). Interestingly, Valkenburg et al. (2021) understand ethics as being focused more on the good reputation of science or an institution, and integrity more at the level of the individual and their commitments and responsibilities. In this chapter, we see both as mutually important and related.

In research and publishing we face ethical and integrity issues at several different levels. These include institutional ethics (i.e., your university), professional ethics (i.e., being a member of a professional association or society), publisher ethics (i.e., many publishers have a code of conduct of their own or they have signed on to international recommendations, such as COPE – Committee on Publishing Ethics, https://publicationethics.org), and, of course, personal ethics. These are all embedded in different national rules relating to ethics, for example, privacy legislation, as well as different research cultures. These relationships have many implications for publishing which have become even more important over time as journals have increasingly formalised their ethics requirements, which may differ substantially from that of the institutions researchers come from. However, these different ethical pressures create a challenging situation for publishing in journals as well as raising broader questions about how these various pressures fit together. Do we have a universal set of publishing ethics? And, is there an ends and means issue when it comes to publishing given the ethical responsibilities and constraints that are faced?

This chapter seeks to respond to such issues and help authors consider some of the ethical and integrity issues that they face in seeking to get their work published. It first provides context with respect to the notion of ethics creep and the regulatory scope of ethics before detailing macro-, that is, general and critical ethical questions, and micro-ethical issues, that is, institutional ethics requirements. The chapter then goes on to discuss publishing ethics, research culture, and sanctionable and aspirational values and norms. The chapter concludes with some recommendations about the importance of ethics in publishing.

ETHICS CREEP AND THE REGULATORY SCOPE OF ETHICS

The regulatory scope of research and publishing ethics has expanded sub-stantially in recent years (Schrag, 2010; Guta, Nixon, & Wilson, 2013; Valkenburg et al., 2021). Haggerty (2004) described this expansion as "ethics creep" whereby there is a growth in the formal systems that deal with ethics in terms of the type of activities that are covered as well as the institutions and regulations that cover those activities. Such concerns are significant and Haggarty (2004, p. 391) suggested, "that one effect of the increasingly formal-ized research ethics structure is to rupture the relationship between following the rules and acting ethically." Indeed, there are clearly concerns that with increased regulation, "ethics" becomes more a case of ticking boxes rather than being genuinely engaged in ethical issues (Spike, 2005; Allen, 2008; Schrag, 2010; Gorman, 2011; Chiumento, Rahman, & Frith, 2020).

There has also long been concern that such ethics creep is geared more to natural science and biomedical conceptions of harm and risk rather than critical social scientific approaches and those engaged in qualitative and community-based research practices (Patterson, 2008; Burr & Reynolds, 2010; Schrag, 2010; Munoz & Fox, 2011; Monaghan, O'Dwyer, & Gabe, 2013). Although from a broader perspective that ties into concerns over the domi-nance of research metrics and rankings for institutions, journals, and individual researchers, the changes to the governance of ethics reflect a desire for greater surveillance and control of the academy in which "trustworthiness is being associated with standardization, competence, continuity and reliability" and "quality assurance links the micro world of the organization with the public world of politics and policy" (Morley, 2003, pp. 5–6). In part, regulatory growth may be seen as a response to genuine concerns over research malprac-tice, exploitation, and lack of consideration for potentially vulnerable popula-tions. However, at the same time, it is undoubtedly affecting how research is undertaken and published and, potentially, where it is published.

A key point to consider in the contemporary publishing environment is that the ethics of doing research and the ethics of publishing such research have now become inseparable. This is because many journal publishers now require ethics declarations to be made as a precondition of publication, sometimes including the relevant university ethics committee approval number. Of course, this may then create issues for those researchers who operate in such jurisdictions, universities, and research cultures where tourism-related social science research does not have such institutional arrangements. In addition, many reviewers also want to see discussion regarding ethical clearance and practice in manuscripts. Ideally, this emphasis on ethics in the publishing process should mean that it is important to think about what we mean by ethical issues and to think about why we should be concerned about them. Or to put it more directly: Are you concerned because you have to be, or because you really are?

RESEARCH INTEGRITY: MACRO- AND MICRO-ETHICAL ISSUES

Another complicating point about ethical issues is that they are very different for each individual piece of research and depend on the place and the circumstances of research. Indeed, in reviewing a decade of studies on research integrity, Aubert Bonn and Pinxten (2019) observe that individual researchers are likely to act differently in particular situations, as their perceptions and expectations will be different. Nevertheless, increasingly general ethics frameworks are placed over the variety of research practices and experiences that exist, although specific ethical issues may arise, especially from the perspective of ethics committees when faced with what they regard as controversial issues and subjects. These may be political, cultural, or business oriented in nature or may, if one is being cynical, be concerned with potentially not causing any embarrassment for universities, rather than upholding the ideal of universities fulfilling a role of the critic and conscience of society. As a result, we can potentially differentiate between macro-theoretical issues that ask more critical questions about the ethical nature of the research we do and the responsibilities of a researcher and the more regulatory micro-ethical issues that are required under ethical governance procedures. These ethical fields do overlap, and while the meta-ethical issues pose important methodological and ethical questions that may be considered by researchers and, sometimes by reviewers, the reality is that the focus of most journals and institutions is on ensuring that the topics have been ticked off.

Some examples of the meta-ethical issues that might arise in tourism-related micro-ethical social science research include:

• The potential of the research and the researcher to either promote or demote certain places or businesses (or even people) (Amore, Hall, & Jenkins, 2017; Bulchand-Gidumal & Melián-González, 2023);

- The sensitivity or permission to do the research and to speak to particular individuals – human situations are rarely politics-free, and researchers can often unwittingly end up involved (Hall, 2011; Amore & Hall, 2022);
- Working with "at-risk" or vulnerable populations or sensitive topics (Canosa & Graham, 2016; Prayag et al., 2016; Ram et al., 2019; Nimri et al., 2021; Ram, 2021; Dodds et al., 2023; Hall et al., 2023);
- The question of how much we can and should expect people to share their thoughts, feelings and time with us, and the accuracy of the voice they are given (Stronza, 2001; Brown, 2005; Hall, 2011; Zhou et al., 2020);
- Privacy and confidentiality, especially with respect to personal information (Hew et al., 2017; Hall & Ram, 2020; Rahmadian, Feitosa, & Zwitter, 2022; Yallop et al., 2023);
- Selection of the method that is used (Smith, 2014; Love & Hall, 2021);
- What are the rights and degree of ownership of data of the communities and individuals who participate in research, in particular the differences between working with communities and individuals rather than working on secondary sources? (Hall, 2011; Love & Hall, 2021); and
- Do the results have consequences or make a difference? (Sæþórsdóttir & Ólafsson, 2010; Stefánsson, Sæþórsdóttir, & Hall, 2017; Sæþórsdóttir & Hall, 2020; Tourism Panel on Climate Change (TPCC), 2023; Tverijonaite et al., 2022, 2023).

Many of the above issues raise questions regarding ethics and decision-making in the research process with respect to what we do. In many ways they also make us think about the contribution of research and, hopefully, of the papers that result. At the micro-ethical scale we are more concerned with the standard questions we face with respect to ethical permissions and regulations. There are a number of general principles that we usually see applied in most formal institutional structures that manage ethics and which reviewers will also often look for in papers as well, especially informed consent.

Informed Consent

It has become a widely recognised principle in research ethics that the researcher should always inform participants of any features of the research that might affect their willingness to take part in the study, that is, inform them of exactly what use the research will be put to, what kind of information will be needed, and where that information will end up. This may be done through oral and/or written communication. Increasingly, institutions require written consent for participation, and publishers/editors require evidence that it has been given. Therefore, informed consent is becoming more legalistic in implementation although this depends on relevant national legislation and regulation, which may include not just research governance but also privacy and other laws. While informed consent may be relatively easy to obtain for interviews and face-to-face qualitative methods, it may be more difficult for online ethnography/netnography, observation studies, or when using publicly available data or sources, that is, newspapers, websites.

Openness and Honesty

Another general principle that is applied is that there should be no deception with respect to the purpose and application of a study. However, this may become an issue in those circumstances when the research seeks to covertly observe or interact with people in as natural a way as possible so as not to influence any process or outcome.

Anonymity and Confidentiality

Concerns over privacy and the identification of research participants has meant that many research projects and associated publications use pseudonyms to hide identities. This may be especially important for research on at-risk populations or in illiberal states. Providing absolute anonymity can be extremely difficult in some cases or situations, while it also requires researchers to be truthful in their reporting. Notions of anonymity and public and private space and identities are also changing and the need for anonymity for what people write online is open to interpretation because of the very blurred boundaries between public and private and the conditions placed by platforms on the use of text and material. The situation is even more complicated because online privacy law changes between jurisdictions. However, increasingly, unless explicit permission has been given, it is appropriate to provide anonymity to research subjects and respondents, unless statements are clearly in the public realm (Wiles et al., 2008).

Confidentiality is not always as easy as it may seem when you get into your study. There may be officials and respondents who may be identifiable in the research because of their position within business or government. Absolute confidentiality is also even harder in the post-Edward Snowden era or even impossible, especially if using online surveys and data sharing (Ross, Iguchi, & Panicker, 2018). In some countries, there are also issues as to what may be accessible in a research programme via freedom of information requests.

Right to Withdraw

All participants should have the right to withdraw from a study. However, this can create problems in terms of how far a study has progressed.

Protection from Harm and Risk

Researchers must endeavour to protect participants from physical and psychological harm, but increasingly business, political, reputational, and other forms of harm and risk appear to be considered (Haggerty, 2004). However, such concerns may also impact what and how research is undertaken. In many countries, for example, conducting social science research on politicians or government activities can be extremely sensitive. In other countries conducting research with children is sensitive. Depending on the research context and jurisdiction, researchers need to be sensitive to and respect the race, gender, sexual orientation, children, cultural, and religious issues of all participants. But does that then mean that some questions may not even be asked because researchers become too concerned as to their potential sensitivity for ethics and research permissions? The broader ethical question in such cases, and in many other instances where potentially sensitive issues exist, relate to the ends and means of doing research and, in other contexts, the balance between public and private interest. However, issues of harm and risk may also have legal implications, therefore these are also concerns that publishers increasingly seek to minimise (Di Minin et al., 2021).

Debriefing and Exit

There is increasing recognition that researchers need to provide feedback to participants in their research and its results. This reflects a viewpoint that we work with people rather than on them and it is especially important in community-based research. From such a perspective, researchers should provide an account of the purpose of the study and its procedures and, ideally, researchers should "report back" their results to those who assisted them or at least make their research publicly available. This usually means more than publishing one's work and putting it online. Instead, it means communicating results in a manner understandable to your audience. However, from a practical perspective researchers need to ensure that in communicating their work they do not breach copyright and publishing agreements.

The above are all considerations of the institutional ethics of research. They are key considerations in doing the research that gets published. However, it is important to consider the particular ethical concerns of the context you are researching in. No two research contexts are the same. But similarly, there are very specific ethical dimensions to publishing research, especially in a team context.

PUBLISHING ETHICS

Ram and Hall (2018) likened the application of ethical rules for publishing to refereeing a football game (Figure 10.1). We will use this analogue here to explain some of the issues involved in moving through the ethical issues involved in publishing. From Ram and Hall's (2018) perspective, manuscript and authors are like players, then we have formal and informal rules of the game provided by publishers and institutions, and we have a series of different individual and institutional officials (referees). Or, to be more precise, "Then the reviewer is the assistant referee in the overall review process (reviewers + editors + guidelines for reviewers and authors) and the editor is the referee who interprets and is charged with enforcing the rules of the game," and who has a range of sanctions available to them.

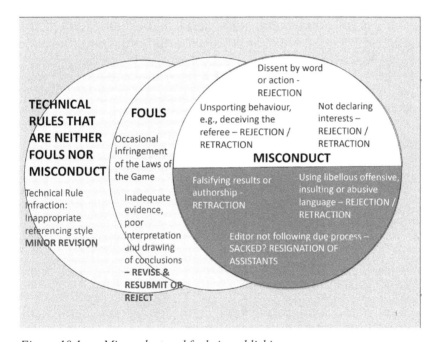

Figure 10.1   Misconduct and fouls in publishing

In terms of the rules of the game, there are "soft rules" or social norms which arise from:

* Research philosophies and schools of thought;

- The research methods and standards of evidence and critique used in fields and disciplines; and
- Disciplinary and national research cultures.

The various "soft rules" act to influence ethical and accepted publishing behaviour and are self-policed in the sense that researchers may seek to meet the social norms of their field to be accepted by their peers. However, as well as "soft rules" there are "hard rules", that is, regulatory, contractual, and professional standards that define research and publishing conduct. These are derived from academic publishers, professional bodies, research funding agencies, and universities, and include policies and codes of ethics or conduct that are required to be met. Most reputable journal publishers, for example, will have clearly stated ethical guidelines that authors, reviewers, editors, and publishers should meet (International Committee of Medical Journal Editors (ICMJE) 2023a, 2023b, 2023c, 2023d, 2023e), as well as their recognition of international and national guidelines and codes of conduct (e.g., Helsinki Declaration on research on human subjects, https:// www .wma .net/ policies -post/ wma -declaration -of -helsinki -ethical -principles -for -medical -research -involving -human -subjects/). In particular, there is emphasis on honesty (provision of complete information, for example, data and analysis, no mis-representation or falsification of data), transparency (any financial or other conflict of interest that affects findings should be revealed) (*Nature*, 2017), and balance (recognition of different literature and perspectives). What is also significant, especially in light of the ethics creep discussed earlier, is that standards from medicine and health research are increasingly being applied across the social sciences and humanities (Schrag, 2010).

Nevertheless, these are ideals which have arguably become less likely to be achieved by papers because of the demands for publishing by institutions. There is therefore more concern over questionable research practices (Fanelli, 2009), as well as falsification, fabrication, and plagiarism (ALLEA, 2017), as a result of the perceived development of a "publish or perish" culture (Tijdink, Verbeke, & Smulders, 2014; Genova & de la Vara, 2019) and its associated incentives which have led to an "erosion of research integrity" (Ellis, 2015, p. 752). To Nichols-Casebolt (2012, p. 16) a "culture of integrity" is one in which ideas of integrity are integrated into education and supervision, mission aims and statements, specific staff and student requirements, policies, and the more informal elements such as the encouragement of discussion of such topics and the setting of appropriate examples. However, the implementation of these elements is unclear in tourism and hospitality graduate education and ongoing staff development beyond the more formulaic elements of ethics permissions and approvals.

According to Sismondo (2008, in Valkenburg et al., 2021, p. 6), "research outcomes are heavily marked by the research context in which they come about". In tourism studies, the implications of different research settings of the researcher and the implications for what is published and where have arguably not been substantively considered. Nevertheless, it is clear that context matters, especially given the pressures that exist to publish, including for some graduate students, as a condition of receiving their PhD, or for staff seeking tenure or promotion.

One useful way of conceiving of these issues comes from Knorr Cetina (1999, p. 10) who argued that research cultures, at the level of research practices, here defined as a "routinized type of [research] behaviour" (Reckwitz, 2002, p. 249) lead to specific styles of knowledge production. She argues that three knowledge production properties can be attributed to research cultures:

1. They are not uniform but may differ across practices and disciplines;
2. Culture comes with a notion of what matters with respect to instrumental, theoretical, and organisational frameworks and associated discourses; and
3. They affect the patterns of meaning through which people communicate, and which are passed on down generations.

Therefore, research ethics and integrity issues are very much embedded in the culture(s) in which we are located and we should be reflecting on these.

SANCTIONABLE AND ASPIRATIONAL VALUES AND NORMS

In considering such matters, Valkenburg et al. (2021) provide a useful way to understand research integrity norms and values in practice. They divide norms and values into those that are sanctionable, that is, there will be unfavourable consequences if you do not fulfil them; and those that are aspirational, that is, these are good to do, but they are not enforceable. The former, sanctionable ethical norms and values, are therefore the domain of institutions and managers while the latter, which are aspirational, lie more in the realm of relationships within an academic community and potential loss of reputation if they are not met. Significantly, in terms of the earlier discussion of institutional ethics and policies,

> sanctionable values lead to liability for the institution, damage for eventual patients or research subjects, or a corruption of the body of scientific knowledge ... Thus, the question whether a value is aspirational or sanctionable also depends on the distribution of benefits, ownership and liability, and hence power, between the researcher and the institution. (Valkenburg et al., 2021, p. 9)

Four values can be identified as sanctionable: avoidance of falsification, fabrication, and plagiarism; provision of fair credit to authorship; transparency; and informed consent and respect for human dignity. Aspirational values include integrity, curiosity, reflexivity, and collegiality and trust. A number of these issues have been touched on already, however we expand on some of these concerns in more detail below.

Falsification, Fabrication, and Plagiarism

Plagiarism in publishing is becoming more difficult because of the growth of software specifically designed to tackle the issue, although plagiarism of unpublished work may occur, for example, from student work or from manuscripts and research grants under review, which is more difficult to track. Falsification and fabrication may be considerably more difficult to identify, especially with qualitative research based on interviews or ethnography. Concerningly, Valkenburg et al. (2021) make the observation,

> If researchers want made-up knowledge to appear credibly, they need intricate knowledge of how their claims will be assessed in the peer-review process. This knowledge is only available in the practice itself, and can only be learnt in the same way other skills are transferred in practice: through mentoring, practising, and various forms of teaching. (Valkenburg et al., 2021, p. 10)

We do not know the extent of falsification and fabrication in tourism research. However, it almost certainly does occur, even if it takes the "milder" form of taking "short cuts" in the research process as well as in responding to reviewers' queries. For example, including references that have not been fully read or have been included at the insistence of a reviewer or a journal editor even though they had nothing to do with the actual development of the research in the first place. Similarly, hypotheses may be rewritten and variables changed if the original analysis did not produce significant results as, although it creates publication bias, significant results may be easier to publish than insignificant ones (Amrhein, Greenland, & McShane, 2019).

Authorship

Many journals now have authorship guidelines and conventions that should be followed. Different disciplines used to have different conventions – for example, references might need to be arranged in alphabetical order and/or ordered by extent of contribution – but increasingly the informal conventions are being pressured by institutional wants. For example, greater credit being given to first authors than others in the allocation of rewards, while Clarivate

Web of Science author profiles now provide details of author position (e.g., first, last, co-authorship) thereby reinforcing the notion that order must be important without the context of why. Such order pressures are also growing at the same time as there is a growth in multiple-authored papers. At the same time, there are issues over the crediting of ideas and contributions. Nylenna (2015), in an article for the Norwegian National Research Ethics Committees, identified three significant problems with respect to unfair authorship and noted that these occurred in potentially almost a third of medical and health papers:

1. Gift authorship: "a situation in which persons with a relatively tenuous association with the project are included on the list of authors, perhaps in the hope that they will reciprocate the favour next time around";
2. Guest authorship: "when particularly well-known or prominent persons are unfairly invited to be included on the list of authors because it is assumed that this will strengthen the project and increase the chance of publication"; and
3. Ghost authorship: "when persons who definitely should be included among the authors are omitted – willingly or unwillingly" (Nylenna, 2015).

The influential ICMJE recommends that authorship be based on the following criteria:

• Substantial contributions to the conception or design of the work; or the acquisition, analysis, or interpretation of data for the work;
• Drafting the work or reviewing it critically for important intellectual content;
• Final approval of the version to be published; and
• Agreement to be accountable for all aspects of the work in ensuring that questions related to the accuracy or integrity of any part of the work are appropriately investigated and resolved (ICMJE, 2023a).

All of the above criteria should be met for authorship. Editing alone does not qualify nor does gaining funding for authorship. Authors should also be able to identify what each co-author has contributed to a work as well as have confidence in the integrity of the contributions of each author (ICMJE, 2023a), although clearly the larger the research team the more difficult this becomes and the more important it is for the research coordinator/lead author to undertake such responsibilities. Those who do not satisfy all four criteria should receive an acknowledgement. "Examples of activities that alone (without other contributions) do not qualify a contributor for authorship are acquisition of funding; general supervision of a research group or general administrative support; and writing assistance, technical editing, language editing, and proofreading" (ICMJE, 2023a). Importantly, it is also not the responsibility of journal editors to manage authorship issues but the corresponding author and the team of authors and, in cases of substantial dispute, the institution.

A more recent issue that has emerged in authorship is the role of artificial intelligence (AI)-assisted technology, such as ChatGPT. Such technology cannot be given authorship given that it is unable to take responsibility for authorship. However, use of AI needs to be fully disclosed in any article and authors need to be able to assert that AI has not led to plagiarism.

CONCLUSIONS: FOLLOWING ASPIRATIONS?

As this chapter has noted, the social sciences, including tourism, have gradually become subject to ethics creep as part of the marketisation and calls for greater control over higher education. As a result, medical and health ethics conventions for research have now become standard in social science publishing, including in tourism and hospitality. This is not necessarily a bad thing in some areas, especially with respect to issues such as authorship, transparency, plagiarism, and the fabrication and falsification of data and results. However, it has also meant greater regulation of research processes and ethics by institutions which has led to concerns that more critical research may not be conducted because of concerns over the reputation of the university or university relationships with funders and government. These impacts may be particularly profound if research is concerned with gender, race, and feminist perspectives, and, in some jurisdictions, research on climate change and the environment. Nevertheless, at the same time there remains continuing institutional pressure to publish, especially in journals of a specific impact or ranking, or in journals included in particular bibliometric databases (Scopus, Web of Science), or as a first author, usually because it is regarded as helping to boost university rankings. If this is the research culture that we are in and pass on, is it no wonder that the wider aspirational values of integrity, curiosity, reflexivity, and collegiality and trust are harder to uphold, and there may be substantial gaps between attitudes and behaviours when it comes to the ethics of publishing.

In seeking to publish, readers may need to balance their personal ethics with those of their institution and of the publisher. Clearly, the most important consideration is that ethical issues are thought about, from the selection of a research topic and how research is done through to writing up and submitting to a journal, and subsequent revisions before acceptance. Each stage has ethical considerations, not all of which are covered by institutional ethics forms, but they all affect researcher integrity in its broadest sense. For example, how to deal with unofficial conversations or the relative importance of an issue? Or, as a research methods class discussing ethics issues might be asked, what is more important to meet, the requirements of the university ethics committee or your own personal ethics? Or, how might your ethics change over time, including during the research process? These issues are significant to getting published and to career satisfaction and development and we hope that you are able to do this while maintaining your integrity.

REFERENCES

ALLEA. (2017). *The European code of conduct for research integrity.* ALLEA – All European Academies.

Allen, G. (2008). Getting beyond form filling: The role of institutional governance in human research ethics. *Journal of Academic Ethics, 6*, 105–116.

Amore, A., & Hall, C.M. (2022). Elite interview, urban tourism governance and post-disaster recovery: Evidence from post-earthquake Christchurch, New Zealand. *Current Issues in Tourism, 25*(13), 2192–2206.

Amore, A., Hall, C.M., & Jenkins, J. (2017). They never said "Come here and let's talk about it": Exclusion and non-decision-making in the rebuild of Christchurch, New Zealand. *Local Economy, 32*(7), 617–639.

Amrhein, V., Greenland, S., & McShane, B. (2019). Scientists rise up against statistical significance. *Nature, 567*(7748), 305–307.

Aubert Bonn, N., & Pinxten, W. (2019). A decade of empirical research on research integrity: What have we (not) looked at? *Journal of Empirical Research on Human Research Ethics, 14*(4), 338–352.

Brown, S. (2005). Travelling with a purpose: Understanding the motives and benefits of volunteer vacationers. *Current Issues in Tourism, 8*(6), 479–496.

Bulchand-Gidumal, J., & Melián-González, S. (2023). Fighting fake reviews with blockchain-enabled consumer-generated reviews. *Current Issues in Tourism*, https://doi.org/10.1080/13683500.2023.2173054.

Burr, J., & Reynolds, P. (2010). The wrong paradigm? Social research and the predicates of ethical scrutiny. *Research Ethics, 6*(4), 128–133.

Canosa, A., & Graham, A. (2016). Ethical tourism research involving children. *Annals of Tourism Research, 61*, 219–221.

Chiumento, A., Rahman, A., & Frith, L. (2020). Writing to template: Researchers' negotiation of procedural research ethics. *Social Science & Medicine, 255*, 112980.

Di Minin, E., Fink, C., Hausmann, A., Kremer, J., & Kulkarni, R. (2021). How to address data privacy concerns when using social media data in conservation science. *Conservation Biology, 35*(2), 437–446.

Dodds, S., Finsterwalder, J., Prayag, G., & Subramanian, I. (2023). Transformative service research methodologies for vulnerable participants. *International Journal of Market Research, 65*(2–3), 279–296.

Ellis, L.M. (2015). The erosion of research integrity: The need for culture change. *The Lancet Oncology, 16*(7), 752–754.

Fanelli, D. (2009). How many scientists fabricate and falsify research? A systematic review and meta-analysis of survey data. *PLoS One, 4*(5), e5738.

Genova, G., & de la Vara, J.L. (2019). The problem is not professional publishing, but the publish-or-perish culture. *Science and Engineering Ethics, 25*(2), 617–619.

Gorman, S.M. (2011). Ethics creep or governance creep? Challenges for Australian human research ethics committees (HRECs). *Monash Bioethics Review, 29*(4), 23–38.

Guta, A., Nixon, S.A., & Wilson, M.G. (2013). Resisting the seduction of "ethics creep": Using Foucault to surface complexity and contradiction in research ethics review. *Social Science & Medicine, 98*, 301–310.

Haggerty, K.D. (2004). Ethics creep: Governing social science research in the name of ethics. *Qualitative Sociology, 27*, 391–414.

Hall, C.M. (Ed.) (2011). *Fieldwork in tourism*. Routledge.

Hall, C.M., Prayag, G., Oh, Y., Mahdavi, M.A., & Xin Jean, L. (2023). Positionality, inter-subjectivity and reflexivity in Muslim minority research. *International Journal of Market Research*, https://doi.org/10.1177/1470785323119498.

Hall, C.M., & Ram, Y. (2020). Protecting privacy in tourism – A perspective article. *Tourism Review, 75*(1), 76–80.

Hew, J.J., Tan, G.W.H., Lin, B., & Ooi, K.B. (2017). Generating travel-related contents through mobile social tourism: Does privacy paradox persist? *Telematics and Informatics, 34*(7), 914–935.

International Committee of Medical Journal Editors (ICMJE). (2023a). *Defining the role of authors and contributors*. https://www.icmje.org/recommendations/browse/roles-and-responsibilities/defining-the-role-of-authors-and-contributors.html.

International Committee of Medical Journal Editors (ICMJE). (2023b). *Disclosure of financial and non-financial relationships and activities, and conflicts of interest*. https://www.icmje.org/recommendations/browse/roles-and-responsibilities/author-responsibilities--conflicts-of-interest.html#two.

International Committee of Medical Journal Editors (ICMJE). (2023c). *Responsibilities in the submission and peer-review process*. https://www.icmje.org/recommendations/browse/ roles -and -responsibilities/ responsibilities -in -the -submission -and -peer -peview-process.html.

International Committee of Medical Journal Editors (ICMJE). (2023d). *Journal owners and editorial freedom*. https://www.icmje.org/recommendations/browse/roles-and-responsibilities/journal-owners-and-editorial-freedom.html.

International Committee of Medical Journal Editors (ICMJE). (2023e). *Protection of research participants*. https://www.icmje.org/recommendations/browse/roles-and-responsibilities/protection-of-research-participants.html.

Knorr Cetina, K. (1999). *Epistemic cultures: How the sciences make knowledge*. Harvard University Press.

Love, T.R., & Hall, C.M. (2021). Decolonising the marketing academy: An Indigenous Māori perspective on engagement, methodologies and practices. *Australasian Marketing Journal, 30*(3), 202–208.

Monaghan, L.F., O'Dwyer, M., & Gabe, J. (2013). Seeking university research ethics committee approval: The emotional vicissitudes of a "rationalised" process. *International Journal of Social Research Methodology, 16*(1), 65–80.

Morley, L. (2003). *Quality and power in higher education*. Society for Research into Higher Education and Open University Press, McGraw-Hill Education.

Munoz, R., & Fox, M.D. (2011). Research impacting social contexts: The moral import of community-based participatory research. *American Journal of Bioethics, 11*, 37–38.

Nature. (2017). Steps towards transparency in research publishing. *Nature, 549*(431), https://doi.org/10.1038/549431a.

Nichols-Casebolt, A. (2012). *Research integrity and responsible conduct of research.* Oxford University Press.

Nimri, R., Kensbock, S., Bailey, J., & Patiar, A. (2021). Management perceptions of sexual harassment of hotel room attendants. *Current Issues in Tourism, 24*(3), 354–366.

Nylenna, M. (2015). *Authorship and co-authorship in medical and health research.* National Research Ethics Committees. https:// www .forskningsetikk .no/ en/ resources/the-research-ethics-library/authorship-and-co-authorship/authorship-and -co-authorship-in-medical-and-health-research/.

Patterson, D. (2008). Research ethics boards as spaces of marginalization – a Canadian story. *Qualitative Inquiry, 14*, 18–27.

Prayag, G., Mura, P., Hall, C.M., & Fontaine, J. (2016). Spirituality, drugs, and tourism: Tourists' and shamans' experiences of ayahuasca in Iquitos, Peru. *Tourism Recreation Research, 41*(3), 314–325.

Rahmadian, E., Feitosa, D., & Zwitter, A. (2022). A systematic literature review on the use of big data for sustainable tourism. *Current Issues in Tourism, 25*(11), 1711–1730.

Ram, Y. (2021). Metoo and tourism: A systematic review. *Current Issues in Tourism, 24*(3), 321–339.

Ram, Y., & Hall, C.M. (2018). Let's talk about the weather [and football]: Disclosing climate change [denial] in tourism publishing. *The 5th International Conference on Climate, Tourism and Recreation CCTR 2018*, Umeå.

Ram, Y., Kama, A., Mizrachi, I., & Hall, C.M. (2019). The benefits of an LGBT-inclusive tourist destination. *Journal of Destination Marketing & Management, 14*, 100374.

Reckwitz, A. (2002). Toward a theory of social practices: A development in culturalist theorizing. *European Journal of Social Theory, 5*(2), 243–263.

Ross, M.W., Iguchi, M.Y., & Panicker, S. (2018). Ethical aspects of data sharing and research participant protections. *American Psychologist, 73*(2), 138–145.

Schrag, Z.M. (2010). *Ethical imperialism: Institutional review boards and the social sciences, 1965–2009.* Johns Hopkins University Press.

Sismondo, S. (2008). Science and technology studies and an engaged program. In E. J. Hacket, O. Amsterdamska, M. Lynch, & J. Wajcman (Eds.), *The handbook of science and technology studies* (3rd ed., pp. 13–31). The MIT Press.

Smith, S.L. (2014). *Tourism analysis: A handbook.* Routledge.

Spike, J. (2005). Putting the "ethics" into "research ethics". *The American Journal of Bioethics, 5*, 51–53.

Sæþórsdóttir, A.D., & Hall, C.M. (2020). Visitor satisfaction in wilderness in times of overtourism: A longitudinal study. *Journal of Sustainable Tourism, 29*(1), 123–141.

Sæþórsdóttir, A.D., & Ólafsson, R. (2010). Nature tourism assessment in the Icelandic Master Plan for geothermal and hydropower development. Part I: Rapid evaluation of nature tourism resources. *Journal of Heritage Tourism, 5*(4), 311–331.

Stefánsson, Þ., Sæþórsdóttir, A.D., & Hall, C.M. (2017). When tourists meet transmission lines: The effects of electric transmission lines on tourism in Iceland. *Energy Research & Social Science, 34*, 82–92.

Stronza, A. (2001). Anthropology of tourism: Forging new ground for ecotourism and other alternatives. *Annual Review of Anthropology, 30*(1), 261–283.

Tijdink, J.K., Verbeke, R., & Smulders, Y.M. (2014). Publication pressure and scientific misconduct in medical scientists. *Journal of Empirical Research on Human Research Ethics, 9*(5), 64–71.

Tourism Panel on Climate Change (TPCC). (2023). *Tourism climate change stocktake 2023*. TPCC.

Tverijonaite, E., Sæþórsdóttir, A.D., Ólafsdottir, R., & Hall, C.M. (2022). How close is too close? Mapping the impact area of renewable energy infrastructure on tourism. *Energy Research & Social Science*, *90*, 102574.

Tverijonaite, E., Sæþórsdóttir, A.D., Ólafsdóttir, R., & Hall, C.M. (2023). Wilderness: A resource or a sanctuary? Views of tourism service providers. *Scandinavian Journal of Hospitality and Tourism*, https://doi.org/10.1080/15022250.2023.2233932.

Valkenburg, G., Dix, G., Tijdink, J., & de Rijcke, S. (2021). Expanding research integrity: A cultural-practice perspective. *Science and Engineering Ethics*, *27*(1), 10.

Wiles, R., Crow, G., Heath, S., & Charles, V. (2008). The management of confidentiality and anonymity in social research. *International Journal of Social Research Methodology*, *11*(5), 417–428.

Yallop, A.C., Gică, O.A., Moisescu, O.I., Coroş, M.M., & Séraphin, H. (2023). The digital traveller: Implications for data ethics and data governance in tourism and hospitality. *Journal of Consumer Marketing*, *40*(2), 155–170.

Zhou, S., Yan, Q., Yan, M., & Shen, C. (2020). Tourists' emotional changes and eWOM behavior on social media and integrated tourism websites. *International Journal of Tourism Research*, *22*(3), 336–350.

11. Gender and publishing
Donna Chambers

INTRODUCTION

When I was tasked with writing this chapter on gender and publishing, I was in the final stages of completing a co-edited text titled *A research agenda for gender and tourism* (Wilson & Chambers, 2023). In this text we brought together a collection of 11 chapters which reflected on gender research and tourism, the many ways that tourism is gendered, the current problematics associated with gender including for women in the Global South, and we also proposed future directions for gender and tourism research. We suggested that these future directions were both theoretical and methodological. Regarding theory, we spoke of the need to enrich, for tourism, theorisations of Black feminism, fourth wave feminism, sex and gender, and the nexus between gender and the environment. In terms of methodology, we urged tourism scholars to engage more fully with feminist methodologies, feminist participatory action research methods and the counter narrative/storytelling techniques utilised by critical race theorists. This edited volume followed previous work that I had published independently and collaboratively on gender and tourism (Chambers et al., 2017; Chambers & Rakic, 2018; Finniear et al., 2020; Chambers, 2021a, 2021b). These publications have all been underpinned by critical gender scholarship, described as the sixth phase of the evolution of gender research in tourism (for a discussion of the six phases of scholarship in gender and tourism, see Wilson & Chambers, 2023).

Against this backdrop, I wondered how I might contribute something novel and useful for the readers of this chapter who are either seeking to publish on matters of gender and tourism, or who feel marginalised because of their gender, in the most highly respected international tourism journals. Of course, I accept that society is still gendered and that given that tourism has become an integral aspect of our social world, gender continues to matter in tourism development. But gender also matters in tourism publications, because of the importance of publishing (both in terms of quality and quantity) to the production and dissemination of tourism knowledge, performance evaluations, funding, salary decisions and promotions. Women's lower productivity in academic publishing has, arguably, had negative impacts on their career development (see Cole & Zuckerman, 1984; Leahey, 2006) and deleterious effects on knowledge production. The mantra of 'publish or perish' is a truism in academia and this is especially problematic for women. Therefore, there is still a great deal of scope for further critical work on gender that needs to be manifested and disseminated in tourism journals and other publication outlets. Indeed, in their review of the scholarship on tourism and gender, Figueroa-Domecq et al. (2015) concluded that:

> despite three decades of study and a recent increase in papers, tourism gender research remains marginal to tourism enquiry, disarticulated from wider feminist and gender-aware initiatives and lacks the critical mass of research leaders, publications, citations and multi-institutional networks, which characterise other tourism sub-fields. (p. 87)

I suggest that eight years after this publication by Figueroa-Domecq et al., there has only been glacial change in tourism gender research.

So, I recognise the need for the production and publication of more critical work on gender and tourism, but I nevertheless struggled with whether I was the appropriate person to provide 'guidance' on *what* more should be published and *how* to publish work in this area. I struggled because I did not want to suggest that there is a particular road that must be travelled to publish work on gender and tourism in top journal publication outlets. I didn't want to appear to be prescriptive or essentialist, which are both antithetical to my feminist ideals.

I want researchers in tourism (particularly women) to feel free to explore the issue of gender beyond established boundaries, beyond Eurocentric paradigms, which it is often quite difficult to do within the institutional strictures of higher education departments and faculties. I recognise the contemporary difficulties in publishing on gender, and its many intersections (including with race, class, sexuality and (dis)ability) given the way in which studies on gender have traditionally been marginalised as legitimate fields of academic enquiry in tourism (Figueroa-Domecq et al., 2015; Khoo-Lattimore & Yang, 2018). This marginalisation of gender work in tourism academia is of course reflective of the hegemonic power relationships in our societies which continue to privilege white, Western, hetero-normative, ableist and patriarchal discourses and practices.

Before proceeding I believe it is important to stress from the outset that researchers seeking to publish on gender and tourism should be reflexive about their own positionality and how this influences their choice of topic, their methodology and their interpretations (Khoo-Lattimore & Yang, 2018). According to England (1994, p. 83) 'reflexivity is self-critical, sympathetic introspection and the self-conscious analytical scrutiny of the self as researcher'. In 2018, I wrote that as a researcher, being honest about your own positionality is:

> not a call to self-indulgence or solipsism. Rather, I believe that tourism research which seeks to produce new knowledges, and which is not deeply self-reflexive in terms of the researcher's own motivations, experiences and situatedness will have limited value in terms of providing honest solutions for the problems that exist in our increasingly complex world. (Chambers, 2018, p. 195)

This call for reflexivity is not novel and has a long tradition in feminist research which acknowledges the situated and embodied nature of the researcher and the social construction of knowledge (see England, 1994; Stanley & Wise, 1979; Wilkinson, 1988).

Therefore, important to this chapter on gender and publishing is the centring of my own reflections on what I believe to be important considerations in this regard, and which have not often been sufficiently explored in the tourism literature. These reflections are necessarily influenced by my own positionality as an African-Caribbean, heterosexual, able-bodied woman whose ancestors were enslaved under British colonialism and who has resided in the seat of empire in Britain for over two decades. I have embraced the work of Black feminists (such as bell hooks, Audre Lorde, Kimberlé Crenshaw, Patricia Hill Collins, Hazel Carby, Una Marson and Claudia Jones) and decolonial scholars (Aníbal Quijano, Ramón Grosfoguel, Walter Mignolo, Arturo Escobar, Maria Lugones, Gloria Anzaldúa and Chandra Mohanty) and have found their work relevant to understandings of the role of gender and its intersections (particularly with race), and how this might be interpreted in the context of tourism. So, the reflections I provide in this chapter are underpinned by my situatedness and are not intended to be in any way prescriptive. Indeed, this chapter will necessarily contain many elisions, incoherences and no doubt, inconsistences.

In terms of the structure of this chapter, it would be remiss of me not to first provide an overview of the status of gender (in)equality in academic publications generally and in tourism. This is not provided to put off researchers (especially women) seeking to advance their academic careers through publishing in top-tier tourism journals, but to provide a basic understanding of the gendered nature of publishing that continues to provide challenges even at the time of writing. This helps to set the stage for my subsequent brief reflection on the link between colonialism and gender that I argue should be more widely problematised in tourism journal publications underpinned by concerns about social justice (see Chambers, 2021a; Cohen & Cohen, 2012). I will then end the chapter with a few contemplations for gender-aware tourism academics who wish to produce high-quality publications on gender and tourism. My hope is that readers of this chapter will be stimulated to (re)consider the gendered nature of publishing and the need for more contributions to the still meagre work on gender and tourism which are critical, reflexive, and theoretically and methodologically informed.

OVERVIEW OF RESEARCH ON GENDER AND PUBLISHING

The international publishing giant Elsevier, as part of its commitment to gender diversity and inclusion, and in support of the United Nations' Sustainable Development Goal (SDG) #5, which focuses on achieving gender equality and 'empowering all women and girls', has published a global report on gender-based representation in research since 2017. In its latest 2020 edition which is based on bibliometric data from the Scopus database as of 6 June 2019, the organisation reported on the gendered nature of academic publications and grant and patent applications across 15 countries and all the then 28 countries of the European Union. The report found that, while there are some geographical and disciplinary differences, there has been significant progress over the last few decades in women's participation in research authorship, in many cases approaching or reaching gender parity with men. However, this is particularly so only with authors who have a short publication history. Where there is a long publication history, men still outnumber women. Indeed, the ratio of women to men as authors decreases over time, resulting in men publishing more, having greater impact and more exposure to international career advancement (Elsevier, 2020, p. 6). What seems evident from this 2020 report is that there is still a general lack of gender parity in academic publishing, and in academic research more broadly, to the detriment of women.

Prior to the publication of this report, academics have reflected on the gendered nature of research productivity (with journal publishing as a primary indicator of research productivity), which has consistently underrepresented women, along with those topic areas (gender!) and methodologies (normally qualitative) that are considered 'feminine'. Explanations for women's underrepresentation in publishing have largely been divided into personal factors (such as age, marital and parental status, position in the institution) and structural factors (including the availability of resources such as time, departmental and faculty prestige, and disciplinary integration) (e.g., see Cole & Zuckerman, 1984; Fox, 2005; Sax et al., 2002; Stack, 2004). Mathews and Andersen (2001) acknowledged that, on average, women publish less than men despite the gap narrowing over the two decades since their 2001 publication. They supported the argument that the factors often cited in explanation of this gender imbalance in publishing are a combination of personal and structural factors including ambition, reputation, merit, institutional support and resources, professional networks and mentoring relationships, research topic and methodology, and time. In an interesting study on the role of personal factors in research productivity, Stack (2004) explored the relationship between gender, children and research productivity, and concluded that 'children are not a strong predictor of productivity, but the influence that they do have followed a gendered pattern' (p. 891).

Over 30 years ago, Grant and Ward (1991) produced a literature-based report which examined the gendered nature of the publication process in sociology during three stages – pre-publication, the phase of seeking outlets for publication and post-publication. They concluded that gendered politics served to disadvantage women at all three stages – in the pre-publication stage women had less access to resources such as time and finances, and women were often in institutions that offered them fewer opportunities to form or join research teams. In the publication seeking phase, the forms and modes of research by women were inconsistent with dominant patterns in the most prestigious sociology journals. Finally, in the post-publication phase, articles written by women and articles written by women on gender issues were less widely read, while the allocation of institutional rewards for publication exhibited gender bias.

McDowell, Singell and Stater (2006) used quantitative analysis of individual and job-level data over four decades to examine the role of networks on the joint decision to publish and co-author amongst economists with PhDs who were members of the American Economic Association. They found that there were gender differences in networks that could help to explain observed gender differences, including lower research outputs for women in comparison to men. They also found that women obtained lower benefits from co-authorship than men. They suggested that from their findings it appeared that, at least in the case of the discipline of economics, 'network formation tends to transition toward gender equality relatively slowly in a male-dominated occupation' (McDowell, Singell & Stater, 2006, p. 167). Mayer and Rathmann (2018) analysed gender differences across several types of academic publications (book chapters, journals) amongst psychology professors in Germany. They found that while there was no significant gender difference in book chapter publications, there were significant differences between men and women in journal publications even when personal and organisational factors were controlled. And these significant differences were to the detriment of women given that peer-reviewed journal publications are more important than book chapters for career advancement and peer recognition. Nakhaie (2002) sought to unpack what was deemed as the 'productivity puzzle' (first defined as such by Cole & Zuckerman, 1984), or why women scientists consistently published less than their male counterparts. To do so they analysed a large Canadian national survey of professors and concluded that over their lifetimes, Canadian female professors published significantly less in refereed and non-refereed articles and reports than their male counterparts. These gender disparities, they suggested, were due to differences in rank, years since PhD, discipline, type of university and time set aside for research.

Huang et al. (2020) argued that while there was extensive evidence that women were underrepresented in most scientific disciplines and published fewer articles throughout their careers, this evidence was fragmented. They therefore undertook a more comprehensive longitudinal study covering the more than half a century between 1955–2010 to assess differences in gender performance. Using bibliometric analysis of the academic publishing careers of over 1.5 million authors covering 83 countries and 13 disciplines, they found that while the participation of women in science (specifically STEM subjects – science, technology, engineering and mathematics) had increased, this had rather paradoxically led to a concomitant increase in gender differences in both productivity and impact. They found that in terms of the number of papers published per year, men and women compared favourably and had equivalent career impact for the same total number of publications. Therefore, they suggested that the identified gender gap between men and women in terms of productivity and impact over the period under study might not be underpinned by gender-specific processes but rather could be largely attributed to gender-specific differences in publishing career lengths and drop-out rates. This finding reflects that of the Elsevier (2020) report mentioned earlier which found that length of career was significant in the context of gender parity in academic publishing. This poses important questions for the sustainability of women's careers in academia.

For her part Leahey (2006), in an earlier quantitative study drawing on secondary data and a web-based survey of academics in sociology and linguistics, argued that what might explain the gender differences in productivity in academia was the importance of the critical intervening variable of research specialisation. That is, according to Leahey, 'Women specialize less than men and thereby lose out on an important means of increasing their productivity' (2006, p. 754). However, Leahey was unable to assess whether research specialisation also had an impact on other career outcomes such as job satisfaction and salary levels. Tower, Plummer and Ridgewell (2007) undertook research on the publication patterns of men and women in the top six journals in the world in the fields of science, business and social science based on data collected from the Thomson ISI index in 2005. Their findings revealed no differences between men and women in terms of productivity of publications when the percentage of women present in the academic workforce was considered. Of note here though is that the participation of women in the academic workforce at the time that this study was conducted stood at only 30–40% and raised further questions about the general lack of gender parity in academic institutions. More recent work has examined research productivity during the COVID-19 pandemic and found that while this increased overall, especially in the first few months after the lockdowns, women had much lower levels of productivity than their male counterparts largely due to having more responsibility for the care of young children (see, for example Cui, Ding & Zhu, 2022; Myers et al., 2020). However, despite what appears to be overwhelming evidence, there are nevertheless a few studies which have disputed these findings indicating that there was no discernible decrease in women's research productivity during the pandemic (see, for example Abramo, D'Angelo & Mele, 2022).

What seems clear from the preceding brief review of the historic and contemporary literature on gender and publishing (as a measure of research productivity) is that there has been no consensus on the extent to which there is gender (in)equality in academic publishing. This seems to vary according to discipline, type of publication outlet (book chapters, journals), and through space (geographic context) and time (academic career lifespan). Where there is evidence of a gender gap in academic publishing this seems to have persisted despite the increasing numbers of women in research (Elsevier, 2020). What seems clear is that there is no single cause and no single solution for this apparent gender gap – in fact, the research is inconclusive. Indeed, what is also evident is that what Cole and Zuckerman (1984) referred to as the 'produc- tivity puzzle' is still pertinent almost four decades later. They had themselves argued then that 'gender per se' cannot explain 'much of the variance in pub- lished productivity … [as] variability between the sexes is not nearly as great as variability *within* each sex' (Cole and Zuckerman, 1984, p. 248, my empha- sis). The relevant questions for readers of this chapter at this point are: what is the situation in tourism? Is there a gender gap in tourism publishing and if so, what is the extent of the gap? What can be done? To address these questions, in the next section I will provide a precis of the tourism literature in this regard.

OVERVIEW OF RESEARCH ON GENDER AND PUBLISHING IN TOURISM

While research on gender and tourism has, arguably, existed since the 1970s (Khoo-Lattimore & Yang, 2018), it can be said to have blossomed from the early to mid-1990s with two key publications – the edited text by Kinnaird and Hall (1994) titled *Tourism: A gender analysis* and the special issue of *Annals of Tourism Research* edited by Margaret Byrne Swain (1995). However, much of the research on gender in tourism focuses on gender as a subject area of study rather than on the gender of the researchers themselves or the extent of gender (in)equality in tourism knowledge production as manifested in academic publications. In a bibliometric analysis using the Scopus database of journal articles published between 1986–2014, Figueroa-Domecq et al. (2017) claimed that tourism gender research was finally 'igniting' based on the increase in publications in this area in 2013 and 2014. They mentioned the key themes/subjects that dominated in this area – the gendered impact of tourism in host communities, gendered consumption and the differences between male and female travel, and gendered labour as sex work (Figueroa-Domecq et al., 2017). It was stark that none of these themes/subjects focused on the gendered nature of academic publishing itself. Indeed, Khoo-Lattimore and Yang (2018) undertook a systematic literature review of the Australian Business Deans Council's (ABDC) Journal Quality List to determine the state of gender research in tourism between 1979–2016, and one of their conclusions was that published work on women in academia was sparse.

However, over a decade ago, Chou and Tseng (2010) used bibliometric tools (from the SSCI and SCI databases) and social network analysis to understand the 'intellectual structure' of tourism research between 1997–2008. Using citation indices (68,037 citations from 2,601 published works) they found that there were four authors who had received the highest number of citations and thus were those who had contributed the most to tourism knowledge production. Interestingly these four authors were all men from Western countries. There was no critical awareness by Chou and Tseng at the time of the extent to which this illustrated the gendered nature of tourism knowledge production (as reflected in the authorship of journal publications) and its underrepresentation of women.

Five years later, the statistical report *The gender gap in the tourism academy* (Munar et al., 2015) was the first to seek to undertake a quantitative mapping of the gendered landscape of tourism academia. This report was the work of a collective of 12 women tourism academics from different countries and ethnicities who were frustrated at the underrepresentation and often invisibility of women in key positions of leadership as they felt that this 'opened up significant questions about the structural impediments and gendered practices at play in the tourism academy' (Munar et al., 2015, p. 1). This mapping exercise drew on two databases of tourism scholars worldwide (the International Centre for Research and Study on Tourism – CIRET – n=3370; and The Tourism Research Information Network – TRINET – n=2178). The evidence revealed that women were underrepresented in many leadership and gatekeeping positions, and that there was an imbalance in the number and influence of women in comparison to men. While this report did not examine the gender ratio in academic publishing per se, it did examine the gendered nature of journal leadership and found that amongst the top 20 tourism journals (according to Google Scholar metrics), only 21% of leading editors were women, 25% were associate editors or similar, and there were no women at all who were founding editors or editors emerita. Importantly, at the time of writing this chapter, the situation has changed somewhat with top tourism journals such as *Tourism Management*, *Journal of Travel Research* and *Annals of Tourism Research* all having editors-in-chief who are women. The extent to which this has translated into more women publishing in these journals needs detailed investigation.

In the same year as the Munar et al. report emerged, Figueroa-Domecq et al. (2015) published what they termed a 'critical accounting of the corpus of tourism gender research in order to provoke debate about its status and about the health of tourism research in general' (p. 88). They used a bibliometric analysis of 466 journal articles on gender research in tourism, found through Scopus and the ISI Web of Science databases and published between 1985–2012. In their analysis, they articulated the main themes and methodologies, the most prolific authors and the most popular journals. Although they did name the most prolific authors, interestingly there was no analysis here of the gender of the authors with published work in the sub-field. A few years later, Nunkoo, Hall and Ladsawut (2017) published a short communication in which they used quantitative analysis to explore the gender of authors and the link between gender and methodology in top social science journal *Annals of Tourism Research* between 1990–2015. They found that over this period male authors constituted more than 65% of all publications although this represented a decline from 80% at the beginning of the period of study. In 1990 women only accounted for 19% of all published articles. By 2015 there was a more equal gender balance between male and female authors representing 50% and 49% of all published authors respectively, with a clear acceleration of female authorships evident over time. Nunkoo, Hall and Ladsawut (2017) also found that there was a positive relationship between the increase in female authorship and the increase in qualitative methodologies and this perhaps somewhat reflects the stereotype of qualitative research as being more 'feminine'. This finding by Nunkoo, Hall and Ladsawut (2017) was focused only on one journal and contradicts the findings of previous work by Figueroa-Domecq et al. (2015) who observed that quantitative studies dominated the empirical work on gender in tourism. Figueroa-Domecq et al. (2015) also argued that the absence of the application of feminist epistemologies could lead to the stagnation of scholarship in this sub-field. Several tourism scholars also lamented the lack of theoretical and critical engagement with feminist epistemologies and methodologies in tourism gender research (e.g., Chambers & Wilson, 2023; Pritchard, 2014; Munar et al., 2017; Chambers & Rakic, 2018).

In another publication, Nunkoo et al. (2019) investigated the extent of gender parity in the citation practices of scholars in the most highly cited articles in tourism research. Using data extracted from Google Scholar, they were able to identify the top ten tourism journals based on their *h*-index as of January 2017. Their results revealed that there was a predominance of male authors and that men tended to engage in more self-citation than women. When other factors were considered, it was evident that the gender of authors was an important indicator of citation counts. It appears that in terms of journal citations there is a lack of gender parity which disadvantages women, and which has implications for the extent of diversity and equity in tourism knowledge production (as manifested through journal publications). Further, Figueroa-Domecq and Segovia-Pérez (2020) questioned whether tourism knowledge production is in fact sexist and the implications for the development of tourism more broadly and gender studies in tourism as a sub-field.

Koseoglu, King and Rahimi (2020) used bibliometric and social network analysis to investigate the gendered nature of publications in tourism and hospitality journals using the Social Science Citation Index (SSCI) and Google Scholar's journal metrics (*h*5-index). Twenty-five journals were included in the study spanning the period from the time of their first publication (the earliest was in 1965) to 2016. The findings of this analysis support those of Nunkoo, Hall and Ladsawut (2017) that female authorships have increased over the period. However, they did find that there were still significant gender imbalances according to geographical location. Amongst their findings was also that women contributed less to higher-impact journals, that amongst the top 50 authors only seven were women, that women collaborated less than men and that this gap had increased over time.

It is notable that Figueroa-Domecq et al. (2015) observed that the research on gender and tourism was Anglo-centric and mostly from Western countries, although there was evidence of a cadre of publications from scholars in Spain and China. However, they acknowledged, as had others in tourism before them like Pritchard, Morgan and Ateljevic (2011), that:

> there remains much work to do to build gender research capacity elsewhere in less research-intensive countries and institutions worldwide and to incorporate multiple worlds and knowledge traditions into the canon of tourism knowledge. (Figueroa-Domecq et al., 2015, p. 96)

They went on to suggest that future research:

> needs scholarship that deconstructs how gender overlaps with other vectors of oppression such as race, ethnicity, dis/ability, class, age, etc. and this would intensify with greater cross-disciplinary exchanges. (Figueroa-Domecq et al., 2015, p. 98)

There is, however, some evidence of tourism gender research in non-Western contexts. According to Vizcaino-Suárez and Díaz-Carrión (2019), tourism gender research started in Latin America at the beginning of the 21st century with central focus on the gendered dimensions of the impact of tourism development for local communities (see Vizcaino-Suárez & Díaz-Carrión, 2019). They performed a bibliometric analysis of publications on gender and tourism published in key Latin American journals and found that qualitative methodologies dominated. Topic areas included: investigations of the unequal power dynamics inherent in tourism development activities and projects, gender and tourism work, the link between tourism and the sex trade from the host perspective, and the gendered impacts of tourism development on host communities. They noted that in Latin American tourism gender scholarship, gender was still seen in binary terms and there were limited publications that focused on non-hetero-normative sexualities. Indeed, Vizcaino-Suárez and Díaz-Carrión argued that tourism gender research was still in its infancy in Latin America. They suggested areas for future research which included 'promoting situated gender knowledge; [and] challenging Eurocentric or post-colonial views' (2019, p. 1100). This alludes to the need for tourism gender research to adopt more decolonial perspectives and I will return to this in the next section.

From this brief overview, it is evident that there is scope for more detailed and critical work to be done on the gendered dimensions of academic publishing in the sub-field of gender research in tourism and in tourism research more broadly, particularly in our contemporary times. While it appears that gender parity in tourism publishing might be more achievable today (the increased number of publications by women in tourism journals and the increase in women as editors-in-chief of top tourism journals might be indications of this), there is little evidence that gender intersectionality is being considered. And here I refer specifically to the marginalisation of Black women in the tourism academy, as both consumers of tourism and producers of tourism knowledge. Several tourism scholars have called for more intersectional approaches to gender research in tourism (e.g., Ladkin et al., 2023; Pritchard, 2014; Mooney, 2018). According to Khoo-Lattimore and Yang (2018), who supported the need for more gender intersectional work in tourism, 'there is a dire need for tourism research to capture the voices of the non-Western and non-Asian travellers' (p. 45). Chambers (2021b) also argued for an intersectional approach to gender in tourism and for the specific manifestation of the voices of Black women. It is evident that there is still a lack of engagement with critical approaches and methodologies such as decolonial and Black feminist epistemologies. It appears that tourism gender research is still colonial. In this context, in the following section I will provide a brief discussion of the link between gender, coloniality and tourism that requires further exploration if we are to widen our knowledge of tourism gender research and enhance the depth and scope of publications in this area.

GENDER AND PUBLISHING: GENDER, COLONIALITY AND TOURISM

Tourism is a reflection and a continuation of the unequal power relationships that existed under colonialism. Tourism can therefore be perceived as a new form of colonialism, that governs the relationship between the tourist-receiving countries of the Global South and the tourist-generating countries of the Global North. This understanding of tourism as neo-colonialism is not new and has been acknowledged previously by many scholars including but not limited to: Britton (1992) who problematised the unequal economic relationship occasioned by tourism between the developed and developing countries with a focus on the South Pacific; Palmer (1994) who analysed tourism in the Bahamas; Echtner and Prasad (2003) who examined a number of myths that had been constructed about the peoples and places in the Global South by destination marketers; and Pratt's seminal 2007 text titled *Imperial Eyes*, which focused on the power that the travel writing of Western scholars had on the ways in which the Third World was produced both discursively and materially.

All of these and other works highlighted, whether explicitly or implicitly, the fact that while colonialism had ended in a political sense, coloniality still exists. While Edward Said's groundbreaking 1978 text *Orientalism* can be said, arguably, to have inaugurated postcolonial theory as a critique of coloni-alism, it was evident that this had not served to sufficiently articulate the power of coloniality and its consequences, especially for knowledge production. There has therefore been, since the 1980s, a renewed call for decolonisation largely emerging from scholars in Latin America, but which has now pervaded several conversations about social and racial justice including in tourism (see, for example Chambers & Buzinde, 2015). But what does coloniality mean? Nelson Maldonado-Torres, Latin American decolonial scholar, defined colo-niality as:

> long-standing patterns of power that emerged as a result of colonialism that define culture, labour, intersubjective relations, and knowledge production well beyond the strict limits of colonial administrations. *Thus, coloniality survives colonisation.* It is maintained alive in books, in the criteria for academic performance, in cultural patterns, in common sense, in the self-image of peoples, in aspirations of self, and so many other aspects of our modern experience. (2007, p. 243, my emphasis)

So coloniality is powerful, it is pervasive, and it survives in all aspects of our social world, including in tourism. Coloniality is intertwined with capitalist economic systems of power (that fuelled the colonial project) within which tourism is integrally enmeshed. Both colonialism and capitalism, as two sides of the same coin, are underpinned by unequal gendered and racialised relationships. And gender and race are socially constructed concepts, which intersect in the lives of Black women, leading to their exclusion from both the discourses of racism and sexism (Crenshaw, 1989). In terms of gender, it is argued that colonialism has reframed this term both in discourse and in practice. And here I draw on the writing of decolonial feminist Maria Lugones (2007) who stated that colonialism:

> imposed a new gender system that created very different arrangements for colonized males and females than for white bourgeois colonizers ... it introduced ... gender itself as a colonial concept and mode of organization of relations of production, property relations, of cosmologies and ways of knowing. (2007, p. 186)

Further, Lugones argued that amongst many Indigenous peoples of the Americas, the existence of intersex people was recognised. However, with the arrival of the colonisers, who feared the sexual nature of Indigenous peoples, sexual dimorphism was constructed 'to serve global, Eurocentred, capitalist domination/exploitation' (Lugones, 2007, p. 196).

Sexual dimorphism, that is the establishment of distinct categories between male and female bodies with the former assuming the dominant position, was integral to the colonial project as a way to control the colonised peoples. Added to this was a racial component which justified the exploitation of Black female bodies. Indeed, under colonialism gender and race intersected and here Black women were placed outside of Western ideas of femininity. Drawing on McClintock (1995), Lugones states that:

> Columbus's depiction of the earth as a woman's breast ... evokes the 'long tradition of male travel as an erotics of ravishment.' For centuries, the uncertain continents – Africa, the Americas, Asia – were figured in European lore as libidinously eroticized ... Within this porno tropic tradition, women figured as the epitome of sexual aberration and excess. Folklore saw them, even more than the men, as given to a lascivious venery so promiscuous as to border on the bestial. (McClintock, 1995, adapted in Lugones, 2007, pp. 204–205)

For her part, Sheller (2003) similarly articulated this trope in the context of the colonies of the Caribbean, seen as inhabited by sexually voracious Black female bodies, at one with these natural, paradisical islands which they inhabited. Indeed, tourism represents Caribbean islands as sites of pleasure and hedonism. Tourism in these islands, Sheller contends, is founded on 'a violent sexual gaze'. According to Sheller:

> Western consumption of 'black' and 'brown' bodies continued in newly mediated forms, which can be traced from 19th century tours 'through the islands, into contemporary forms ranging from package holidays to sex tourism'. (2003, p. 156)

There are very few tourism scholars who have engaged with the intersection between race and gender underpinned by decolonial theory. There is certainly scope for more of this work, as a cursory examination of the gender research published in tourism journals has scarcely revealed any publications that engage with Black feminism *and* decolonial theory despite the call for more critical work in tourism that manifests the voices of those from marginalised communities (Pritchard, Morgan & Ateljevic, 2011). Exceptions here include Lee (2017) and Chambers (2021b).

The point is that in seeking to research and publish work on gender and tourism, it is important to understand two central arguments – the first is the way in which our predominant knowledge about gender as dimorphic has been shaped by colonialism; and second is how colonialism has had a significant influence on the way Black women are (re)presented in and through tourism. And I would suggest that interrogating and problematising the link between colonialism, gender and tourism using decolonial and Black feminist theorising can provide fruitful avenues for further research in the field and can add significantly to our knowledge about gender and tourism.

CONCLUDING REMARKS

Exploring gender and publishing within the confines of a book chapter with strictures of word count has proven challenging. So what I have provided in this chapter is an overview of the status of gender (in)equality in publishing generally and more specifically in the context of tourism. I have approached this from two perspectives – first, the extent of gender parity in published work primarily in academic journals, and second, the extent to which gender is a subject of study in publications in tourism. In terms of the former, I have demonstrated that there is no consensus in the wider academic community on the nature and extent of gender parity and there are also discrepancies about the causes of identified gender (in)equalities. In tourism there is limited research which has focused on the gendered nature of academic publishing but where this exists it seems apparent that there is a gender gap which disadvantages women, although this has been decreasing over time. In terms of the latter perspective, gender remains a relatively marginal subject within tourism research publications. The still meagre research on gender in tourism that has been published often fails to take account of gender as a complex and multifaced construct, and specifically intersectionality (especially that between gender and race) has been scarcely discussed. Gender is often conceptualised as binary and this, I have argued, is a colonial legacy. I have also suggested that the coloniality of tourism research has resulted in the very limited manifestation of Black women's voices using Black feminist and decolonial theories although with some exceptions. As such, gender research in tourism is not sufficiently inclusive and this has serious implications for tourism knowledge production and issues of social and racial justice in tourism academia.

It would appear from my discussions in this chapter that things are quite grim for women, and particularly Black women, in tourism academic publishing and tourism knowledge production. However, there is still room for change and as such I would like to provide some concluding thoughts on how to achieve gender parity in tourism knowledge production and academic journal publications which readers of this chapter might find useful:

Gender Parity in Tourism Publishing

1. In looking for publication outlets for your work it is important to check the values of the journal in terms of equity, diversity and inclusion. Is there information on the journal website about these issues? Similarly check the editor-in-chief and the editorial board of the journal – is there apparent gender parity? What is the situation with gender intersectionality amongst the members of the editorial team? If you are unable to find answers to these questions, then challenge the editors about the reasons for this and what their action plan is to progress gender intersectional equity.

2. Find collaborative and supportive networks that can lead to co-publications. Research has found that men tend to collaborate more than women, and this has been detrimental for women (see Koseoglu, King & Rahimi, 2020). Collaboration can increase the quality and quantity of your journal publications and, as has been discussed, this is a key measure of research productivity. Consider, as Chandra Mohanty has claimed that 'ideas are always communally wrought, not privately owned' (2003, p. 1).

3. Currently, our higher education institutional system reifies journal publications and especially publications in journals with high-impact factors. While you are working on navigating this system (refer to points 1 and 2 above), I would urge you to think more long term and become an advocate for change in terms of what is valued as 'productive' research (with a collective of other change makers). Studies (e.g., Mayer & Rathmann, 2018) have demonstrated that there are significant differences in journal publications between men and women with the former having more publications while women are better represented in terms of book chapters. Productive research should be valued in terms of its impact (on pedagogy or on society) and not because of the outlet within which it is disseminated. The hegemony of journal publications in measurements of research productivity has disadvantaged women and more so women of colour who are either silenced or not heard in the academy (see, for example Myers, 2002). What is required according to Hall (2011, p. 26) is 'changing the rules of the game, something which the individual and collective repre-

sentatives of tourism studies have not been very good at doing … The greatest challenge to tourism scholars may be to stop playing the game altogether'. Journal publications will, of course, remain important, but we need to work together to ensure that a wider array of publication formats are also valorised.

Gender Parity in Tourism Research

4. It is important to strengthen the theoretical and methodological foundations of tourism gender research. I have highlighted the importance of gender intersectionality and in this regard of applying Black feminism and decolonial theory to deepen the criticality and diversity of work. It is important in tourism to recognise the pervasive nature of coloniality, and its impacts on tourism and gender and how this serves to marginalise and delegitimise Black women within the tourism canon.
5. Related to the above point, it is necessary to consider knowledges that are produced at other gender intersections including class, (dis)ability, sexuality and those produced in languages that are not English. It is important here to open up tourism gender knowledge production to worlds and knowledges otherwise (Escobar, 2007).
6. Reflexivity is central to research on gender, and it is necessary to include your positionality in your research publications. Indeed, feminist research demands that the researcher locate themselves within the text. That said, not all gender research draws on feminist epistemologies and there are other critical approaches that might be adopted and adapted (see Pritchard, 2014). But regardless of the research approach taken, I would argue that it is not possible to disassociate the researcher from the research and publications on gender and tourism must recognise the situated nature of knowledge. It is reflexivity, after all, that allows us to question the nature and extent of gender parity in tourism academic publishing and to devise creative and sustainable solutions for social justice.

REFERENCES

Abramo, G., D'Angelo, C.A. & Mele, I. (2022). Impact of Covid-19 on research output by gender across countries. *Scientometrics*, 127(12), 6811–6826.
Britton, S.G. (1992). The political economy of tourism in the Third World. *Annals of Tourism Research*, 9(3), 331–358.
Chambers, D. (2018). Tourism research: Beyond the imitation game. *Tourism Management Perspectives*, 25, 193–195.
Chambers, D. (2021a). Are we all in this together? Gender intersectionality and sustainable tourism. *Journal of Sustainable Tourism*, 30(7), 1586–1601.

Chambers, D. (2021b). Reflections on the relationship between gender and race in tourism. In P. Dieke, B. King & R. Sharpley (Eds.) *Tourism in development: Reflective essays* (pp. 233–244). Wallingford: CABI.

Chambers, D., & Buzinde, C. (2015). Tourism and decolonisation: Locating research and self. *Annals of Tourism Research*, 51, 1–16.

Chambers, D., Munar, A., Khoo-Lattimore, C. & Biran, A. (2017). Interrogating gender and the tourism academy through epistemological lens. *Anatolia*, 28(4), 501–513.

Chambers, D., & Rakic, T. (2018). Critical considerations on gender and tourism: An introduction. *Tourism, Culture and Communication*, 18(1), 1–8.

Chambers, D., & Wilson, E., (2023). Conclusion to a research agenda for gender and tourism. In E. Wilson & D. Chambers (Eds.) *A research agenda for gender and tourism* (pp. 219–239). Edward Elgar Publishing, Cheltenham, UK and Northampton, MA, USA.

Chou, L., & Tseng, H. (2010). Exploring the intellectual structure of contemporary tourism studies. *Journal of Quality*, 17(2), 159–178.

Cohen, E., & Cohen, S.A. (2012). Current sociological theories and issues in tourism. *Annals of Tourism Research*, 39(4), 2177–2202.

Cole, J.R., & Zuckerman, H. (1984). The productivity puzzle. *Advances in Motivation and Achievement*, 2, 217–258.

Crenshaw, K. (1989). Demarginalizing the intersection of race and sex: A black feminist critique of antidiscrimination doctrine, feminist theory and antiracist politics. *University of Chicago Legal Forum*, 1(8), 139–167.

Cui, R., Ding, H. & Zhu, F. (2022). Gender inequality in research productivity during the COVID-19 pandemic. *Manufacturing & Service Operations Management*, 24(2), 707–726.

Echtner, C.M., & Prasad, P. (2003). The context of third world tourism marketing. *Annals of Tourism Research*, 30(3), 660–682.

Elsevier (2020). *The researcher journey through a gender lens*. https://www.elsevier .com/connect/gender-report.

England, K.V. (1994). Getting personal: Reflexivity, positionality, and feminist research. *The Professional Geographer*, 46(1), 80–89.

Escobar, A. (2007). Worlds and knowledges otherwise. *Cultural Studies*, 1(2–3), 179–210.

Figueroa-Domecq, C., Palomo, J., Flecha, M.D., Segovia-Pérez, M. & Vico, A. (2017) Is the tourism and gender research area igniting? A bibliometric analysis. *Revista Turismo & Desenvolvimento*, 2(27/28), 173–175.

Figueroa-Domecq, C., Pritchard, A., Segovia-Pérez, M., Morgan, N. & Villacé-Molinero, T. (2015). Tourism gender research: A critical accounting. *Annals of Tourism Research*, 52, 87–103.

Figueroa-Domecq, C., & Segovia-Pérez, M. (2020). Application of a gender perspective in tourism research: A theoretical and practical approach. *Journal of Tourism Analysis: Revista de Análisis Turístico*, 27(2), 251–270.

Finniear, J., Morgan, N., Chambers, D. & Munar, A. (2020). Gender-based harassment in tourism academia: Organizational collusion, coercion and compliance. In P. Vizcaino, H. Jeffrey & C. Eger (Eds.) *Tourism and gender-based violence: Challenging inequalities* (pp. 30–44). Wallingford: CABI.

Fox, M.F. (2005). Gender, family characteristics, and publication productivity among scientists. *Social Studies of Science*, 35(1), 131–150.

Grant, L., & Ward, K.B. (1991). Gender and publishing in sociology. *Gender & Society*, 5(2), 207–223.

Hall, C.M. (2011). Publish and perish? Bibliometric analysis, journal ranking and the assessment of research quality in tourism. *Tourism Management*, 32, 16–27.

Huang, J., Gates, A.J., Sinatra, R., & Barabási, A.L. (2020). Historical comparison of gender inequality in scientific careers across countries and disciplines. *Proceedings of the National Academy of Sciences*, 117(9), 4609–4616.

Khoo-Lattimore, C., & Yang, E. (2018). Tourism gender studies. In C. Cooper, S. Volo, W. Gartner & N. Scott (Eds.) *The SAGE handbook of tourism management: Applications of theories and concepts to tourism* (pp. 38–48). London: SAGE.

Kinnaird, V., & Hall, D.R. (1994). *Tourism: A gender analysis*. Chichester: Wiley.

Koseoglu, M.A., King, B. & Rahimi, R. (2020). Gender disparities and positioning in collaborative hospitality and tourism research. *International Journal of Contemporary Hospitality Management*, 32(2), 535–559.

Ladkin, A., Mooney, S., Solnet, D., Baum, T., Robinson, R. & Yan, H. (2023). A review of research into tourism work and employment: Launching the *Annals of Tourism Research* curated collection on tourism work and employment. *Annals of Tourism Research*, 100.

Leahey, E. (2006). Gender differences in productivity: Research specialization as a missing link. *Gender & Society*, 20(6), 754–780.

Lee, E. (2017). Performing colonisation: The manufacture of Black female bodies in tourism research. *Annals of Tourism Research*, 66, 95–104.

Lugones, M. (2007). Heterosexualism and the colonial/modern gender system. *Hypatia*, 22(1), 186–219.

Maldonado-Torres, N. (2007). On the coloniality of being. *Cultural Studies*, 21(2–3), 240–270.

Mathews, A.L., & Andersen, K. (2001). A gender gap in publishing? Women's representation in edited political science books. *PS: Political Science & Politics*, 34(1), 143–147.

Mayer, S.J., & Rathmann, J.M. (2018). How does research productivity relate to gender? Analyzing gender differences for multiple publication dimensions. *Scientometrics*, 117(3), 1663–1693.

McClintock, A. (1995). *Imperial leather: Race, gender, and sexuality in the colonial contest*. London: Routledge.

McDowell, J.M., Singell Jr., L.D. & Stater, M. (2006). Two to tango? Gender differences in the decisions to publish and coauthor. *Economic Inquiry*, 44(1), 153–168.

Mohanty, C.T. (2003). *Feminism without borders: Decolonizing theory, practicing solidarity*. Durham, NC: Duke University Press.

Mooney, S. (2018). Illuminating intersectionality for tourism researchers. *Annals of Tourism Research*, 72, 175–176.

Munar, A., Biran, B., Budeanu, A., Caton, K., Chambers, D., Dredge, D., Gyimóthy, S., Jamal, T., Larson, M., Lindström, K., Nygaard, L. & Ram, Y. (2015). *The gender gap in the tourism academy: Statistics and indicators of gender equality*. Discussion Paper.

Munar, A.M., Khoo-Lattimore, C., Chambers, D. & Biran, A. (2017). The academia we have and the one we want: On the centrality of gender equality. *Anatolia*, 28(4), 582–591.

Myers, K.R., Tham, W.Y., Yin, Y., Cohodes, N., Thursby, J.G., Thursby, M.C., Schiffer, P., Walsh, J.T., Lakhani, K.R. & Wang, D. (2020). Unequal effects of the COVID-19 pandemic on scientists. *Nature Human Behaviour*, 4(9), 880–883.

Myers, L. (2002). *A broken silence: Voices of African American women in the academy*. Westport, CT: Greenwood Publishing Group.

Nakhaie, M.R. (2002). Gender differences in publication among university professors in Canada. *Canadian Review of Sociology/Revue canadienne de sociologie*, 39(2), 151–179.

Nunkoo, R., Hall, C.M. & Ladsawut, J. (2017). Gender and choice of methodology in tourism social science research. *Annals of Tourism Research*, 63, 207–210.

Nunkoo, R., Hall, C.M., Rughoobur-Seetah, S. & Teeroovengadum, V. (2019). Citation practices in tourism research: Towards a gender conscientious engagement. *Annals of Tourism Research*, 79, https://doi.org/10.1016/j.annals.2019.102755.

Palmer, C.A. (1994). Tourism and colonialism: The experience of the Bahamas. *Annals of Tourism Research*, 21(4), 792–811.

Pratt, M.L. (2007). *Imperial eyes: Travel writing and transculturation*. London: Routledge.

Pritchard, A. (2014). Gender and feminist perspectives in tourism research. In A. Lew, C.M. Hall & A. Williams (Eds.) *The Wiley Blackwell companion to tourism* (pp. 314–324). Chichester: John Wiley & Sons.

Pritchard, A., Morgan, N. & Ateljevic, I. (2011). Hopeful tourism: A new transformative perspective. *Annals of Tourism Research*, 38(3), 941–963.

Said, E. (1978). *Orientalism: Western concepts of the Orient*. New York: Pantheon.

Sax, L.J., Hagedorn, L.S., Arredondo, M. & DiCrisi, F.A. (2002). Faculty research productivity: Exploring the role of gender and family-related factors. *Research in Higher Education*, 43, 423–446.

Sheller, M. (2003). *Consuming the Caribbean: From Arawaks to zombies*. London: Routledge.

Stack, S. (2004). Gender, children and research productivity. *Research in Higher Education*, 45, 891–920.

Stanley, L., & Wise, S. (1979). Feminist research, feminist consciousness and experiences of sexism. *Women's Studies International Quarterly*, 2(3), 359–374.

Swain, M.B. (1995). Gender in tourism. *Annals of Tourism Research*, 22(2), 247–266.

Tower, G., Plummer, J. & Ridgewell, B. (2007). A multidisciplinary study of gender-based research productivity in the world's best journals. *Journal of Diversity Management (JDM)*, 2(4), 23–32.

Vizcaino-Suárez, L.P., & Díaz-Carrión, I.A. (2019). Gender in tourism research: Perspectives from Latin America. *Tourism Review*, 74(5), 1091–1103.

Wilkinson, S. (1988). The role of reflexivity in feminist psychology. *Women's Studies International Forum*, 11(5), 493–502.

Wilson, E., & Chambers, D. (2023). *A research agenda for gender and tourism*. Edward Elgar Publishing, Cheltenham, UK and Northampton, MA, USA.

12. Writing for English language versus other language journals

Serena Volo

INTRODUCTION

Research outputs – no matter where the study was conducted – cannot be detached from the global complex system and practice of academic dissemination (Crystal, 1997; Lillis & Curry, 2010). In this system, the dominance of English is quite well documented (Sharifian, 2009). Indeed, academic research meant to reach worldwide scientists has been – and most likely will continue to be – published in English, the dominant language to disseminate scientific knowledge (Gibbs, 1995; Kirkpatrick, 2009). A relevant portion of scientific studies focuses on understanding the politics and the impact of English dominance in the global academic publications and evaluation systems. Indeed, this prominent linguistic choice influences the overall scientific marketplace and the performances of scholars for whom English is neither their native nor their official or dominant language of communication (Gibbs, 1995; Lillis & Curry, 2010). The supremacy of English over other languages has occurred throughout time, and while – in some countries – journals are using the native local language, rarely do these journals and their published articles find resonance in the international scientific community. This reality poses several challenges to non-Anglophone authors wanting to contribute to English-medium publications.

Similarly, in our field, the most valuable platforms to circulate knowledge coming from theoretical and applied tourism research are peer-reviewed journals published in English (McKercher & Tung, 2015; Zehrer, 2007). In addition, scholars, editors, institutions, universities, libraries and evaluators are keen to consider English as "academic lingua franca" thus reinforcing the privileged position of Anglophone writers. Nevertheless, at a more pragmatic level, tourism scholars come from different regions of the world and carry very diverse language backgrounds and scholarly opportunities. Furthermore, with the expansion of our field of research (McKercher & Tung, 2015), competition for publications space has grown considerably and editors tend to disregard contributions that are poorly written. Thus, it remains paramount to ensure that the writing style and language competences of non-English native authors are enhanced so as to allow these researchers to contribute to the global scholarly debate.

Hence, this chapter provides an overview of the issues that non-native English authors face when writing for English language journals and offers a set of suggestions to support the enhancement of their writing style. The chapter is divided into four parts. The first part provides an outline of English as scientific language. The second part describes the difficulties of thinking, writing and disseminating in a non-native language. The third part presents suggestions on writing structure, style and clarity. The fourth and final part discusses "the art of writing" for top English language journals.

THE EVOLUTION AND RELEVANCE OF ENGLISH IN OUR FIELD OF RESEARCH

Using Kachru's circles of linguistic capability (1992, 2001), most pioneers of tourism research can be easily identified as belonging to the so-called "inner circle" of the English language – that is, native of countries such as the United Kingdom, the United States and Australia. A handful belong to the "outer circle" – scholars from countries with a colonial relationship with United Kingdom – and a few are non-English speakers, mostly based in mainland Europe. These non-Anglophone scholars – constituting the so-called "expanding circle" of English users – are those using English as an instrumental foreign language for researching, teaching and writing purposes. The situation has changed across decades and considering the development of tourism scholarship worldwide, it is possible to track the coping mechanism put in place by non-Anglophone authors in their approach to English writing. Indeed, tourism researchers of different generations have had diverse approaches to this issue. Older generations relied on human translators and expected to retain the writing style of their native language. This approach was certainly accepted and respected in the early years of tourism scholarship, with some journals even offering multilingual abstracts. As tourism research further developed in the 1990s and became a mainstream research field (McKercher & Prideaux, 2014), the global education and research systems confirmed the supremacy of English with its politics of knowledge production and dissemination (Erling & Seargeant, 2013; Lillis & Curry, 2010). Thus, before the turn of the millennium, young tourism scholars had the chance to be exposed to international teaching and researching environments and, therefore, could acquire a greater level of fluency and a closer relationship with the language. Standard language tools, automated grammar and spelling checks were also available to facilitate improvements in written text. Likewise, contemporary debates would include the possibility for today's scholars to use generative artificial intelligence (AI) and large language models (LLM) tools to copy-edit articles so as to improve readability and language. This short narrative, on the evolution that has occurred over the past 50 years, shows the shift in the approach to English writing and briefly outlines that the number of opportunities to improve one's written text has expanded.

While considering our field as multilingual, McKercher (2022) noticed the leadership role of English journals in tourism, hospitality and events (188 in 2021), coupled with a large number of Spanish and Portuguese language journals (66 in total in 2021) and 62 in various other languages. Specialist journals wanting to appeal to the global market tend to be published mostly in English, irrespective of the discipline, whereas generalist journals and titles with a narrow geographic focus are mostly based in non-English speaking countries. Furthermore, it is important to notice that English is also the language to conduct research. Indeed, given the nature of tourism, hospitality and leisure, scholars often conduct research using English as a medium of communication, as both the supply and demand side of the sector function – at international level – mostly in English. Thus, scholars wanting to conduct research that goes beyond their geopolitical space will encounter tourists, or other players in the field, with whom to engage in surveys, interviews and other empirical activities, and with these subjects, scholars will most likely communicate in English as "tourism lingua franca". Beside the need to communicate with research subjects, English competence is also desirable when engaging with the scientific community. It is used to collaborate with co-authors and scholars of other mother-tongues and to participate in those "academic power circles" that set the evaluation mechanism in most countries – and beyond – and that ultimately influence the trajectories of knowledge produced, published and recognised as valuable (Lillis & Curry, 2013). Therefore, despite some recent attempts to reframe the importance of English in academic contexts (Curry & Lillis, 2022; Navarro et al., 2022), scientific collaboration among members of international teams and disciplinary networks happens in English and results in English written outputs.

WRITING FOR ENGLISH LANGUAGE VERSUS OTHER LANGUAGE JOURNALS

Mastering a language to produce scientific text is a complex matter. Undeniably, Anglophone scholars retain a privileged position in the English-dominated publication landscape. Indeed, as acknowledged by Tribe (2010, p. 29), "the English language operates a difficult obligatory passage point for many researchers". While, many non-Anglophone tourism scholars are actively and successfully engaged with academic English writing, a large share of the market is made up of scholars who have neither the fluency nor the resources to reach the levels required by journals. In less developed countries, resources – libraries, funding and writing support – are lacking. Consequently, scientific outcomes from those contributors have already lower chances of reaching the wider public and this has consequences for knowledge production and dissemination more generally (Lillis & Curry, 2010), as it reduces the global scope of research. Supporting local research using non-English languages and offering publication opportunities to these scholars can be effective but will not necessarily fit the current academic marketplace. Thus, there is a need for resources that aim at supporting non-Anglophone authors in the production of text for English journals.

It is also important, in our scholarly community, to conceptually frame the issue of writing for English language journals versus other language outlets, as, after all, this is the issue of disseminating knowledge in a non-native language and to a wider audience and, likewise significant, it is the matter of gaining recognition and being rewarded institutionally. This reinforces the concept that the English language is not just a functional medium of communication of scholarly pieces, but an agent that connects scholars to specific, and often different and multiple, identities as a result of choosing it in this particular situation (Curry & Lillis, 2022). In this context, it is therefore important to remember that training and support in paper writing can be offered in different forms. Indeed, peer writing groups, writing support units and discipline-specific writing workshops can offer learning opportunities to non-Anglophone authors. In addition, within the academic written production there is a need to examine and recognise the contribution offered by various "literacy brokers" such as "editors, reviewers, academic peers, and English-speaking friends and colleagues, who mediate text production in a number of ways" (Lillis & Curry, 2006, p. 4). Indeed, together with a clear recognition of the issues faced by non-Anglophone scholars, there is the imperative to find effective solutions and to provide appropriate support.

IN SEARCH OF STRUCTURE, STYLE AND CLARITY

Structuring a scientific article is an essential step in academic writing. Like in many other types of writings, the aim is to make sure that the central research message can reach the targeted audience in the best possible way. A few essential tips can help writers with this task. Most tourism, hospitality and events journals offer detailed guidelines on the structure that submissions should follow and often these propose some writing tips. Editors usually strongly encourage the use of such guidelines and more recently have also provided additional support to authors proposing specific seminars and webinars, often offered during academic conferences. These occasions, while mostly focusing on generic aspects of paper writing, offer unique chances to discuss structure, style and clarity from an English language perspective.

Among the most common suggestions offered to non-English writers are those of keeping a standard structure, creating flow, and maintaining a coherent and logic narrative. One could argue that in all native languages such characteristics are also valued. This is true. However, what makes structure, flow and narrative work well in each language is quite different as it is shaped by linguistic, historical and cultural aspects. Therefore, it is strongly advisable for authors to get familiar with the concepts of structure, flow and coherency of narrative in English, thus trying to detach from those typical of the native language. An additional suggestion is often that of critically reading some sample articles of the preferred English outlets, and even compare and contrast the different structural aspects of papers written in English journals versus other language journals.

One aspect that can help non-Anglophone authors to improve their writing is that in most English journals the structure of writing is similar, and this structure and the related requirements are also similar to those of basic English compositions or essays. Among the most common issues that non-native English writers face are those related to the use of appropriate tenses, active versus passive forms in specific and suitable occasions, and structure of sentences and paragraphs. In particular, common pitfalls for non-Anglophone writers include incorrectly shifting tenses in a unit of text such as a paragraph; use of redundant words, judgmental adjectives or "false friends"; inappropriate length of sentences – according to the native language for some writers too long, for others too short – unsuitable position of the core message versus the supporting information within a sentence or paragraph; and improper paragraph constructions.

In this vein, some useful readings in composition would be essential to improve the basic principles governing English writing. Some volumes that should populate the tourism writer's library are, for example: Williams (2000); Strunk and White (2007); Griffies, Perrie and Hull (2013); Trimble (2000); Rankin (2001); Zinsser (2006); and, of course, the discipline's publication manuals (e.g., APA or similar). These volumes offer, often in a succinct space, the principal requirements of plain English style. Trimble's book (2000), an accessible reading that can be used as a self-teaching tool, offers writers an opportunity to learn how to engage in stylistic concepts with appealing original examples. Williams (2000) focuses on the differences between writing correctly and writing clearly, and offers a detailed guide with numerous examples and exercises to improve one's style and enhance clarity. Griffies, Perrie and Hull (2013) emphasise the importance of presentation and language, stating that "clarity in writing reflects on clarity in thought" (p. 20). Proper and clear language allows the reader to understand the core message of the research, positively impacting on knowledge transmission in one's field. Poor language quality – involving inappropriate grammar, spelling mistakes or inaccurate language usage – often impedes or delays publication. Zinsser (2006) also focuses on the relevance of simple and direct language, clutter free and parsimonious word choices, and insists on the importance of fine-tuning and merciless pruning of text. Strunk and White (2007) offer a brief yet very informative compendium of rules to improve writers' style; they notice how most mistakes come from "commonplaces of careless writing" and suggest the substitution of vague general statements with specific, unambiguous alternatives. Finally, Rankin (2001) focuses on academic writing, offering plenty of real-life stories gathered during writing groups dedicated to different disciplinary fields and writing types – such as curricula, journal articles, grant proposals and book chapters.

"THE ART OF WRITING" FOR TOP ENGLISH LANGUAGE JOURNALS

The previous sections discuss – with different perspectives – the complexity of the scholarly publishing endeavour in English language journals. In most social sciences, English academic writing has a somewhat standardised structure, form and style, and this is accepted within the specific disciplines. The consistency indeed allows readers, across countries and decades, to access the knowledge presented in scientific papers and use it to build newer research. Therefore, owing to the needs of global users of scientific writing, tourism scholars have more and more invested in perfecting their English for publication purposes. Nevertheless, writing remains complex and good scientific writing is an art. In our field, English language journals, and their gatekeepers – publishers, editors, reviewers – request that research papers are carefully constructed manuscripts complying with the scientific genre. Indeed, adhering to the technical, practical details of the journals and their guidelines is essential to pave the road to publishing in most English tourism journals, and mastering the art of writing is paramount in successfully positioning research in the top journals in our field.

   Engaging in finding one's own academic English writing "voice" is a rewarding albeit demanding endeavour. Few essential aspects can be identified in this process. It is useful to learn the difference between the requirements of writing linear narratives in English versus those non-linear sequences typical of conducting research and perhaps also distinctive of one's native language. It is beneficial to attempt, from the beginning of the research project, to draft and craft the storyline in English written form, ensuring later that it is an accurate representation of the research process but that it also respects the linearity of scientific writing. It is advisable to use available automated language tools but keeping in mind the need to tailor the writing style to that of different journals and their audiences. Furthermore, it is essential not to assume that what is logical, clear, stylish and structured in one's native language would also be in English, as English has its own rules of logic, clarity, style and structure to be followed. Finally, as most of the mentioned writing resources reiterate, reading and polishing the written text should be considered an important aspect of each research project. Journals' gatekeepers can discern between writing styles and, in most cases, despise the careless writers and appreciate the meticulous efforts of non-Anglophone authors.

CONCLUSION

This chapter introduced the issues that non-Anglophone authors face when writing for English language journals. It first discussed the origins, evolution and politics of English as the dominant language in scientific writing and in tourism publications, and it then related them to the needs of negotiating one's own language with the rewards offered by producing scientific knowledge in English. After discussing the difficulties of thinking, writing and disseminating in a non-native language, suggestions on writing structure, style and clarity were offered. The final part briefly discussed "the art of writing" for top English language journals.

A note from the non-Anglophone author: With a little twist on the perspective, one could notice the linguistic value of multilingual – or at least – bilingual authors, versus the monotonous language reality of Anglophone writers. Then, *au revoir, auf Wiedersehen, arrivederci*!

REFERENCES

Crystal, D. (1997). *English as a global language*. Cambridge, UK: Cambridge University Press.
Curry, M.J., & Lillis, T. (2022). Multilingualism in academic writing for publication: Putting English in its place. *Language Teaching*, 1–14.
Erling, E.J., & Seargeant, P. (2013). *English and development: Policy, pedagogy and globalization* (Vol. 17). Bristol: Multilingual Matters.
Gibbs, W.W. (1995). Information have-nots: A vicious circle isolates many third world scientists. *Scientific American*, 8–9.
Griffies, S.M., Perrie, W.A. & Hull, G. (2013). Elements of style for writing scientific journal articles. *Publishing Connect, Elsevier*, 20–50.
Kachru, B. (1992). *The other tongue: English across cultures*. Champaign-Urbana: University of Illinois Press.
Kachru, B. (2001). World Englishes. In R. Mesthrie (Ed.), *Concise encyclopedia of sociolinguistics* (pp. 519–524). New York: Elsevier.
Kirkpatrick, A. (2009). English as the international language of scholarship: Implications for the dissemination of "local" knowledge. In F. Sharifian (Ed.),

English as an international language: Perspectives and pedagogical issues (Vol. 11) (pp. 254–270). Bristol: Multilingual Matters.

Lillis, T., & Curry, M.J. (2006). Professional academic writing by multilingual scholars: Interactions with literacy brokers in the production of English-medium texts. *Written Communication*, 23(1), 3–35.

Lillis, T., & Curry, M.J. (2010). *Academic writing in a global context: The politics and practices of publishing in English*. London: Routledge.

Lillis, T., & Curry, M.J. (2013). English, scientific publishing and participation in the global knowledge economy. In E.J. Erling & P. Seargeant (Eds.), *English and development: Policy, pedagogy and globalization* (pp. 220–242). Bristol: Multilingual Matters.

McKercher, B. (2022). The rise and potential fall of some tourism journals. *Annals of Tourism Research Empirical Insights*, 3, 100049.

McKercher, B., & Prideaux, B. (2014). Academic myths of tourism. *Annals of Tourism Research*, 46, 16–28.

McKercher, B., & Tung, V. (2015). Publishing in tourism and hospitality journals: Is the past a prelude to the future? *Tourism Management*, 50, 306–315.

Navarro, F., Lillis, T., Donahue, T., Curry, M.J., Reyes, N.Á., Gustafsson, M. & Motta-Roth, D. (2022). Rethinking English as a lingua franca in scientific-academic contexts: A position statement. *Journal of English for Research Publication Purposes*, 3(1), 143–153.

Rankin, E. (2001). *The work of writing: Insights and strategies for academics and professionals*. The Jossey-Bass Higher and Adult Education Series. San Francisco, CA: Jossey-Bass.

Sharifian, F. (Ed.) (2009). *English as an international language: Perspectives and pedagogical issues* (Vol. 11). Bristol: Multilingual Matters.

Strunk Jr, W., & White, E.B. (2007). *The elements of style illustrated*. Harmondsworth: Penguin.

Tribe, J. (2010). Tribes, territories and networks in the tourism academy. *Annals of Tourism Research*, 37(1), 7–33.

Trimble, J.R. (2000). *Writing with style: Conversations on the art of writing*. Des Moines, IA: Prentice Hall.

Williams, J.M. (2000). *Style: Ten lessons in clarity and grace*. New York: Addison Wesley Longman.

Zehrer, A. (2007). The justification of journal rankings – a pilot study. *Scandinavian Journal of Hospitality and Tourism*, 7(2), 139–156.

Zinsser, W. (2006). *On writing well: The classic guide to writing nonfiction*. New York: Harper Perennial.

PART IV

PUBLISHING AND ACADEMIC CAREERS

13. Crafting a publications career

Garry Wei-Han Tan and Dimitrios Buhalis

THE IMPORTANCE OF PUBLISHING IN AN ACADEMIC CAREER

Publishing stands out as an important component of an academic career (Buckley, 2019). However, in reality, not all manuscript submissions will be accepted, let alone progress to the revise-and-resubmit stage. Engaging in the publication process is unquestionably challenging, requiring significant time and intrinsic motivation. Yet, it remains a must, given that a good track record of scholarly publications stands out as an important fixture in the academic landscape. Consequently, many studies have attempted to explore various methodologies for evaluating hospitality and tourism journals over the last decade (Okumus et al., 2018; Ertaş & Kozak, 2020). Today's academic reality is characterized by an increasing pressure to 'publish or perish' (McKercher & Tung, 2015). This indicates that academics must consistently contribute to academic publications, otherwise they will jeopardize their academic standing in the community. There are many reasons why academics should publish in their academic careers. These include knowledge dissemination, career advancement, credibility and recognition, and societal impact.

Knowledge Dissemination

Publishing a scientific paper is essential in the facilitation of knowledge dissemination. It is crucial as it acts as a channel through which scientific works are communicated, guaranteeing their acknowledgement within academic circles. McKercher (2020, p. 12) states that 'academic journals have been, continue to be and will remain the dominant platform to disseminate high-quality research'. By sharing their research output, an academic plays a role in expanding knowledge. This, in turn, will help to build the knowledge of other academics by building upon their previous work, furthering scientific progress. A recent viewpoint article published in the *Annals of Tourism Research* reported 10,752 refereed tourism, hospitality and event articles in 272 journals published in 2021 (McKercher and Dolnicar, 2022). Publishing allows a researcher to advance a particular work by improving methodologies, uncovering potential weaknesses through constructive critique, and engaging in ongoing discussion to enrich the work's dimensions. Through this process, the publication helps to create a more robust work and facilitates linkage between theoretical contributions and real-world applications.

Career Advancement

Publishing a paper goes beyond scholarly endeavours but is also important for academic and professional growth. The act of publishing remains an essential factor in academic progression. It is often stated that journal publications are an important indicator of the research productivity of an academic. This is evident when many universities worldwide evaluate publication records when deciding on promotion and tenure. Law, Chan, and Zhao (2019) indicated that publications are used for recruitment, promotion, appraisal, and tenure in measuring academic activities in the hospitality and tourism sector. Therefore, the number, quality, and impact of these publications are vital in decision-making as they provide an overview of the academic's productivity and influence within their field. Similarly, a good track record of publication can help secure academic positions.

Credibility and Recognition

Publishing helps cement an academic's credibility and validates their research findings (Buckley, 2019). As peer-reviewed journals are subjected to double-blind reviews by experts in the field, publishing helps build evidence of academics' work within their respective areas and helps cultivate their standing and profile. Publications also extend to research funding. Specifically, they are essential for improving the prospect of applying for research funding (Lopes et al., 2017). A published work leads to an ideal research profile and a recognition status as an authoritative figure within a particular area. Such recognition helps to increase the chances of securing research funding. This accolade of expertise also leads to opportunities for consultative engagements and collaboration with other academics.

Societal Impact

Publication holds the key to translating theoretical knowledge into evidence-driven decisions (Lopes et al., 2017). They are essential for addressing real-world challenges and shaping effective policy formulation. The dissemination of research through accessible and widely distributed channels can help influence governments, businesses, and various organizations, resulting in favourable societal effects. Academics contribute to the advancement of society by transforming their studies for positive change within society (Kozak, 2020).

STRATEGIC CONSIDERATIONS FOR ACADEMIC PUBLISHING

There are many motivations prompting academics to publish throughout their careers, and all factors must be carefully weighed. Determining what, in collaboration with whom, where, why, and to what extent you publish are essential considerations within the academic landscape (see Table 13.1).

What to Publish?

Academic publishing goes beyond just journals. It also includes monographs, working papers, books, newspaper articles, and conference papers. Therefore, it is essential to decide what to publish based on the aims of your research goals. The objective for PhD students and early career researchers is to publish work closely related to their dissertations. This can be in the form of converting thesis content into journal articles. Publishing your thesis establishes your profile and solidifies your core areas among the academic community. These publications can take the form of conference and journal articles. Ertaş and Kozak (2020) emphasized that academics commonly disseminate their research outputs through conference papers, academic journals, and books. There are many advantages to publishing at conferences. Conference papers are published more quickly when compared to journal articles and can be a valuable addition to your CV. A conference paper is a good way to receive feedback on your work and is essential for future improvement. Additionally, some conferences are closely related to scholarly societies or journals, often leading to invitations for extended article submissions post-conference. Attending conferences also helps to build connections with other scholars within your field, which may result in future collaboration. However, it is essential to be cautious regarding predatory conferences. Predatory conferences refer to poorly organized conferences with minimal or no peer review, primarily aimed at making money from the registration fees.

Another form of publication is a refereed journal. It includes original research papers and can be in the form of qualitative, quantitative, or mixed methods. The structure typically consists of an introduction, literature review, hypotheses, methodology, data analysis, discussion, implication, and conclusion, spanning between 5,000 and 12,000 words, depending on the requirements of the journal. Full, original research papers are often important in one's academic career. On the other hand, Hu et al. (2023) highlighted the concept

Table 13.1   Strategic considerations for publishing

Category	What to publish	With whom you publish	Where you publish	How frequently you publish	Why you publish
PhD student	Conference Journals	Supervisor	Generic/specialized journals In-house journals Indexed journals (WoS/Scopus)	1–2 indexed journals	Graduation Job recruitment
Early career researcher	Conference Journals	Supervisor/ Cross-faculty collaboration	Generic/specialized journals Indexed journals (WoS/Scopus) Journal quality list (ABDC/ABS)	2–3 indexed journals	Career advancement Networking Credibility Funding opportunity
Young academic	Conference Journals	Supervisor Cross-faculty collaboration International collaboration	Generic/specialized journals Indexed journals (WoS/Scopus) Journal quality list (ABDC/ABS)	2–5 indexed journals	Career advancement Networking Credibility Funding opportunity
Senior academic	Conference Journals	Multidisciplinary collaboration Industry collaboration Cross-generational collaboration	Generic/specialized journals Indexed journals (WoS/Scopus) Journal quality list (ABDC/ABS/FT-50)	5–10 indexed journals	Establishing reputation Credibility Impact and influence
Retired	Conference Journals	Multidisciplinary collaboration Industry collaboration Cross-generational collaboration	Generic/specialized journals Indexed journals (WoS/Scopus) Journal quality list (ABDC/ABS/FT-50)	5–10 indexed journals	Establishing reputation Credibility Impact and influence

of review articles. Review articles are often accomplished through summarization, analysis, and comparison of existing published articles in a field. They are often considered secondary literature, as they do not present new data. The authors further categorized review articles into five types: critical reviews, qualitative thematic reviews, quantitative systematic reviews, meta-analysis reviews, and mixed-method reviews. As they advance in their academic careers, senior/retired academics can contribute through perspective/opinion articles. Perspectives, or short notes, are usually by invitation and present a personal standpoint within a specific field. The article usually comments on the strengths and weaknesses of a topic (see Dwivedi et al., 2022; Koohang et al., 2023; Tan et al., 2023). Ertaş and Kozak (2020) argued that while various publication types exist, most academics focus on research articles due to their more significant impact.

With Whom You Publish

Collaboration plays a vital role in shaping an academic's career because of the complexity of knowledge, which is becoming increasingly interdisciplinary. Many factors come into play when considering collaborative ventures. The reputation of potential collaborators presents an important criterion. Working with collaborators with good track records in publishing amplifies the visibility and credibility of the author's work. Additionally, collaborating with academics with specific expertise and skills can help address any shortcomings in the research, fostering a well-rounded paper. Bibliometric analysis papers, for example, can provide a list of influential and top authors in a specific area (Leong et al., 2021). Some collaborators usher in benefits, including access to facilities, data, funding, and networks. Researchers should consider this added value, as they can tap into the benefits. Collaboration with academics in different areas can help develop new insights and novelty.

For PhD students, early career researchers, and young academics, co-authoring papers with one's supervisor is advisable. Collaborating with your supervisor provides many opportunities to learn from a more experienced mentor, which will help speed up your learning curve and research skills. A supervisor also accelerates skill acquisition and helps widen various networks. Collaborating with their supervisor will allow young scholars to build their network within the academic community and expand their professional relationships. There are other reasons to co-author with your supervisor. Supervisors are more likely to have established their publication credibility in the specific domain through their published works. This mentorship will make it easier for young academics to publish in reputable journals by co-authoring the paper together. Finally, supervisors may also access various resources, including funding and facilities. Young academics need access to these resources, allowing them to undertake more ambitious projects that might otherwise remain beyond their reach.

In a broader context, engagement with international collaborators is also important for young academics. Partnering with international collaborators from different backgrounds and countries will bring diversity to research and provide opportunities beyond geographical constraints. Specifically, collaborating with leading international figures within their research field can elevate the academic's reputation and profile. Young academics are also encouraged to collaborate within their institutions by working with colleagues from various departments. Cross-faculty collaboration can foster different methodologies, ideas, and perspectives. For senior academics, they carry with them years of experience and knowledge resulting from their academic journey. For example, a senior/retired academic specializing in tourism could collaborate with another peer in information systems to pursue an array of research objectives from multiple viewpoints. Embracing a multidisciplinary view can lead to groundbreaking findings. Engaging with younger researchers also gives senior/retired academics a fresh perspective on their work. Senior academics can tap into newer methodologies and ideas while facilitating mentorship for young scholars. Finally, engaging with industry partners brings tangible outcomes such as intellectual property, copyrights, and technology transfer. The collaborations are important not only to bridge the gap between theory and application but also to foster innovation with practical implications.

Where You Publish

The decision of where to publish your manuscript is essential, as it has a significant impact on visibility and citation potential. The choice hinges on whether to submit to a generic journal tailored to a broader readership or opt for a specialized journal with a niche readership. For instance, consider journals like *Tourism Review*, which have a generic focus, contrasting with specialized journals such as *Tourism Geographies* with wider audiences. Law, Chan, and Zhao (2019) commented that specialized journals are less popular because of their focused topics and tend to receive fewer citations than generic journals. Some universities offer journals perfectly suited for PhD candidates to publish their work. Additionally, it is also worth exploring emerging journals, both local and international, as potential venues. McKercher (2020) highlighted a trend with specialist journals focusing on tourism geography, human resources, financial management, marine environments, and geotourism.

However, making an informed choice demands careful evaluation. It is important to ensure that the prospective journal aligns with your work by perusing similar articles in the journal or looking at past issues. Does it resonate with your target readership? Also, it is important to scrutinize the journal's scope and coverage for guidelines on what the prospective journal is looking for to ensure suitability. Aligning your methodology and concepts with the journal's context is also imperative. In addition, it is important to cite articles from your target journals to establish a 'conversation', showcasing the relevancy of your work. For PhD students, consulting with their supervisor for suggested journals is essential. As your academic journey advances, the reputation of the journal gains importance. As a general rule, aim for the most prestigious journal within your field that you think you can get into. Cunil et al. (2023), however, argued that there is no consensus in the literature indicating which metric is the most ideal for evaluating the quality of a research output. Certain universities consider metrics like the impact factor to assess a journal's success. Clarivate Analytics, for example, publishes journal citation reports and ranks journals based on impact factors. Journals in Quartile 1 hold more esteem than those in Quartiles 2, 3, and 4 (Ertaş & Kozak, 2020). Papers submitted to higher quartile journals may require a longer time to write as you need to build a more robust argument regarding theory and methodology. The metric is calculated by dividing the citations received by articles within the journal by the total number of articles published in a given time frame. However, the impact factor fluctuates annually and varies across disciplines. Certain specialized journals (e.g., *Tourism Management*) have a greater number of researchers, leading to higher citation rates and impact factors (Law, Chan, & Zhao, 2019).

It is also important to exercise caution, refraining from considering the impact factor as the sole requirement when deciding whether to submit your paper. Certain reputable tourism journals have relatively low impact factors. Law, Chan, and Zhao (2019, p. 755), for example, argued that reputable journals such as 'International Journal of Hospitality & Tourism Administration and Journal of China Tourism Research, are out of sight'. Similarly, some universities consider CiteScore (Scopus) for ranking. An academic can also consider a special issue as a venue to submit their work. A special issue is a collection of articles that concentrate on a specific area within the journal's scope and may offer less competition than regular issues. Certain universities consider journals listed on quality lists, such as those from the Australian Business Deans Council (ABDC) and the ABS (Association of Business Schools). The ABDC hierarchy includes A*/A/B/C, while ABS encompasses 4*/4/3/2/1. For professorship promotion, certain universities might prioritize articles published in A*/A journals. For further information, use resources like Harzing Publish or Perish. As your academic journey advances, it is essential to consider journals ranked in the *Financial Times'* Top 50 Journals (FT50) and the UT Dallas Top 24 Leading Business Journals (UTD24), and/or journals with A/A* (ABDC) or level 4*/4/3 (ABS) rankings.

Apart from the above, judgment also depends on the academic's endorsement of whether a journal is good and makes significant contributions to a specific domain, and also whether the professor would take pride in showcasing their work in that journal. Law, Chan, and Zhao (2019) argued that some scholars have adopted subjective judgment by relying on the views of industry experts and top scholars in the hospitality and tourism sector to make judgments. Interestingly, McKercher (2020) argued that researchers will no longer feel obligated to refer to the top journals in their respective fields. Instead, they will seek articles about their interests. In other words, the significance of the journal itself may diminish compared with the significance of the specific article in the journal. Senior academics might also consider practitioner journals aligning with their field of expertise. Amid this selection process, it is essential to avoid predatory journals, as these represent one of the biggest red flags in the academic world. Alrawadieh (2020) stressed that many young and inexperienced early career researchers often fall prey to predatory journals. Predatory journals are deceptive entities that mask themselves as legitimate publications and often do not go through a rigorous peer-review process. Often, they levy publication fees, concealed as legitimate processing charges, and lack transparency in their editorial process, such as the turnaround time (McKercher & Tung, 2015). Alrawadieh (2020) added that these journals promote questionable special issues, lack clear contact information, and report fake impact factors. Predatory journals could also mimic the titles of well-established journals. As a result, the broader academic community may call the findings published in these journals into question, potentially ruining the reputation of those publishing in them within their discipline. Therefore, publishing in such journals has consequences, as it could damage the researcher's reputation and credibility. Tung and McKercher (2017) argued that publishing in such journals may lead to careers being blocked when review panels recognize the poor credibility of such journals. It is essential to check the credibility of unfamiliar publishers and journals by cross-checking resources that maintain the list of predatory journals (e.g., Beall's List) or checking with senior academics in your institutions before submission (Alrawadieh, 2020).

How Frequently You Publish

The decision on how frequently one should publish depends on various motives. For instance, an individual pursuing a PhD is often compelled to publish because of the requirements set by the university for the conferment of a doctorate degree. For aspiring post-doctoral applicants, a PhD candidate should also consider publishing early to build their academic profile. Additionally, early career researchers/young academics must take into account the number of publications as they transition from a fixed-term to a permanent position or seek advancement in their academic careers. There are also distinct standards when it comes to promotion in different countries and institutions. In some contexts, a rise to Associate Professor may necessitate approximately seven publications in journals indexed by the Web of Science (WoS), where the individual needs to be the main or corresponding author. On the other hand, the attainment of a professorship might demand around 15 such publications. The number, however, can differ significantly among institutions, and therefore it is essential to consult with the promotion and tenure committee within one's university to find out more about the requirements. While the number varies, some universities prioritize journals indexed by Scopus to enhance their world ranking, such as in the QS World University Rankings. Other universities emphasize WoS-indexed journals for the purpose of the Times Higher Education World University Ranking. Many university councils presently gauge the performance of their universities against the number of publications produced. Buckley (2019) stresses that many universities put emphasis on rating and ranking as they serve as an indicator of prestige to the general public. This prestige, in turn, confers functional power.

Regardless of the type of rankings, an academic should not only aspire for quantity but also the quality of publications. Young researchers should aim for a production rate of 2–3 papers annually. Publishing in high-impact journals, however, is unpredictable. Peer-review procedures take time, and acceptance is far from guaranteed. According to Ertaş and Kozak (2020), acceptance rates of top-tier journals have decreased to 5% on a regular basis. Certain esteemed journals may take a longer turnaround time, close to a year. Thus, having a few submissions can enhance the likelihood of securing at least one successful publication annually. The publication number is also influenced by various factors, including the article processing charges (APC) associated with publishing. Open-access journal publications, such as gold and platinum open access, come with certain costs. While certain universities allocate funds to cover those charges, others may not provide such support. Nevertheless, open-access journals are just one avenue for publishing. Academics also have the option to submit their work to non-open-access journals. Finally, the frequency of publications is determined by the expectations of the respective universities and may change over time. It is common to expect the number of publications to vary across regions and academic cultures. Advancement in one's academic career often leads to an increased number of publications.

Why You Publish

There are many reasons why you should publish. For PhD students, publishing could be a requirement so they can be awarded their PhD. Often, universities will set a number of required published papers for graduation. A good publication record can also help secure academic contracts and post-doctorate positions (Tung & McKercher, 2017). Many universities use the number of publications to measure the competency of academics during recruitment. Similarly, for early career researchers and young academics, publishing is essential for career growth and is often one of the requirements for promotion or tenure (Law, Chan, & Zhao, 2019). Tenure committees, for example, may expect early career researchers and young academics to publish in high-impact publications. Quality, as indicated by the journal reputation, and citation metrics, may play a significant role in measuring the productivity of an academic. Publishing is also a form of knowledge dissemination and a contribution to the scholarly community (Lopes et al., 2017). By sharing their work, an academic can share their ideas, findings, and insights with peers worldwide. This may lead to constructive comments and feedback. This will help accelerate and advance scientific understanding, facilitate knowledge exchange, and enable other researchers to further progress your work. Successful publication can also bring more funding or grants for your institution (Lopes et al., 2017). Publishing also helps foster academic collaboration among young academics. Often, publication will lead to invitations for seminars and conferences, which will lead to engagement with other experts from different institutions and countries. This could potentially lead to collaborations. For senior and retired academics, apart from the reasons mentioned above, publishing is often a form of recognition that helps build the credibility of their findings (Buckley, 2019). Often, the more you publish in your area, the better you build your profile, leading to opportunities for consultancies. Finally, publishing is a form of contribution to society. Publishing is essential for policy formulation and to address real-world issues. Books and research papers can shape opinions and influence organizations, businesses, and governments in their decision-making.

CONCLUSION

Publishing comes with a series of challenges, encompassing factors like time limitations and a rigorous peer-review process. Many academics are also faced with internal barriers that prevent them from writing for publication. However, it remains essential for securing promotions, achieving tenure, and obtaining grant funding. Beyond these pragmatic motivations, publishing is a pursuit for sharing research findings and contributing indispensably to advancing knowledge within the global community. This chapter has attempted to highlight the critical significance of publishing within an academic career and the many reasons (e.g., what, whom, where, how, and why aspects) academics should publish at various junctures of their academic journey.

REFERENCES

Alrawadieh, Z. (2020). Publishing in predatory tourism and hospitality journals: Mapping the academic market and identifying response strategies. *Tourism and Hospitality Research*, *20*(1), 72–81.

Buckley, R. (2019). Tourism publications as newly tradeable commodities: Academic performance, prestige, power, competition, constraints and consents. *Annals of Tourism Research*, *74*, 121–133.

Cunil, O.M., González, L.O., Santomil, P.D., & Forteza, C.M. (2023). How to accomplish a highly cited paper in the tourism, leisure and hospitality field. *Journal of Business Research*, *157*, 113619.

Dwivedi, Y.K., Hughes, L., Kar, A.K., Baabdullah, A.M., Grover, P., Abbas, R., & Wade, M. (2022). Climate change and COP26: Are digital technologies and information management part of the problem or the solution? An editorial reflection and call to action. *International Journal of Information Management*, *63*, 102456.

Ertaş, M., & Kozak, M. (2020). Publish or perish: The proportion of articles versus additional sections in tourism and hospitality journals. *Journal of Hospitality and Tourism Management*, *43*, 149–156.

Hu, T., Chen, Y., Chen, H., & Zhang, Y. (2023). Tourism research progress: Comparing tourism literature reviews published in English WoS and Chinese CNKI language journals. *Tourism Review*, *78*(6), 1361–1386.

Koohang, A., Nord, J.H., Ooi, K.B., Tan, G.W.H., Al-Emran, M., Aw, E.C.X., & Wong, L.W. (2023). Shaping the Metaverse into reality: A holistic multidisciplinary understanding of opportunities, challenges, and avenues for future investigation. *Journal of Computer Information Systems*, *63*(3), 735–765.

Kozak, M. (2020). Historical development of tourism journals – a milestone in 75 years: A perspective article. *Tourism Review*, *75*(1), 8–11.

Law, R., Chan, I.C.C., & Zhao, X. (2019). Ranking hospitality and tourism journals. *Journal of Hospitality & Tourism Research*, *43*(5), 754–761.

Leong, L.Y., Hew, T.S., Tan, G.W.H., Ooi, K.B., & Lee, V.H. (2021). Tourism research progress – a bibliometric analysis of tourism review publications. *Tourism Review*, *76*(1), 1–26.

Lopes, I., Silva, J.A., Castela, G., & Rebelo, E. (2017). Knowledge transfer through journals. In N. Scott, M. De Martino, & M. Van Niekerk (eds.), *Knowledge transfer to and within tourism* (Bridging Tourism Theory and Practice series), vol. 8, 271–288.

McKercher, B. (2020). The future of tourism journals: A perspective article. *Tourism Review*, *75*(1), 12–15.

McKercher, B., & Dolnicar, S. (2022). Are 10,752 journal articles per year too many? *Annals of Tourism Research*, *94*, 103398.

McKercher, B., & Tung, V. (2015). Publishing in tourism and hospitality journals: Is the past a prelude to the future?. *Tourism Management*, *50*, 306–315.

Okumus, F., Zhao, X.R., Van Niekerk, M., & Law, R. (2018). The importance of having a balanced rating index for ranking academic journals. *Journal of Hospitality & Tourism Research*, *42*(7), 1170–1181.

Tan, G.W.H., Aw, E.C.X., Cham, T.H., Ooi, K.B., Dwivedi, Y.K., Alalwan, A.A., Balakrishna, J., Chan, H.K., Hew, J.J., Hughes, L., Jain, V., Lee, V.H., Lin, B., Rana, N.P., & Tan, T.M. (2023). Metaverse in marketing and logistics: The state of the art and the path forward. *Asia Pacific Journal of Marketing and Logistics*, *35*(12), 2932–2946.

Tung, V.W.S., & McKercher, B. (2017). Negotiating the rapidly changing research, publishing, and career landscape. *Tourism Management*, *60*, 322–331.

14. A perspective on official research performance evaluation in tourism

Rhodri Thomas

INTRODUCTION

The UK government first introduced performance evaluation of university research in 1986 as a means of allocating research monies. It did so via what was then termed the Research Assessment Exercise (RAE), which subsequently became the Research Excellence Framework (REF). At the time, the linking of research funding to demonstrable research performance represented a radical departure from existing practice. The expectation was that this new approach would lead to an increase in the volume of research and an improvement in quality as higher education institutions engaged in a competition for funding by improving performance. Several countries subsequently adopted performance-based research funding systems (PBRFS), perhaps most notably Australia, Hong Kong, Indonesia, Malaysia, New Zealand and a growing number of European countries (Hermanu et al., 2022; Ta et al., 2021; Zacharewicz et al., 2019). Many higher education evaluation and national ranking systems that do not 'qualify' as PBRFS also display some of their characteristics (Pardo-Guerra, 2022).

This chapter considers the characteristics of PBRFS and what they mean for academic researchers. The nuances of national systems are not examined (the emphasis of each often changes) and few concrete suggestions about academic practice are offered. Instead, by revealing the operation of PBRFS, readers will be able to develop bespoke approaches to career planning that also reflect personal circumstances and outlook. Clearly, values and personal dispositions will influence the decision making of individuals; some will seek out ways of maximising the metrics associated with their work while others might resist what they might see as distorting and damaging pressures. Perhaps most will navigate a middle way.

It is appropriate to acknowledge the context within which national research policy development takes place and the diversity of the higher education sector, both within and between countries. National research policies as they relate to PBRFS are inflected with broader neoliberal discourses that conceptualise universities as being engaged in market-oriented competition for students, staff and income (including research income) or, at least, that market-type (competitive) mechanisms are an effective way of distributing resources (Smythe, 2017; Jones, 2022). This, of course, contrasts with systems where the state intervenes by, perhaps, linking student numbers with the perceived needs of the economy and society.

Against this backdrop, public policy narratives tend to emphasise notions of transparency and fairness, whereby funding decisions reflect performance or merit. As the source of funding is from general taxation, it is often held that research monies should increasingly also generate non-academic impacts so that economic and social welfare are enhanced. The adoption of corporate managerial practices is a logical corollary if institutions are to 'do well' in such systems (Davis & Farrell, 2016).

The debates about the consequences of neoliberal approaches to higher education are rehearsed elsewhere (see for example Smythe, 2017; Jones, 2022). It is germane to note, in passing, that the growth in volume of universities over recent decades, and their contrasting missions, influences how organisations relate to research policy (for an account of the variety, see Watts, 2017). This implies that caution must be exercised when making generalisations about universities and performance-based research funding regimes.

The spread of performance-based university research funding, nevertheless, has consequences for the work of many academics. As others have pointed out, promotion prospects are often tied to what institutions regard as important, and 'importance' often relates to how research and related activities will be evaluated. Thus, an individual's ability to publish, their capacity to attract research grants and – increasingly – their capability to generate non-academic impact have become prominent yardsticks (Bastow, Dunleavy & Tinkler, 2014; Pardo-Guerra, 2022; Whitfield, 2023). These, in turn, suggest that to be successful, academic researchers need to develop a range of skills that extend beyond research.

THE CHARACTERISTICS OF PERFORMANCE-BASED RESEARCH FUNDING SYSTEMS (PBRFS)

Prior to exploring the (potential) response of academics to the policies spawned by national PBRFS, it is important to appreciate their parameters. This avoids conflating various other forms of research evaluation that may also influence the practices of academics. These include the international ranking of research by non-official or commercial organisations such as the Academic Ranking of World Universities (the so-called Shanghai ranking, https://www.shanghairanking.com/rankings/gras/2022/RS0513) or those constructed by the Times Higher Education (https://www.timeshighereducation.com/world -university-rankings), both of which are influenced substantially by research performance.

Hicks (2012) provides a useful starting point for defining PBRFS by listing five essential criteria:

- Research quality is the focus of evaluation and not that of degree pro-grammes, for example;
- Research evaluation is *ex post* rather than considering research proposals or funding applications (such as those required by research councils);
- Research outputs are central to the evaluation, rather than research student (PhD) numbers and external grant funding;
- Government funding is informed by the research evaluation exercise;
- It is a national system of evaluation.

The agencies responsible for the evaluation of research performance vary from ministries of state to dedicated arms-length agencies who then inform those responsible for budget allocations. Timelines for evaluation also differ in terms of frequency of evaluation and are not stable (i.e., they change as national PBRFS evolve). Some, such as those in Australia and Norway, used to require annual data to inform budget allocations, whereas in New Zealand and Hong Kong, assessments were held every three years. Intervals in the UK are usually longer (up to seven years) (Hicks, 2012).

The rationale used for the introduction and maintenance of PBRFS has common elements. Drawing on the work of others, Hicks (2012) identifies six aspects to be the most prevalent rationales: (1) improving the productivity of researchers (increased volume of outputs without additional investment); (2) encouraging strategic research planning in universities by offering them the discretion to determine how funding should be used (unlike 'responsive mode funding' which prescribes the projects to be funded); (3) promoting stronger links between researchers and the wider population; (4) strengthening the ability of universities to be 'agile' and responsive to emerging agenda; (5) gaining efficiencies by limiting the role of government to research policy formulation rather than policy formulation and delivery; and finally (6) strengthening accountability by focusing on outputs and outcomes rather than structures, processes and narratives.

Within these broad ideas, most systems also emphasise selectivity and the funding of excellence. This means rewarding those that perform well with additional resources so that they can continue to engage in research that deliv-ers the benefits anticipated by officials. For many, the egalitarian language is little more than a veneer that fails to acknowledge the historic advantage of some institutions (i.e., those who have traditionally attracted government

funding) or that evaluation is inevitably superficial and confirms existing hierarchies (Bishop, 2021). Moreover, it is suggested that those operating in fields
or disciplines that are seen as marginal (or are perhaps marginalised) also fail
to attract significant impact (Thomas, 2018).

Some forms of PBRFS are bureaucratically intense and expensive to
operate. By one estimate, the UK's 2014 exercise cost almost £250m or some
$310m (USD) and accounted for approximately 2.4% of the total expected
budget of the research funding agencies (Else, 2015). Cost estimates of the
most recent exercise have yet to be published. Clearly, the cost of PBRFS
depend upon their methods of evaluation.

National systems of research performance evaluation fall broadly into three
categories: ones where the unit of evaluation is the university (e.g., several
countries in Europe), the department – though the term is used loosely to
encompass clusters of expertise organised accordingly (e.g., Australia, the UK
and Hong Kong) – and, perhaps most dauntingly on face value, those systems
that operate at the level of the individual (e.g., Spain and New Zealand). Time
frames range from annually to six or seven years.

Predictably, the design of evaluations varies. Some use the number of papers
published and/or citations as key dimensions of performance. These and other
bibliometric approaches have tended to be used mainly for university-level
evaluations (Hicks, 2012). For many, bibliometric-led evaluation of research
outputs fails to replicate the 'richness' of the peer-review model (e.g., Grove,
2022) but adds a layer (perhaps a veneer) of objectivity.

PERFORMANCE-BASED RESEARCH EVALUATION IN TOURISM

Several commentators have pointed to the growing maturity of research in
tourism. The number of journals in the field – now estimated to be more than
200 (www.ciret-tourism.com/index/listes_revues.html) – is often used as con-
firmatory evidence. Perhaps of greater significance is its inclusion as a district
and separate field in official evaluations. As the three PBRFS described below
show, there is yet no consensus on where tourism should be aligned within
broader cognate areas. In the UK, for example, it is positioned as part of
a unit of assessment that includes sport, whereas in New Zealand it is grouped
with marketing which is situated within a broader category of business and
economics.

This official recognition has not prevented some influential commentators
from suggesting that tourism research is at the periphery of the research policy
landscape (e.g., Airey et al., 2015). It is noteworthy that the 2014 assessment
of research performance in the UK included tourism within the title of a unit

for the first time and that this was repeated for the 2021 exercise. The unit is entitled 'Sport and Exercise Sciences, Leisure and Tourism' (Unit 24).

Commenting on the growing maturity of the field, the review at the end of the 2014 assessment stated:

> Tourism research had improved noticeably since RAE2008 … the panel was pleased to see greater and more effective engagement with theory and outputs with considerable methodological rigour. There was an increase in original, significant and rigorous overview papers reviewing the field and testament to the maturing nature and contribution of the subject area. The sub-panel also assessed world-leading tourism research that employed innovative methods of analysis of large and new datasets. The sub-panel was pleased to see a larger number of submissions from event management researchers (even though) … this field is still at an earlier stage of maturity (REF, 2015, p. 117).

The position of tourism research has a different history in Australia. Thus, the number of submissions made by universities in 2012 with tourism as formal units of evaluation was lower than previously. The suggestion is that university strategists limited the number because ratings for tourism were lower than other areas in business and management with none achieving the top score (Airey et al., 2015). As is shown below, the level of performance changed in 2018 as two units excelled.

PBRFS AND TOURISM AS ILLUSTRATED BY ERA (AUSTRALIA), PBRF 2018 (NEW ZEALAND) AND REF 2021 (UK)

Australia

Australia's PBRFS is entitled Excellence in Research for Australia (ERA). As its title implies, its aims are to promote and reward excellence in all types of research undertaken by Australian higher education institutions.

As the official documentation notes, the objectives of ERA are to:

- Establish an evaluation framework that gives government, industry, business and the wider community assurance of the excellence of research conducted in Australia's higher education institutions;
- Provide a national stocktake of discipline-level areas of research strength and areas where there is opportunity for development in Australia's higher education institutions;
- Identify excellence across the full spectrum of research performance;
- Identify emerging research areas and opportunities for further development;

- Allow for comparisons of Australia's research nationally and internationally for all discipline areas (ARC, 2019).

The evaluation of research varies slightly by discipline or field of study (units of evaluation) but is underpinned by a concern with research quality, research volume and the non-academic value of research. From these, a set of principles is used to inform the judgement of expert panels of reviewers. The principles encompass quantitative measures that are internationally recognised, thus allowing for comparability between countries which also extends to comparability between disciplines. In a similar vein to other systems of evaluation, there is a concern to ensure that the ability of institutions to game the system is minimised or eradicated. The so-called ERA 2018 Discipline Matrix operationalised these principles for particular subjects, though there is disquiet in some quarters over the transparency of their application (https://www.timeshigher education.com/blog/do-australias-era-discipline-assessments-really-measure -research-excellence).

This section draws on the State of Australian University Research 2018–2019 report (https://dataportal.arc.gov.au/ERA/NationalReport/2018/ pages/section3/15/1506/). It reports the outcome of the most recent national research performance evaluation (the next was taking place at the time of writing). Tourism as a field was located within the broader subject category of 'Commerce, Management, Tourism and Services'. The grading system used for this evaluation was as follows: 5 equates with 'well above world standard'; 4 reflects research performance that is 'above world standard'; 3 indicates that average performance in the grouping evaluated is at world standard; 2 and 1 suggest research that is below or well below world standard. These scores relate only to research quality.

Thirteen institutions submitted a tourism grouping to the most recent evaluation exercise. Between them, they amounted to 173 full-time equivalent staff (FTE) who had produced 2,440 outputs and generated a research income of almost $6m (AUD). There were no patents or commercial income reported. Sixty-three per cent of outputs were in the form of journal articles, followed by 23% as book chapters and 11% as conference papers.

Two of the submitted units were awarded a top rating (5), one was rated as 4, followed by eight in the 3 category. None received a score of 1. This represented a general improvement in performance in the field, according to the growth in volume of institutions submitting to tourism, and an increase in the number gaining the top score (for details of rankings, see: https://www .universityrankings.com.au/tourism-rankings-2/). As there is usually a gaming of PBRFS, some institutions may have decided to allocate outputs to other fields for tactical advantage.

New Zealand

Research performance evaluation in New Zealand, entitled the Performance-Based Research Fund (PBRF), focuses on the evidence portfolios (EPs) of individual researchers. Each EP contains details of outputs (70% weighting) and other aspects of research performance (research contribution) (30%), and is evaluated by a panel comprised of national and international peers. The panel evaluates EPs against agreed quality standards. To achieve an A rating, the EP would contain evidence of world-class outputs and high levels of peer esteem. A C rating, by contrast, would indicate quality assured outputs and some level of peer esteem, perhaps including contributions at institutional level. An R rating would reflect performance that falls short of the minimum expected standards of research quality and contribution (TEC, 2019).

Table 14.1   Percentage of EPs awarded funded categories by subject area, 2018, 2012

SUBJECT AREA	YEAR	A	B	C	C(NE)
	2018	6.6%	38.1%	34.6%	20.8%
Accounting and Finance	2012	10.5%	30.1%	42.2%	17.3%
	Variance	-3.9	+8.0	-7.6	+3.5
	2018	8.5%	43.3%	37.3%	11.0%
Economics	2012	12.6%	41.8%	33.6%	12.0%
	Variance	-4.1	+1.5	+3.7	-1.0
Management, Human Resources, Industrial	2018	8.8%	50.4%	30.0%	10.8%
Relations, International Business and Other	2012	5.3%	40.3%	42.8%	11.7%
Business	Variance	+3.5	+10.1	-12.8	-0.9
	2018	8.4%	41.5%	28.9%	21.3%
Marketing and Tourism	2012	8.9%	37.7%	37.1%	16.3%
	Variance	-0.5	+3.8	-8.2	+5.0

Source: https://www.tec.govt.nz/assets/Publications-and-others/PBRF-2018/268776b02d/Report-of-the-Moderation-and-Peer-Review-Panels-PBRF-2018-Quality-Evaluation-12-09-2019.pdf , p. 26.

The report produced by the Business and Economics Panel noted a narrowing in the performance gap between subjects since the 2012 evaluation (see Table 14.1). Some of this, they suggest, could be accounted for by the greater use of journal metrics in the earlier evaluation exercise. The emphasis on quality of individual outputs, rather than the status of the journal within which work is published, probably helped improve scores for fields where there are few top-quality journals. Interestingly, the report also noted that for Marketing and Tourism, there was an increase in the number of EPs awarded the grade associated with early career researchers. This was taken as a healthy sign for the field. Further, more researchers than previously were awarded the top two grades (TEC, 2019). Unfortunately, it is not possible to separate those in marketing from those in tourism.

United Kingdom (UK)

The purpose of the most recent Research Excellence Framework (REF) was to attain:

• Accountability for public funding of research and identify its value;
• Data enabling comparison of institutional performance by different stakeholders; and
• Information to assist in decisions on research funding allocations (REF, 2022).

REF assessed three aspects of research quality: the quality of outputs (60% weighting); the quality of the non-academic impact of research (25% weighting); and the quality of the research environment (15% weighting).

The criteria for assessing the quality of outputs were originality, significance and rigour. Unit 24 attracted 185,594 outputs from universities in REF 2021. Without an intricate assessment of each submission, it is hard to estimate how many of these related to tourism (interested readers with sufficient time could gain access to the data if they so wished because all institutional submissions are available on the REF 2021 website).

Impact was defined as 'the effect on, change or benefit to the economy, society, culture, public policy or services, health, the environment or quality of life, beyond academia'. It was evaluated via a number of case studies submitted by institutions. The number of case studies per institution depended upon the size of the institutional submission (i.e., number of FTEs). The criteria for evaluating impact were 'reach' and 'significance'.

The research environment was assessed to establish how effective universities were in supporting research and facilitating non-academic impact. The formal criteria were 'vitality' and 'sustainability'. In addition to a narrative statement, submissions included number of PhD students and grants secured.

Sub-panel 24 encompassed research that was undertaken by some 1,452 FTEs. Of these, some 15% were early career researchers. Individual submissions ranged from 6.5 FTEs to 94.9 FTEs. The average was 24 FTEs. The results of REF for Unit 24 are reproduced in Table 14.2.

Sixteen universities submitted tourism outputs to Unit 24 and a further eight submitted work to Unit 17 (Business and Management Studies).

Table 14.2   REF results for Unit 24

SUB-PANEL 24: SPORT AND EXERCISE SCIENCES, LEISURE AND TOURISM					
Quality Profiles (FTE weighted) for the UOA					
	%4*	%3*	%2*	%1*	% Unclassified
Output	28.7	55.1	15.1	0.8	0.3
Impact	44.1	40.8	13.6	1.5	0.0
Environment	37.5	39.2	19.5	3.7	0.1
Overall	34	49	15	2	0

Source: REF, 2022, p. 170.

In spite of the steady but sustained decline in the number of universities in the UK with dedicated tourism departments, the assessors noted an improvement in the quality of research since the last REF. In addition, the summary report states:

> Tourism research is still largely underpinned by concepts from social sciences and applied management. The sub-panel noted the use of more sophisticated and innovative methodological rigour compared with REF 2014. There continued to be an increase in rigorous literature review papers which used sophisticated bibliometric methods. Research areas that were particularly strong included outputs related to policy, planning and development, the impact of tourism, sustainability, climate change, wellbeing, consumer behaviour, and the use of technology in tourism, particularly as related to phone tracking, Big Data, Artificial Intelligence, and wearable technology. (REF, 2022, p. 175)

It is perhaps somewhat paradoxical that in addition to highlighting improvements in quality, the panel drew attention to what they saw as 'an over-reliance on outputs submitted to a small number of highly regarded tourism journals' (REF, 2022, pp 175–176).

Although impact case studies relating to tourism were submitted, most of the impact case studies focused on physical activity/exercise and health and sports injury/sports medicine. Indeed, some 60% of claimed impacts related to sport. This may be because developing strong impact case studies is challenging in tourism (Thomas, 2018).

Public policy debates about the next REF (2028) are now beginning to emerge. It seems that outputs will diminish in overall importance but that a measure of academic impact may be introduced (some have speculated that this may be measured via citations data), and that both non-academic impact and research environment will be elevated. This implies that individual academic researchers in tourism will need to continue to focus on high-quality outputs but redouble their efforts to undertake work likely to inform decision-makers. In addition, they might expect a collegiate and supportive research environment if their institution is to do well in this assessment (UKRI, 2023).

CONCLUSION: THE EMERGENCE OF ACADEMIC SUPER-HEROES?

Few would doubt that PBRFS have affected how academic researchers approach their work (for perspectives in contrasting systems, see Li, 2021; Thomas, 2018). For some, PBRFS are best understood as manifestations of neoliberal systems of higher education which constrain their academic freedom. Bottrell and Manathunga (2019), for example, have assembled a collection of essays from academics who have negotiated their work in different types of university. Grant (2019), within that volume, discusses what she describes as a system where 'careerism' has come to dominate discussions of academic careers. Her autoethnographic study provides rich insight into how she navigated the pressures to 'perform' and addressed the challenging ethical issues she identified. Similar employment-related matters have been discussed in the context of tourism by Thomas (2022). His research undertaken in the UK found substantial evidence of an academic community primarily concerned with their own performativity. This he explained via the notion of affective subjectification whereby academic researchers become 'manageable subjects' (rather than independent critically minded researchers).

Alternative ways of considering PBRFS are perhaps more appropriate for the purposes of this book. Hay (2017), for example, utilises the notion of super-hero to offer guidance on how to operate within a modern higher education system. The advice on offer is broadly based to assist individuals in securing a post and then advancing their career. They advocate the acquisition of 'soft' skills that encompass networking, public relations and mentoring, as well as teaching and research skills. In the context of this chapter, their assessment might be seen as partial. They acknowledge the need for high-quality output but downplay the influence public policy – in this case research policy – has on how people are judged and, in turn, what they might prioritise. The importance attached to research impact as part of many PBRFS, for example, now has a direct impact on academic work for those operating in those systems (Thomas, 2018).

Another way of looking at the practical implications of operating within a PBRFS is provided by Pitt and Mewburn (2016, p. 88) who ask 'What do academic employers really want from the PhD now?' The premise of their question is that studying for a PhD represents the best 'training' for an academic career yet, they suggest, PhD curricula are not informed by employment-related research. Their paper reports an attempt to remedy this deficiency by offering insights gleaned from their exploratory scrutiny of a set of job adverts in Australia. They note the following:

> These job adverts provide a window into Australian university employers' expectations for the new academic worker – where 'new' has a dual meaning, reflecting both those 'new' to working within academia and signifying a shift towards a 'new' academic who is simultaneously autonomous and a team player. This new academic we see figured in the data is a multi-talented, always ready and available worker that we have started to label the 'academic super-hero', capable of being everything to everyone and leaping over 24 KSC (key selection criteria) in a single job application … At any moment our hero must be ready to deal with the multiple uncertainties that beset the higher education sector in Australia, all the while collecting business cards for that next round of student placements, soothing hurt feelings and smiling graciously at the crowds of prospective students at Open Day while publishing prodigiously and creating innovative learning opportunities for their students across multiple media. (Pitt & Mewburn, 2016, p. 99)

The daunting scenario they paint will resonate with many because of the breadth of expectation. It led some commentators to suggest, for example, that expecting teaching-oriented academics to produce research work of world-class quality is akin to inviting a bowler in a cricket team to focus on batting (Anonymous, 2023). Nevertheless, as chapters of this book have explained, learning lessons, and developing individual strategies for key aspects of an academic's role, may ease the potential stress of these demands and enable individuals to enjoy rewarding academic careers.

REFERENCES

Airey, D., Tribe, J., Benckendorff, P. and Xiao, H. (2015). The managerial gaze: The long tail of tourism education and research. *Journal of Travel Research*, 54(2), 139–151.

Anonymous (2023). Universities' REF policies are hitting non-researchers for six. *The Times Higher Education*, 14 March. https://www.timeshighereducation.com/opinion/universities-ref-policies-are-hitting-non-researchers-six.

Australian Research Council (ARC) (2019). *State of Australian university research 2018–19: ERA national report*. Canberra: Australian Research Council. https://www.arc.gov.au/evaluating-research/excellence-research-australia/past-era-evaluation.

Bastow, S., Dunleavy, P. & Tinkler, J. (2014). *The impact of the social sciences*. London: Sage.

Bishop, S. (2021). Is the benefit of the REF really worth the cost? *The Times Higher Education*, 28 April. https://www.timeshighereducation.com/opinion/benefit-ref-really-worth-cost.

Bottrell, D. & Manathunga, C. (2019). *Resisting neoliberalism in higher education volume I: Seeing through the cracks* (pp. 119–134). London: Palgrave Macmillan.

Davis, J.A. & Farrell, M.A. (2016). *The market oriented university. Transforming higher education*. Cheltenham, UK and Northampton, MA, USA: Edward Elgar Publishing.

Else, H. (2015). REF 2014 cost almost £250 million. *The Times Higher Education*, 13 July. https://www.timeshighereducation.com/news/ref-2014-cost-250-million.

Grant, B.M. (2019). Wrestling with career: An autoethnographic tale of a cracked academic self. In Bottrell, D. & Manathunga, C. (Eds.) *Resisting neoliberalism in higher education volume I: Seeing through the cracks* (pp. 119–134). London: Palgrave Macmillan.

Grove, J. (2022). 'Avoid all-metric approach to REF', says review. *The Times Higher Education*, 12 December. https://www.timeshighereducation.com/news/avoid-all-metric-approach-ref-says-review.

Hay, I. (2017). *How to be an academic superhero: Establishing and sustaining a successful career in the social sciences, arts and humanities.* Cheltenham, UK and Northampton, MA, USA: Edward Elgar Publishing.

Hermanu, A.I., Sari, D., Sondari, M.C. & Dimyati, M. (2022). Is it necessary to evaluate university research performance instrument? Evidence from Indonesia. *Cogent Social Sciences*, 8, 2069210.

Hicks, D. (2012). Performance-based university research funding systems. *Research Policy*, 41, 251–261.

Jones, S. (2022). *Universities under fire: Hostile discourses and integrity deficits in higher education.* London: Springer.

Li, J. (2021). The global ranking regime and the reconfiguration of higher education: Comparative case studies on research assessment exercises in China, Hong Kong, and Japan. In Welch, A. & Li, J. (Eds.) *Measuring up in higher education* (pp. 177–202). Singapore: Palgrave Macmillan.

Pardo-Guerra, J.P. (2022). *The quantified scholar: How research evaluations transformed the British social sciences.* New York: Columbia University Press.

Pitt, R. & Mewburn, I. (2016). Academic superheroes? A critical analysis of academic job descriptions. *Journal of Higher Education Policy and Management*, 38(1), 88–101.

Research Excellence Framework (REF) (2015). *Research Excellence Framework 2014: Overview Report by Main panel C and Sub-panels 16-26.* https://2014.ref.ac.uk/media/ref/content/expanel/member/Main%20Panel%20C%20overview%20report.pdf.

Research Excellence Framework (REF) (2022). *Overview report by Main Panel C and Sub-panels 13 to 24.* Bristol: REF. https://ref.ac.uk/media/1912/mp-c-overview-report-final-updated-september-2022.pdf.

Smythe, J. (2017). *The toxic university: Zombie leadership, academic rock stars and neoliberal ideology.* London: Springer.

Ta, G.C., Halim, S.A., Azman, N., Komoo, I. & Mokhtar, M. (2021). Evaluating research performance of research institutes within Malaysian universities: An alternative assessment framework. *Tertiary Education and Management*, 27, 331–349.

Tertiary Education Commission (TEC)/Te Amorangi Mātauranga Matua (2019). *Report of the moderation and peer-review panels PBRF 2018 quality evaluation. PBRF 2018 quality evaluation.* Wellington: TEC. https://www.tec.govt.nz/assets/Publications-and-others/PBRF-2018/268776b02d/Report-of-the-Moderation-and-Peer-Review-Panels-PBRF-2018-Quality-Evaluation-12-09-2019.pdf.

Thomas, R. (2018). *Questioning the assessment of research impact. Illusions, myths and marginal sectors.* London: Palgrave Macmillan.

Thomas, R. (2022). Affective subjectivation or moral ambivalence? Constraints on the promotion of sustainable tourism by academic researchers. *Journal of Sustainable Tourism*, 30(9), 2107–2120.

UK Research and Innovation (UKRI) (2023). *Early decisions made for REF 2028.* https://www.ukri.org/news/early-decisions-made-for-ref-2028/.

Watts, R. (2017). *Public universities, managerialism and the value of higher education.* London: Palgrave Macmillan.

Whitfield, J. (2023). A bit of everything. *London Review of Books*, 45(2), 19 January.

Zacharewicz, T., Lepori, B., Reale, E. & Jonkers, K. (2019). Performance-based research funding in EU Member States – a comparative assessment. *Science and Public Policy*, 46(1), 101–115.

15. Journal rankings: tourism management's *idée fixe*

Nigel Morgan and Annette Pritchard

INTRODUCTION

Despite the advent of the post-truth age (Ahlstrom-Vij, 2023), society remains hugely dependent on knowledge creation. The key challenges now facing humanity, such as the climate crisis and the transition to a low carbon future, cannot be solved without expert advice; and expert advice and sound decision-making can only be based on a foundation of high-quality evidence. The more reliant society is on such evidence, the more important the reliability and trustworthiness of research become. Thus the credibility of research, always vital to the academic community, is now also crucial to a wider audience of publics, stakeholders and funders. The cornerstone of academic rigour has long been peer review, which, for its many flaws and subjectivities (Smith, 2006), is seen to maintain the integrity of scholarship by filtering out poor quality research, determining the validity, significance and originality of a study, and improving the quality of work deemed of sufficient quality for publication. In turn, peer review is the foundation of the hierarchical academic publication system of journals, the rankings of which have assumed increasing importance as part of the overall shift to a metric-driven neoliberal academic environment in many countries (Standing & Atkinson, 2018; McCann et al., 2020) and the increasing external surveillance of research quality (Hall, 2011; Tourish & Willmott, 2015). Publication in highly ranked journals is therefore the principal route to academic promotion and prestige in many academic disciplines and fields, including that of tourism management. This chapter critically reflects on journal rankings. It discusses the ranking methodologies, their flaws and partialities, and considers how our field's fixation with journal rankings is skewing its development and the careers of its scholars.

THE MIRAGE OF MEASUREMENT OR RANKING METHODOLOGIES

Different organizations and databases use different methodologies to rank academic journals, although the methodologies and criteria used in journal rankings are not always transparent or easily accessible. This lack of transparency makes it difficult for researchers to understand how rankings are determined and to critically evaluate their validity and reliability. The rankings may also overlook journals that publish groundbreaking or innovative research but have lower citation rates, and new journals or emerging (sub)fields are not usually adequately represented in existing rankings, which take time to update and may not reflect recent developments in the academic community. This can limit researchers' ability to identify and publish in journals that are appropriate for their research interests and audiences. Additionally, rankings typically favour journals from certain countries (usually more economically developed ones), languages (especially English) and disciplines (particularly established ones). Journal rankings often prioritize journals within specific disciplines or sub-disciplines, which can discourage interdisciplinary research, as researchers may feel pressured to publish in high-ranking journals within their own discipline rather than seeking outlets that bridge multiple fields, thereby keeping disciplines separate and isolated (Rafols et al., 2012). All this leads to an incomplete and partial representation of the academic landscape.

It is important to note that the different rankings are a product of the power dynamics of the contemporary globalized, marketized higher education system (Canaan & Shumar, 2008). They also reflect the fact that scientific impact is a multi-dimensional subjective construct and is influenced by government and institutional policy contexts. Indeed, the institutional context of government evaluations of research quality increasingly determine which metrics are applied, with subsequent effects on performance evaluation, career development and the future direction of tourism management (Hall, 2011). Different rankings may emphasize different aspects and criteria and thus will have inherent limitations. Some common criteria include citation counts, impact factor (IF), peer-review process and editorial board reputation, while others may prioritize journals with a higher publication frequency. Many journal rankings focus on the narrow set of criteria of citation counts or IF, which are both deeply flawed measurements of the quality and significance of the research published in a journal. Originally invented as a tool to help university librarians decide which journals to purchase, a journal's impact factor soon became used as a measure for judging academic success, despite continued concerns over its limitations (Callaway, 2016).

Traditional journal impact factors (JIFs) are determined by Clarivate Analytics using the simple metric of the yearly mean number of citations of articles published in the last two years in a given journal, as indexed by Clarivate's Web of Science. The more frequently a journal is cited, the higher its IF and the higher its IF, the more influential the journal is assumed to be (Allen, 2019). There are other models used to evaluate journal rankings, which feature a wider selection of metrics, but all of them use the number of citations journals receive as their basis, including the SNIP (Source Normalized Impact per Paper) and CiteScore rankings. SCImago Journal Rank (Scopus, Elsevier) assesses journals based on the number of citations and weights these citations based on the ranking of the journals where they are published. Citations appearing in leading journals are therefore more 'valuable' than citations from less significant journals (Allen, 2019). Despite their prevalence, much has been written on the misuse of the IF in judging publications, scholars and research work, critiquing journal IFs as ambiguous, opaque and unreliable (e.g., Brembs, Button & Munafò, 2013). Regardless of these misgivings, over time, a journal's IF has been seen to correlate with quality, and the mean IF of papers in a journal is assumed to suggest that all papers published in that journal are of similar quality. By this process, IF has become regarded as a proxy measure of journal prestige and researchers and evaluators often judge a paper on the basis of where it is published rather than the significance of its content (Casadevall & Fang, 2015), often without even reading it (Tourish & Willmott, 2015).

Despite its widespread application, the use of journal IF to measure the quality and impact of individual papers is statistically flawed. The high IF of the top-tier journals in any field results from their ability to attract a few very highly cited papers, but publication outlet is a poor predictor of the number of citations an individual article will receive. 'Thus, for most authors, the benefits of publishing in high-IF journals result more from their association with other papers in the same journal that happen to be highly cited' (Casadevall & Fang, 2015, p. 1). Moreover, using citation as a measure of research impact is itself highly problematic and has been critiqued within tourism (as in other fields) (e.g., Pritchard & Morgan, 2007, 2017). Indeed, as Jamal, Smith and Watson (2008, p. 68) comment: 'citation frequency is not an indicator of academic scholarship or leadership. There are several reasons why it cannot be considered a good substitute for scholarly value and should not be considered as a basis for assessing journals.' Highly cited papers are not necessarily important in a fundamental sense. For example, review articles tend to be more highly cited than conceptual papers or those advancing disruptive innovation (Ioannidis, Boyack, Small et al., 2014), whilst citations flow disproportionately towards established scholars to whom others wish to pay homage or from whom others wish to gain associated recognition (Jamal, Smith & Watson, 2008; Pritchard & Morgan, 2007, 2017).

Some journal rankings rely heavily on the reputation of the journal's editorial board or the perceived prestige of the journal. However, these factors may not accurately reflect the rigour and quality of its peer-review process. A journal with a prestigious editorial board may still have inconsistencies or flaws in its review process, while a lesser-known journal may have a rigorous, thorough and efficient review process. The peer-review systems of every journal are different in at least some detail; although many tourism journals follow the classic system whereby the editor looks at the paper and sends it to two reviewers whom the editor thinks know something about the subject. If both advise publication the editor accepts it and if both advise against publication the editor rejects the paper. Whilst a simplification, this process is little better than tossing a coin, since the level of agreement between reviewers on whether or not a paper is publishable is little better than one would expect by chance (Smith, 2006). The journal review system is extremely slow, highly subjective and opaque, prone to bias, cliquey and easily abused, often a lottery, and it runs on free labour from already overworked academics at enormous opportunity costs (Morey et al., 2016; Smith, 2006). 'So peer review is a flawed process, full of easily identified defects with little evidence that it works. Nevertheless, it is likely to remain central to … journals because there is no obvious alternative' (Smith, 2006, p. 182).

THE USE AND ABUSE OF JOURNAL RANKINGS

There are many problems with tourism management's obsession with journal rankings, but perhaps its most damaging effect is its influence on how researchers work and what they choose to study. Rankings are often amalgamated into guides, such as the *Academic Journal Guide* produced by the Chartered Association of Business Schools, the self-styled 'voice of the UK's business and management education sector' (https://charteredabs.org) or the *Journal Quality List* produced by the Australian Business Deans Council (https://abdc.edu.au). The use of these types of guides as performance management tools in business schools (where many tourism academics are located) to prepare for external research quality assessments (e.g., the UK Research Excellence Framework, https://www.ref.ac.uk) has been described as an example of Foucault's (1977) notion of 'disciplinary practices'. Despite years of critique, such guides have been used, often insensitively and ruthlessly, to 'inform calculations and career-defining decisions about the allocation of teaching and administration duties as well as those concerning appointments, probation, promotion and retention' (Tourish & Willmott, 2015, p. 38).

Journal rankings thereby contribute to and cement a politicized, competitive environment where researchers and institutions are driven to prioritize publishing in high-ranking journals to enhance their reputation and secure funding. The resultant organizational culture rewards individualism, extreme competitiveness and acute self-interest, and under-values collegiality and academic emotional labour; at its worst, it can encourage clientelism, side-deals, cronyism, careerism and impression management (Leathwood & Hey, 2009; Thornton, 2013; Finniear et al., 2020). At the very least, it promotes a highly stressful environment (especially for early and mid-career scholars) and skews research output, as researchers are incentivized to publish on mainstream topics in journals with high-impact factors rather than pursuing innovative or niche research, often to the detriment of specialist journals and topics (Jamal, Smith & Watson, 2008). For early career scholars seeking to publish their work and establish a reputation, the high rejection rates and long publication lead times for the top three tourism journals, *Annals of Tourism Research*, *Tourism Management* and *Journal of Travel Research*, are hugely stressful (Jamal, Smith & Watson, 2008). Indeed, the pressure to publish in these and other top-tier tourism journals, alongside the burden to compete for research funding, together with increasing workloads, isolation, career and financial insecurity, and interpersonal conflicts, significantly contributes to a lack of work–life balance in academia, which has one of the highest rates of mental illness and burnout when compared with other occupations (Lau & Pretorius, 2019; Urbina-Garcia, 2020).

Whilst rankings remain and continue to be used to measure and manage academic performance, scholars, especially those new to publishing, are advised to seek feedback from experienced researchers, mentors and colleagues in the field. They may have insights and recommendations regarding the credibility, reputation and efficiency of specific journals, which can help scholars make informed decisions about where to submit their research. Journal reputation and credibility are crucial factors when deciding where to publish and it is relatively simple to identify the most widely recognized and respected journals within the tourism academic community. The *Annals of Tourism Research*, *Tourism Management* and *Journal of Travel Research*, and increasingly the *Journal of Sustainable Tourism*, have strong reputations for their history, impact and the quality of the research they publish (Pechlaner et al., 2004). We should do well to remember, however, that journal rankings are just one tool among many for evaluating the quality and impact of academic journals, and a very flawed tool at that. Finally, be wary of choosing a journal based on impact factor alone since, ultimately, the quality and significance of our research should be our primary focus, rather than solely relying on journal rankings. You may want to consider an open access journal, which can increase the dissemination of your work and boost its exposure to non-academic audiences. The downside of publishing in an open access journal is that you have to pay 'article processing charges' and you need to be wary of predatory, ultra-low-impact journals interested only in this publication fee.

It is important to exercise judgment when deciding where to publish our research and we should ask ourselves some key questions. For example, do you read articles published in the journal you are targeting and has it published papers on your topic and using your methodology? If you are aiming to publish in high-impact journals, then remember that manuscript rejection is common and many top-tier journals have high rejection rates, ranging upwards from 60% to over 90%. However, take encouragement from evidence and experience, which suggest that authors who are committed to publishing and know how to handle a rejected manuscript do have a reasonable chance of achieving publication success. Over 60% of published papers have been rejected at least once and around half of all rejected manuscripts are published within two years (Woolley & Barron, 2009).

CONCLUSION

The hierarchical publication system or journal ranking system remains central to the tourism academic community, which is closely tied to business and management schools in many countries. The 'uses' of journal rankings are hotly debated across many disciplinary areas, and especially in business and management schools, typically the most highly commercialized departments of many universities, which presage 'a likely image of their future' (McCann et al., 2020, p. 433). Journal rankings exert an enormous influence on where tourism researchers publish, on what they publish in order to attain their career goals and, eventually, on who reads the research that they publish. Publications in the most prestigious journals lead to rewards, promotion and influence; many universities actively reward researchers publishing in the top-tier journals and covertly or overtly discourage other contributions, for example in lower ranked journals or edited books. It has been said that never before has there been such systemic control wielded over researchers, 'a situation that can be compared to the exertion of overt political control over academia or even to past eras in which religious demands constrained research' (Allen, 2019, pp. 33–34). This has far-reaching consequences as it serves as a mechanism for manipulating what and how we research, what is deemed of value to the field, who are seen as its star researchers and leaders, and ultimately the future of tourism research itself.

The field has therefore created a self-imposed zero-sum game, in which its most feted academics are those who have proved most skilful in directing their research agenda, theoretical frameworks and choice of method to what best fits in the 'top' journals. That those journals constantly demand novelty from their contributors also damages the field's ability to consolidate knowledge – a cumulative process so vital in producing a corpus of knowledge for theory-building (Khan, 2019). Such a skewed academic landscape pays scant attention to the notion that papers should be valued by their contribution to the field, neither by the standing of the journal they appear in nor by their number of citations or hits; or that high-quality and high-impact work, which engages meaningfully with the deepening problems of our time (e.g., of sustainability and social justice) is also found outside of the prestigious journals. While journal impact factors and rankings are here to stay and will continue to influence researcher behaviour, at least in the short term, we should not confuse journal impact factors with creating research with genuine impact. Ultimately any publication metrics are meaningless if the research we produce does not make a positive difference to society. Whilst most tourism journals demand that the papers they publish include consideration of implications for tourism management/policy, the uncomfortable reality is that very few academic papers make any contribution to either and are written in such a way that few practitioners or policy-makers would read them.

What does the future hold for our field's academic journals and their rankings? As more people use search engines and social media as their primary vehicle for searching for and receiving information, other ways of measuring research engagement and impact may come to the fore. For example, Altmetric scores are becoming increasingly important for measuring how much attention an individual article receives online and are able to capture broader global interest in the research beyond merely academic interest. For individual journals, rather than ranking systems, which produce a single journal guide or list, perhaps we could develop a more nuanced measurement, which could take account of different types of journal orientations (such as theoretical, empirical and applied/practical journals) and specializations (disciplinary and topic-related) (Jamal, Smith & Watson, 2008). Ultimately, perhaps all research will eventually be published in open access journals or perhaps journals will be abandoned altogether, in favour of 'a library-based scholarly communication system' (Brembs, Button & Munafò, 2013). Just as other sectors have been restructured by disruptive digital transformation, perhaps that still lies ahead for academic journals and publishing houses.

REFERENCES

Ahlstrom-Vij, K. (2023). Do we live in a 'post-truth' era? *Political Studies, 71*(2), 501–517.

Allen, K.A. (2019). What is the actual impact of measuring academic notions of impact? *The Educational and Developmental Psychologist, 36*(2), 33–34.

Brembs, B., Button, K. & Munafò, M. (2013). Deep impact: Unintended consequences of journal rank. *Frontiers in Human Neuroscience, 24*(7), 291.

Callaway, E. (2016). Beat it, impact factor! Publishing elite turns against controversial metric. *Nature*, *535*, 210–211.

Canaan, J.E., & Shumar, W. (2008). Higher education in the era of globalization and neoliberalism. In *Structure and agency in the neoliberal university*, (pp. 3–30). London: Routledge.

Casadevall, A., & Fang, F.C. (2015). Impacted science: Impact is not importance. *MBio*, *6*(5), e01593-15.

Finniear, J., Morgan, N., Chambers, D. & Munar, A.M. (2020). Gender-based harassment in tourism academia: Organizational collusion, coercion and compliance. In P. Vizcaino-Suarez, H. Jeffrey & C. Eger (eds.), *Tourism and gender-based violence: Challenging inequalities* (pp. 30–44). Wallingford, UK: CABI.

Foucault, M. (1977). *Discipline and punish*. London: Penguin.

Hall, C.M. (2011). Publish and perish? Bibliometric analysis, journal ranking and the assessment of research quality in tourism. *Tourism Management*, *32*(1), 16–27.

Ioannidis, J., Boyack, K., Small, H. et al. (2014). Bibliometrics: Is your most cited work your best? *Nature*, *514*, 561–562.

Jamal, T., Smith, B. & Watson, E. (2008). Ranking, rating and scoring of tourism journals: Interdisciplinary challenges and innovations. *Tourism Management*, *29*(1), 66–78.

Khan, M.A. (2019). Building theories for hospitality discipline: An attempt to describe and elaborate required processes and procedures. *Journal of Hospitality & Tourism Research*, *43*(5), 619–632.

Lau, R.W.K., & Pretorius, L. (2019). Intrapersonal wellbeing and the academic mental health crisis. In L. Pretorius, L. Macaulay & B. Cahusac de Caux (eds.), *Wellbeing in doctoral education: Insights and guidance from the student experience* (pp. 37–45). Singapore: Springer.

Leathwood, C., & Hey, V. (2009). Gender/ed discourses and emotional sub-texts: Theorising emotion in UK higher education. *Teaching in Higher Education*, *14*(4), 429–440.

McCann, L., Granter, E., Hyde, P. & Aroles, J. (2020). 'Upon the gears and upon the wheels': Terror convergence and total administration in the neoliberal university. *Management Learning*, *51*(4), 431–451.

Morey, R.D., Chambers, C.D., Etchells, P.J., Harris, C.R., Hoekstra, R., Lakens, D. & Zwaan, R.A. (2016). The Peer Reviewers' Openness Initiative: Incentivizing open research practices through peer review. *Royal Society Open Science*, *3*(1), 150547.

Pechlaner, H., Zehrer, A., Matzler, K. & Abfalter, D. (2004). A ranking of international tourism and hospitality journals. *Journal of Travel Research*, *42*(4), 328–332.

Pritchard, A., & Morgan, N. (2017). Tourism's lost leaders: Analysing gender and performance. *Annals of Tourism Research*, *63*, 34–47.

Pritchard, A., & Morgan, N. (2007). De-centring tourism's intellectual universe or the dialectic between change and tradition. In I. Ateljevic, A. Pritchard & N. Morgan (eds.), *The critical turn in tourism studies* (pp. 12–28). London: Routledge.

Rafols, I., Leydesdorff, L., O'Hare, A., Nightingale, P. & Stirling, A. (2012). How journal rankings can suppress interdisciplinary research: A comparison between innovation studies and business and management. *Research Policy*, *41*, 1262–1282.

Smith, R. (2006). Peer review: A flawed process at the heart of science and journals. *Journal of the Royal Society of Medicine*, *99*(4), 178–182.

Standing, K.E., and Atkinson, K.Y.M. (2018). 'Changing the culture' – A feminist academic activist critique. *Violence Against Women*, available from: http://researchonline.ljmu.ac.uk/9733/.

Thornton, M. (2013). The mirage of merit: Reconstituting the 'ideal academic'. *Australian Feminist Studies*, *28*(76), 127–143.

Tourish, D., & Willmott, H. (2015). In defiance of folly: Journal rankings, mindless measures and the ABS guide. *Critical Perspectives on Accounting*, *26*, 37–46.

Urbina-Garcia, A. (2020). What do we know about university academics' mental health? A systematic literature review. *Stress and Health*, *36*(5), 563–585.

Woolley, K.L., & Barron, J.P. (2009). Handling manuscript rejection: Insights from evidence and experience. *Chest*, *135*(2), 573–577.

16. Careers, citations, bibliometrics, and impact: perspectives of new and emerging researchers

Bailey Ashton Adie, Alberto Amore, Richard S. Aquino, Tim Baird, Dorothee Bohn, C. Michael Hall, Fahimeh Hateftabar, Sara Naderi Koupaei, Tyron Love, Lan Lu, Hamed Rezapouraghdam, Samaneh Soleimani, and Chris Zhu

INTRODUCTION

Publishing, doing a PhD, and developing an academic career do not occur in a vacuum. Even if it is not explicitly articulated, academic research, where academics publish, and their careers are guided by values and interests. The paths that people take in their publishing are therefore influenced by a wide range of factors, many of which are outlined in this book. However, what people publish cannot be isolated from what else is happening in their career, what they have to teach, where they work, and, just as importantly, where they want to work.

This chapter brings together invited contributions from new and emerging academics with respect to their experiences and how publishing demands affect their careers and life, and vice versa. The provision of such experiences is important as it conveys the reality of publishing from a real-world context with respect to the pressures we face, especially when starting on the academic ladder. Authors were given a broad scope with respect to their contributions and the results are provided below with only very minor editing. They have also been presented anonymously, or rather collectively, because although there are clearly different perspectives, emphases, and interpretations, there are also commonalities in the contributors' experiences. Nevertheless, as the reader will see, there are a number of common themes that emerge. Following the perspectives of the different contributions the chapter will discuss some of the main issues that emerge and their implications, including some of the darker aspects of the pressures of publishing (Fanghanel, 2012; Fleming, 2020, 2021).

MEETING THE HOSPITALITY AND TOURISM DISCIPLINE: A PERSPECTIVE FROM PHD STUDENT

Hospitality and tourism are important disciplines that have contributed significantly to the understanding of the global economic recovery and the development of tourist psychology (Gössling, Scott, & Hall, 2020; Hall, 2014; Truong & Hall, 2013). As an emerging scholar in the hospitality and tourism disciplines, it is of great relevance for early career researchers (e.g., PhD students) to understand the disciplines. As a PhD student in hospitality and tourism, I believe that there are several points that can help us develop early in our student careers.

First, in the selection of research interests, when I look at the Google Scholar professional citation rankings, I found Professor Colin Michael Hall, ranked first, and then Professor Rob Law and Professor Dimitrios Buhalis, ranked second and third respectively. Their main research interests are sustainable tourism and smart tourism. The recent hot phenomenon of the very popular Metaverse and ChatGPT also validates the forward-looking nature of their research interests, as both the Metaverse and ChatGPT can be used to make tourism more sustainable using information technology. More importantly, their research topics have a lot of practical and applied value rather than just being theoretical and academic contributions. In other words, the choice of research interest should always be relevant, not only to promote the development of tourism and hospitality disciplines, but more importantly, to help stakeholders become more reflective on the values that tourism and hospitality disciplines bring to society and the nation. Thus, a good research interest may be more important than effort for early career scholars.

Second, the paper's storytelling and research methods are also significant. With the current rapid development of interdisciplinary convergence, many new research methods are gradually emerging in the tourism discipline (Zhu & Fong, 2022). Some of the early scholars may believe that traditional questionnaire-based research methods (e.g., SEM) have fallen out of fashion, and instead they pursue more diverse research methods. For me, I admit that a diverse research approach does have the potential to enhance the publication of an article. However, when I go back to the essence of writing, I believe that writing an article is telling a story and you need not only your peers to be able to understand your values and views on the tourism and hospitality phenomenon, but also readers who are not tourism and hospitality professionals should still be able to gain insights from your points. For a true and inspiring story, it should be that with a simple description, that other readers from different backgrounds can understand what you are trying to say and thus know your point of view. Conversely, if there are too many highly specialized words or complex research methods, although peers may be interested, readers from different professions or even subscribers to the journal may just abandon a valuable piece of work because they may be bored by these unfamiliar methods. Therefore, I think it is important for early academics to tell a story in order to inspire readers from different backgrounds. And finally, choosing the right journal based on that story rather than writing for the purpose of publishing in a high-impact factor journal is paramount.

Why is a good story more essential than a high-impact journal? For me, if I don't understand what research methods need to be used to accomplish the research question and furthermore how to string the question and the research methods together into a good story, publication is simply out of the question. Therefore, in the early years of a PhD student, the most important thing should be to know how to write a paper or tell a good story. Only in this way can one have the opportunity to publish an article with a high-impact factor. If, however, I cannot tell a story, the probability is that I will receive a rejection, which creates a lot of pressure to publish. Therefore, this is where I would like to emphasize that it may not be right to focus on publishing in high-impact journals without building a solid foundation (e.g., telling a good story), which in turn can create a lot of pressure to publish. Of course, every PhD student will be under pressure to publish. But I believe that only by learning the most basic research questions, research methods, and other story components will I have a chance to write a good story and finally publish it. In short, publishing is a process of continuous learning and reflection.

Finally, the most important thing for early career researchers is an attitude of learning and hard work. I am sure that many famous scholars have experienced frustrations and challenges when they were young, such as being rejected, not having their ideas published, and a bundle of other problems. But I would say that studying something or a discipline comes from your inner recognition of them and the role you see them playing in the development of society. Thus, publishing an article is not only a hobby, but also a job and a sense of responsibility. More realistically, we need to make some progress in the subject to be better able to get a job and support our families and lives in the future. So, from this perspective, while early career academics will encounter many challenges in terms of professional learning and publication, it is these realities and a sense of social responsibility that will continue to drive early career researchers to become better academics and contribute to society in the longer term.

All in all, the development of the hospitality and tourism discipline will require groups of all ages to work together. And as an important part of the future of academia, there is significant research value in focusing on the development of early career scholars. PhD students have different understandings of hospitality and tourism due to different cultures and backgrounds. Hospitality and tourism are important social disciplines that help societies to develop economically, connect tourists around the world, and, most importantly, help disadvantaged regions develop their economies, reduce unemployment, and improve education. With this sense of social responsibility and the future development of the hospitality and tourism discipline, I believe that it is important for an early career researcher to have this sense of values and mission. Whenever I think about this, some of the challenges and problems I experienced as an early career researcher become motivation for me to move forward on my academic path.

IMPACT FACTORS, IMPACTFUL RESEARCH, AND CAREER IMPACTS: A VICIOUS CIRCLE?

When I was first approached to write a paper on tourism, sustainability, and regional development, I must confess I had zero knowledge on *what* and *where* to publish. To me, being invited as co-author of a publication from a professor was all the incentive I needed. Things changed in the moment I moved to New Zealand to enrol for the PhD. One week into the program, I was made aware of rankings, metrics, impact factors, and which journals to target for publication. There is no doubt that this added information was extremely useful to streamline relevant journals and works for the literature review of my research proposal. However, I soon realized that I had to go beyond citation scores and metrics for tourism journals to develop an original contribution and, most importantly, keep an open mindset to research in the field. In my early years following the PhD, I got formal and informal praise for the research done and my daring to challenge preconceived ideas about tourism. Part of this outside-of-the-box thinking is because I do not fully adhere to the idolatry of rankings, impact factors, citations scores, and indexes.

Yet, journal metrics and impact factors are part of the academic life. Five years after the completion of the PhD, I find myself in what can be best described as a vicious circle encompassing publishing companies, journals, editorial boards, colleagues, departments, and universities. Each of the involved parties value and use indicators for their own purpose. There are internationally recognized metrics as well as national indicators that universities and research councils use as benchmarks. Regardless of which metrics and indicators are used, publishing in top-ranked journals is important for your academic visibility, your department, your co-author network, and your career advancement.

I understand that publishing relevant empirical and conceptual papers in top journals helps build your credibility and visibility. The question, however, is how to rise and establish yourself as a scholar in the fiercely competitive "publish or perish" bazaar. According to a review by McKercher and Dolnicar (2022), a total of 10,752 papers in tourism, hospitality, and event studies were published in 2021. This figure alone should make us reflect on the over-abundance of studies and research disseminated in just one year. If we estimate the percentage of rejections and the pervasive practice of resubmitting papers down the journal rankings ladder, you can deduce that the number of papers submitted for consideration were between 100,000 and 150,000(!)

Rankings and indexes are, to me, a necessary evil to closely keep in consideration in my journey to academic recognition. At the same time, I carefully position my research and target journals based on *what* I want to convey and the audience of the journal. This might be seen as counter-effective considering the trends highlighted above. Some of you may say I am a dreamer and that there are structural forces that will inevitably overcome my current stance about metrics. However, in a crucial phase in which key scholars and current editors-in-chief publicly express concerns on the implications of the publish or perish culture, it is important to find a balance between the pertinence of my research, aim, and scopes of journals and metrics.

Unfortunately, I do not have a recipe or a proved formula supporting my belief. If I had one, I would have published it in a journal instead of writing down this commentary. This platform, however, provides me with the opportunity to share my own experience as an academic globetrotter in four different university systems in the last ten years (Italy, New Zealand, the United Kingdom, and Finland). Overall, there are three key reflection points that apply to both my niche research area and the wider field of tourism:

1. The pursuit of research excellence is a thin line between genuine advancement of knowledge and performative display of allegedly "impactful" research that is only validated by journal rankings and impact factors. As a researcher in the early stages, you will find yourself in a dilemma between contributing to conceptually and empirically innovative studies that take time to be completed, reviewed, and published or small studies reaffirming the status quo that will most likely be published in a shorter period and build up your own citation score.
2. Try not to abide to the dogmatic rhetoric of impact factors and rankings. Acknowledge their relevance to support your publication strategy to advance your career. At the same time, be mindful of where you want to publish, the editorial line of the journals, and the composition of the editorial board. Publishing is still a craftwork involving different people in the "getting published" journey.
3. Impact factors, H-index, number of citations, and number of publications are mere performance indicators that do not fully shed light on the actual

quality or relevance of research published. The display of these indicators on social media (especially LinkedIn) by academics over the last few years tells us nothing about the research itself and causes more harm than good to the collegiality and dialogue that nurtures the academic debate.

Finally, as a scholar fresh out of the PhD, I want to provide a reflection on a recent debate regarding the use of ChatGPT in the publication of papers and journal articles and the implications for current and future tourism scholars. I have observed and taken note of those who championed ChatGPT and already used it to publish a paper. There are also changing rules by the publishing companies and universities on the use of AI-generated text. I am deeply concerned of the implications of ChatGPT in the pervasive publish or perish culture of academia. As a community, we should carefully reflect on our role as creators of knowledge and enablers of debate and the implications of this technological innovation to the future of tourism research.

PUBLISH (IN A*) OR PERISH

The type (or title) of the journal research is published in serves as one indicator of quality. Especially amongst tourism and management scholars based in Australasia, the quality of the academic publication is guided by the Australian Business Deans Council (ABDC) Journal Quality List. Popularly adopted by business schools in the region to evaluate their faculties' research quality (e.g., Grossmann, Mooney, & Dugan, 2019), this list assigns a letter grade to 2,680 listed journals as an indicator of quality (ABDC, 2023): A* being the highest category (7.4% of listed journals); A being the second highest category (24.4% of listed journals); B being the third highest category (31.9% of listed journals); and C being the fourth highest category (36.3% of listed journals). Publication agendas and promotion criteria are increasingly driven by this list, urging academics to aim to publish in "elite" A* or A journals at the least. Working as a full-time academic in a university based in this region, the same institutional expectations apply to me.

I used to never care about the grade or ranking of the journal where I published my research, especially when I was a doctoral student. Back then, I mainly cared about how my research would create real-world impact – in the industry, communities, and for individuals involved in my work – and contributions to knowledge. Secondary to this was the aim of publishing journal articles out of my PhD thesis. After all, I needed to present a decent list of publications in my CV that would make me "marketable" enough for when I applied for academic jobs. I view publishing in A* journals as more of a personal challenge rather than a critical aspect of my career as a tourism academic. But the "game" is continuously changing.

Reflective Thoughts

Increasingly, we see PhD candidates, especially those based in Australian institutions, publishing about three to four articles in A* journals even before graduating. This makes the competition for the already scarce full-time permanent lecturing roles in tourism more competitive. I consider myself lucky enough to have secured my lecturing position in New Zealand without any A* journal publication when I was hired. When I applied for my current role, I was based in New Zealand and the borders were closed due to the pandemic. This meant I did not have to compete with candidates with a much deeper publication list based elsewhere. Given this, I felt I had to publish an A* article to prove myself worthy of the position.

Since joining my current university, I am being mentored by senior colleagues who have rich expertise in publishing in highly ranked and graded journals. As an early career researcher (ECR), they advised me to publish my best work in high-quality journals in tourism early on in my career rather than focusing on quantity. They are always willing to look at my work and provide generous feedback before I submit any article. I consider myself privileged to have my mentors, and to be working with people in my department who have the knowledge, experience, and generosity to support me in publishing in highly graded journals. With the publication "game" becoming more intense as A* journals compete to be the best in their fields, publishing in these journals becomes more difficult, especially for ECRs who are not based in "elite" institutions (e.g., Grossmann, Mooney, & Dugan, 2019) or who do not have the connections that will help them to do so.

Beyond the pressure to publish in A* journals, I have experienced different benefits in doing so. Any academic who published in these journals knows it is not easy. I improved my skills in crafting articles suitable to the level expected in those journals. Apart from the practical skills, we cannot deny that there is some form of prestige in publishing in these outlets as perceived by peers. When I published an article in one of the reputable tourism journals, one colleague who is also a friend and an ECR sent me a congratulatory message. They wrote: "Congratulations on your paper! I'm jealous. It [publishing in that journal] is a culmination of being a tourism scholar."

I realized publishing in certain tourism journals could mean finally "making it" in tourism academia. Thus, to paraphrase the popular phrase, "publish or perish", I feel that the situation now, at least amongst tourism academics, is: "publish in A* or perish" or if I am to be more (or less) harsh, "publish in A* or you don't exist".

On "Humble Brags" and "Publication Envy"

Reflecting on my friend's message, I realized that a post on social media about an achievement could be a source of (publication) envy for others, adding to the pressure and mental health issues already faced by PhD students and ECRs. Academic Twitter, LinkedIn, and Facebook are full of "celebratory" posts that start with: "I am pleased to announce that my new article is published in [insert journal name] (ABDC A*; Q1; IF: [insert IF score])."

I'm not saying getting published in these journals should not be celebrated. It's about how to frame social media posts. These so-called "humble brags" on social media could place attention away from the impact of the work towards the title and grading of the journal. People outside of academia do not care about journal grades: they care about the usefulness of the research for them. Thus, we should be mindful about announcing new publications on social media, and highlighting findings of the research rather than the title of the journal it is published in.

Concluding Thoughts

Journal rankings and grading are in place to ensure publication quality. One's work should be impactful (in practice and theory) and novel enough to be published in these journals. Staying true to my role as an academic, I need to continuously do impactful research and, thereafter, publish in highly graded journals. While I enjoyed several benefits in doing so with the help of my mentors, publishing in these journals can add challenges to PhD students and early career researchers, especially if their institutions' priorities are driven by these sorts of journals and if they lack the resources and mentorship to publish in them.

WHY METRICS (DON'T) MATTER

The academic debate on metrics is hotly contested, with arguments made both for and against their use, especially when it comes to journal rankings and personal citation counts. Ultimately, though, this debate on the use of metrics is just that, a debate. While internally, many academics may push back against this numerical over-simplification of academic research, practically, many often reinforce this system by relying on personal citation counts, H-indices, and i-10 indices as shorthand markers of "quality" work. This is not to say that all academics fall into this trap, but more that, as with all change, some are doing more than others. But what does this mean practically, particularly for those in the job market or earlier in their careers and trying to plan for promotion? Well, predominantly it means that, as of right now, metrics do count, that is, until they don't. Entry-level job openings will require top-tier publications along with a host of other requirements. The bigger your H-index, the more impressive you look. Will this get you the job though? It might get you an interview, but, sadly, academic hiring processes are often incredibly arbitrary, especially in countries that lack transparent hiring practices. All the -isms are still very much evident in academia, resulting in not only hires who do not always meet the job criteria but also may very much be a mirror of the department as a whole.

In terms of internal promotions, metrics are a double-edged sword. In some academic contexts, metrics are increasingly being used by university management as overt employment controls. More specifically, metrics are sometimes weaponized to punish individuals who aren't viewed as "adding value" to the university's research portfolio, ultimately exerting managerial power over what are considered acceptable research topics. In practical terms, this means that those who are researching novel but niche areas which are not a "priority" focus for universities may find their research time taken away as their research is deemed as not having enough impact. On the flipside of this, some academics game the system through a variety of methods, including:

- Citation rings;
- Exchanges of gift authorship;
- Salami slicing research papers to increase outputs;
- Excessive self-citation; and
- While reviewing, requesting multiple citations of their own work, especially if irrelevant to the manuscript.

This is done for a variety of reasons, from a desire for early promotion to trying to avoid teaching and service expectations as well as, in some case, pure ego. In systems where publications = money for the university, these individuals may rise quickly up the ladder, regardless of the actual impact of their research, both theoretically and practically.

So, what, within this apparent doom and gloom scenario, where the only way to "win" is to play the game, can any one academic do? Well, there are several options, all of which require you to reject this idea that metrics mean anything apart from a requirement for your CV. First, when you write, you can cite relevant works, regardless of where they are published or who published them, which will have the additional benefit of helping to potentially prioritize marginalized voices. Second, focus on doing work that you care about, regardless of whether the topic is currently *en vogue* and/or highly citable. Third, engage in good practices as both a researcher and peer reviewer. Publish in the most relevant journals and don't just submit to the ones with the best citation rates or the highest rank. Prioritize quality in your own work and others and, if you can, call out bad behaviour in publishing. If you want to focus on research that has direct impact over theoretical impact, do it. Focus on what makes your work worth doing. I should note that it is likely that none of this will help with employment, particularly with the way that academia is heading. In fact, it may actually hinder promotions or even finding a more permanent post. But, at the end of the day, are you ok buying into a system that promotes overwork, stress, and unhealthy competition to build up a collection of numbers that ultimately mean little? Or would you rather do something meaningful, for yourself and/or others, and pay the price in prestige?

THE EXPERIENCES OF EARLY CAREER RESEARCHERS ON THE EFFECTS OF CITATIONS, BIBLIOMETRICS, AND NOTIONS OF IMPACT ON THEIR WORK

Citations can provide scholars the feeling of acknowledgement and they can work as a mechanism of appreciating their contribution to the field, but they also can carry the weight of pressures and expectations. It is apparent that bibliometrics and citation metrics increasingly have an influence on academic careers, impacting choices about opportunities for employment, advancement, and financing. The pressure to produce highly cited research or to publish a certain number of articles, however, can result in prioritizing subjects and research methods that are more likely to garner attention rather than embracing the broad spectrum of academic inquiry. It can also compromise the psychological well-being of the academicians. In the following I will share my experiences in two different work environments where opposing credits were given to my research attempts. I will also share my feedback received from the students and the newly emerged culture of publishing or perishing in academia at the end.

I have personally felt the demoralizing and depressing impacts of an academic climate at a private university where citations and publications were given little weight during my academic career. After receiving my PhD, I began working at a private university and discovered that these criteria had no bearing on the hiring and tenure processes. I had a true enthusiasm for research and for making a contribution to the area, therefore the lack of focus placed on citations and publications left me feeling underappreciated and unhappy. This experience strengthened my conviction that research should be respected and recognized because it is an important component of academic careers and advances knowledge.

On the other hand, I had fierce competition for a position in a public institution during my second academic career. The selection procedure's emphasis on scholarly articles stands out as one distinctive feature. I realized that my chances of success may be considerably impacted by having a publishing record. Hopefully, in addition to meeting other qualifications, my publishing history aided in my ability to get that job. Citations did not, however, play a part in getting that position.

In recent years, I've noticed that our students have become more divided due to the emerging publish-or-perish culture. One group is just concerned with producing as many papers as they can, frequently at the price of giving less attention to acquiring knowledge, developing creativity, and enhancing critical thinking. These students place a higher priority on quantity rather than quality. They are in a rush to be part of the trend as soon as possible without allocating time to acquiring actual knowledge in their respective subjects for the sake of building their academic résumés. This phenomenon inhibits intellectual development and deters them from seeking information for its own sake.

Another group of students, on the other hand, are discouraged and frustrated by this publication-centred environment. They believe they cannot compete in a field and cope with the stress where the quantity of publications is dominant. Despite their aptitude and sincere enthusiasm in their professions, such students get dissatisfied with academia and opt to finish their program with the unpleasant memories of competition for publications.

In learning from these experiences, I believe that it is critical to achieve a balance between promoting productivity and fostering intellectual curiosity in order to create a healthy academic atmosphere. This will foster an atmosphere in which academics in their early careers may flourish and pursue substantial contributions to their subject areas while also feeling intellectually fulfilled. Institutions may play a critical role in creating such an atmosphere that encourages and promotes creative research by encouraging junior researchers to pursue novel approaches rather than by focusing on the number of publications. Furthermore, encouraging multidisciplinary cooperation and supporting unorthodox research concepts might aid in ending the replication loop and motivate young researchers to undertake really transformational lines of investigation.

BEING A PHD STUDENT AND THE DIFFICULTIES OF PUBLICATION

To provide some sort of context to the issues of publication from a doctoral student perspective, it is appropriate to provide some background to my own PhD journey as an international student. Unfortunately, studying in another country as an Iranian female student and without any financial support at times had many problems. My master's degree in tourism was completed in North Cyprus exactly when my country (Iran) was in the worst condition economically and politically, which created substantial pressure to find a job if I wanted to stay there and continue my education with a PhD. Clearly, finding a job in a small country like North Cyprus was not easy, given that the salary from such work cannot meet your daily expenses and cost of doing a PhD there. I applied for a PhD scholarship and fortunately, before my visa expired, I received a 50% scholarship which meant that I still had to pay half of the tuition fees. I started to work hard to obtain a full scholarship and after the first semester I received one, although under the condition of publication. In addition, a full-time scholarship student must work in the department every day from 8 a.m. to 5 p.m. and they must attend and help in any function that the department has during semester. The PhD curriculum in North Cyprus is based on courses and a thesis which requires seven courses to be completed before starting the thesis. These seven courses took three semesters (one and half years) and in the fourth semester the student should submit their proposal and at the end of the semester students attend a qualification exam which is kind of confirmation for their proposal. In addition, every PhD student needs at least one SSCI article for their graduation. This is in addition to the publication requirements of the scholarship. For both PhD and scholarship, book chapters are not acceptable forms of publication (i.e., what I am writing now will not count). So, how can a PhD student publish articles under these tough conditions?

By providing the above story, I strive to give a short account of my journey to become a PhD student. However, I believe that being a PhD student is the beginning of a tougher process in the academic world. There are different reasons for everyone for publishing research, such as graduation or finding a job or opportunity in another country, but the path to reaching this goal can be challenging. I am a non-Anglophone PhD student in an English language university and by providing some of my personal difficulties in this process, I want to highlight that there are numerous factors, including non-academic ones, that influence what we try and publish.

Writing is considered by some academics as hard work, and requires adequate preparation, time, quality of reasoning, expertise, and energy, but obviously it is even tougher for novice non-Anglophone researchers when English is the major language used by scholars in the journals that meet university scholarship and doctoral requirements. Non-Anglophone researchers face the challenge of failure and rejection of articles during their publication process due to improper use of English and they may have to take assistance from third-party editing services, which is a cost they will often have to bear themselves. Nevertheless, it is equally important that articles are written properly for the ease of reviewers and readers.

Another serious challenge is designing or finding research topics or fields because articles should ideally express their author's passion, and his/her depth of involvement, otherwise they may fail. So, it is essential to identify a field of research based on our passions and interests. However, we should also recognize that many researchers sometimes have to work on unimpressive research topics for some personal reasons such as lack of job, need for money, or a lack of other publishing opportunities. Nevertheless, working on your personal interests provides better results and personal feelings.

Another barrier for PhD students is identification of an adequate journal outlet. With myriad journals available in every field of science, it becomes difficult for researchers to identify the best journal to submit their manuscript to, although in some cases this is determined by external factors such as requirements for an SSCI journal for graduation. Furthermore, going from article submission to a final peer-review decision can be an opaque and lengthy process, during which time the same article should not be submitted to another journal even if, as a graduate student, you need to be published as soon as possible to either graduate or fulfil scholarship requirements. Also, given that once a manuscript is published it will represent years of hard work, it becomes particularly important to choose the right publisher. However, there are challenges here as there are some journals with a relatively high acceptance rate that will seemingly publish without many revisions but these may not be acceptable for some universities.

To wrap up, although I may not have enough experience to state all of the difficulties in the PhD journey with respect to publishing, because every university, person, and PhD has their own rules, strategies, and perspective, obtaining publications in the current competitive academic world is very tough. In addition, I can advise to all novice and non-Anglophone researchers, that if you/we have a distinctive goal for your/our future and really want to be a successful researcher and lecturer, you/we just have to keep going, be patient, and never give up, which are the only ways to achieve our goals.

REFLECTIVE WRITING

As an aspiring novice researcher, embarking upon the nascent stages of my scholarly trajectory, I humbly acknowledge that there lies a vast realm of knowledge yet to be acquired. The insights I now share predominantly derive from the valuable lessons gleaned through my personal missteps encountered along the way. I believe that the realization of more favourable results would have been within reach had I averted some of the missteps I encountered. Nevertheless, these challenging missteps have served as valuable stepping stones towards a deeper understanding of the research process and my career development. Thus, while I cannot rewrite my own past, I aim to share some advice from my experience in the early stages of my career. My intention is to provide this advice in the hope that it can facilitate a smoother journey for others.

First and foremost, I want to emphasize the importance of focusing on a specific research topic and the benefits it brings. It is crucial to choose one or two subjects that genuinely interest us and dedicate ourselves to them. Reflecting on my own experiences, I realize that one of my biggest mistakes was working on multiple topics instead of concentrating on one. Focusing on a limited number of topics can yield better results for novice researchers like me. By immersing ourselves in a singular area of study, we can develop a comprehensive understanding of subject matter, enhancing the depth and quality of our research. This concentrated focus allows us to explore various aspects and nuances, developing expertise within the chosen field. By narrowing our scope, we can use our time, energy, and resources more efficiently, avoiding scattered efforts.

In addition to a deeper understanding, focusing on a limited number of topics helps in building a cohesive body of work. This coherence is valuable when developing a thesis or producing a series of related articles. By selecting a singular theme, we establish a narrative thread that connects our research endeavours, enhancing the impact of our work. This approach fosters a sense of purpose and direction, making a meaningful contribution to the academic community.

While seasoned scholars may adeptly navigate multiple topics, I have come to realize that novice researchers, like myself, can greatly benefit from concentrating on a limited number of subjects. Through deep immersion in a chosen area of interest, we can produce focused, rigorous, and impactful research. This approach not only facilitates the accumulation of knowledge and expertise but also resonates with the academic community, ultimately propelling the advancement of our field.

The scholarly world presents other substantial challenges for early career professionals, including intense competition and issues with relationships and collaboration. Working independently often leads to decreased motivation and increased procrastination. However, despite the prevalent individualism and competitiveness in academia, building a strong support network is a valuable strategy for managing job pressures and finding fulfilment in research. To overcome these challenges, seek out compatible partners for collaboration and engage in joint efforts. Collaborative research offers numerous advantages, such as boosting efficiency, facilitating extensive learning opportunities, and ensuring adherence to timelines, as well as potentially preventing demotivation and idleness that often accompany independent work and solitary endeavours. Therefore, I suggest actively engaging with fellow scholars who share similar interests and can offer guidance, and perhaps ultimately collaborating as co-authors. By participating in conferences and symposia at various levels, you can exchange valuable feedback on ongoing and upcoming research endeavours. By approaching these interactions with an open mind and respecting differing perspectives, while still confidently expressing your own ideas, you can enrich your academic journey and gain both energy and benefits.

Moreover, as an early career researcher, I often find myself grappling with numerous challenges in publishing and advancing my career. The magnitude of these challenges creates a daunting and demanding environment that can be discouraging at times. It is widely recognized in the academic community that the number of publications as a first author and the prestige of the journals they are published in hold significant importance when evaluating the accomplishments of early career researchers. This awareness further amplifies the pressure we face to produce a substantial body of work in order to gain recognition and opportunities for growth. The urgency of publishing and its impact on career prospects, along with the competitive nature of the field, adds stress and uncertainty to our journey as we strive for stability and progress. Moreover, due to the high competition, there may be a temptation to sacrifice quality for quantity and start publishing articles of lesser quality. However, it is important to resist this temptation and prioritize the quality of our work. While the quantity of publications is important, it is equally crucial to ensure that each publication demonstrates rigour, impact, and contribution to the field. Also, it is crucial to remember that the challenges we encounter are not unique to us alone. Many others have faced and overcome similar obstacles on their academic paths. Therefore, it is important for us to build a supportive network and community where we can share our experiences, seek advice, and find encouragement.

The path to securing a job following the completion of a PhD is frequently characterized by unpredictability and can present unexpected challenges, leaving individuals uncertain about their next course of action. One of the primary challenges I faced upon graduating was the scarcity of academic job openings within the field of tourism in France. In contrast, there were more promising prospects in related areas such as marketing and economics. In hindsight, I believe that if I had thoroughly explored employment opportunities during my PhD, I could have directed my research towards the interdisciplinary domain of tourism and marketing as this would have expanded the scope of job possibilities available to me upon completing my studies. Therefore, I recommend regularly assessing the labour market, maybe even in different countries, while pursuing a PhD so as to better position publications and interests in light of where employment opportunities are available.

As an early career researcher, I have a long path ahead of me and numerous opportunities for growth. Throughout my journey thus far, I have shared a few lessons that I have learned. I sincerely hope that my personal experiences along this journey resonate with readers and provide an advantage in navigating present or future academic endeavours.

MY PUBLISHING JOURNEY AS A PHD STUDENT AND GRADUATE

While I was so excited that I got a scholarship to pursue my studies in a PhD program, my understanding of the hurdles along the way was so limited. Especially as an international student with English as a foreign language, the experience felt like a dive without knowing how to swim. There were many aspects to consider in academic life – learning how to teach, research, publish, network, apply for grants, and many more. Despite the beauty of researching something you love, I constantly heard the voice that I needed to be more. I wanted to learn and do everything perfectly, but teaching and researching well takes a lifetime, even if someone devotes all their time to it. Knowing the road map and knowing where to start was a big challenge. It is simple to say that you seek help, but the real challenge is knowing what kind of help you need and who can help you. Besides, I could see all of the professors were busy receiving tons of emails from students and early career researchers to either be their mentor or help them with their publications which was another challenge for me considering that I wouldn't say I liked to connect people just with a hope of getting some benefit. I would have loved to communicate with people only for human interactions and I feel that everyone is worthy of respect regardless of their positions.

After graduation, the more challenging part started. I was seeking a job with a résumé without significant publication or answering the selection criteria, with all the jobs demanding publication in high-quality journals and successful grant outcomes. As it is tough to get a full-time position meeting all these criteria, most graduates, including myself, start taking contract teaching positions to earn income. On the other hand, as teaching itself is quite different and requires expertise, less time remains for publication. Assuming anyone with a PhD can teach needs to be corrected, as teaching differs from researching. Someone who has a PhD is an expert in that field, but they are not necessarily able to transfer and teach their knowledge to others. A tremendous amount of time, energy, and learning is needed to become an expert in teaching. Therefore, another big challenge for a recent graduate such as myself was how to teach well, how to mark the assignments with valuable feedback, and at the same time, focus on my research and publication. This critical time when you need as many publications as possible in a short time is when fewer resources and less time and support are available. Time goes by, and it gets harder and harder to focus on the research you once were passionate about and wanted the whole world to know about it. Sooner rather than later, you understand that you are not alone, and most graduates, especially international students, feel the same way. Although you wish you were alone in this pain, you realize that if others could overcome these hurdles, you can do so too, especially since you came a long way to get your PhD, although it seems you are at the beginning of your journey.

Another hurdle that I faced was the publication journey itself. The long process of paper reviews, especially in good journals, makes the wait towards reaching goals even more intolerable. As a graduate, you hear from professors to publish your best idea in a good journal without breaking down your content into pieces, but when applying for jobs, the panel asks about the number of publications. Therefore, the immediate struggle is deciding which way to go – one impactful publication in an outstanding journal which may take up to two years to get published after rounds of reviews, or slicing up the research and publishing it in two or three less demanding journals to meet the requirements of the job applications in a shorter amount of time.

Besides, researching journals themselves to understand which journal should be chosen for an article is another learning curve not addressed in any academic program I know of. I assume it simply is something that comes with experience. Putting this issue aside, learning the best way and approach to adjust a journal article based on a new journal's requirements is another struggle, especially when some of the most time-consuming tasks seem very irrelevant, such as changing the referencing style! Such a process will reduce a researcher's enthusiasm to devote meaningful time to something that doesn't necessarily add further value.

Based on the experience I got, here are some ways that helped me to overcome these hurdles to some extent:

- Showing my genuine interest in my research and discussing it passionately with others or at conferences. Nothing is more important than feeling you add value to society and wanting others to join you.
- Always trying to find out how best I can serve others. Is there any PhD student needing my help with their proposal, data collection, or data analysis? You will be surprised how satisfying it is to help others achieve their goals. Just remember that your help should be genuine without any expectations. In the first week of my job, I remember overhearing one of my colleagues talking with someone about their struggles with some data analysis software. I stepped in and shared how they could solve the issue. Later that week, they asked me to join their team as a co-author and to date, we have published four articles. This approach of collaboration has helped me with my other struggle of publishing one piece or a few. Ultimately, I decided to publish a meaningful and impactful article derived from my thesis in one journal and collaborate with other colleagues, and even other PhD students, to publish other articles in maybe less impactful journals for

a faster turnaround allowing me to meet the requirements of publication quantity for job applications.

- Despite having less experience, always try to find a win–win situation when seeking help from experts. For example, if you want to submit a grant application, start writing it yourself and then seek help from an experienced professor to help you complete it and ask him to give you the honour to be on the application. We should always remember that all academics in universities have targets to meet. Also, it is always good to offer help if they organize a conference to alleviate some mundane tasks or promote their event. It would be a learning experience for you and free up some of their time to help others such as us.

- Proactively learning new skills is another way to help in becoming success-ful in the publication domain. We should not assume that because our thesis was qualitative, we only know how to do qualitative research. Learning new research skills, software, and different data analysis approaches will create more opportunities. This learning effort applies to learning more about the journals and taking some time to go through the purpose and structure of the journals, especially with reading articles in our interest domain. Plus, utilizing referencing software may save some time in meeting the requirement of the journals.

- Last but not least, I constantly repeat to myself: "always remember that your value doesn't depend on your grades or position, or how many publi-cations you have or how successful you are, or how famous or rich … YOU always matter the most".

"I AM A NAME, AND NOT A NUMBER!" A REFLECTION ON THE LIFE OF AN EARLY CAREER RESEARCHER

Introduction

The journey as an early career researcher can be a daunting one. Aside from the usual sigh of relief once you get a permanent position in academia, there is the added pressure of the numbers game that the neoliberalization of the university system presents. This can run counter to the feelings that those more empathetic researchers might feel as they try to marry the demands of quality tertiary-level pastoral care and teaching responsibilities with meeting the KPIs (key performance indicators) that their institution might demand of them. Throw in disruptions like a global pandemic, and the goalposts of expectation continuing to shift, and sometimes these expectations can feel unrealistic as early career researchers try to remain relevant, impactful, and of a balanced mind whilst they too navigate the uncertainty produced by such events.

This reflection will first provide some context in terms of my own early career research journey, before highlighting both the reality and impacts of what I feel have been some of the barriers that I have had to negotiate along the way. Whilst it is designed to be more cathartic than depressing, the reflexive nature of this piece might resonate with others who have been in a similar position. If not, take me off your Christmas e-card list (assuming I was even on there in the first place).

The Context

Timing is everything in academia; I learnt this immediately after I obtained my PhD at the end of 2019. At the time I was running multiple teaching contracts to be able to survive as I applied for lecturer roles within my chosen discipline. Then, you guessed it, the pandemic hit. Teaching contracts literally disappeared overnight, hiring for lecturing positions was temporarily frozen, and international travel to present your research was filed under the "Fantasy" section in the local bookstore. This did nothing for my own levels of anxiety, and it was with great relief that I finally landed a full-time lecturing position in July 2020. I literally had only five days where I was an unemployed PhD graduate as the gap between the teaching contracts and the start of this new position intersected.

The Reality

Settling into the new position was easy; contracting for the institution I was now working for in the past meant that I was familiar with not only the systems, but also some of the political dynamics which existed within the walls of the building that I now worked from. It was also good not running multiple contracts, and my mind was now clear to focus on one job and prove my value as both a researcher and a teacher. What I was not prepared for were the uncontrollables; COVID-19 meant that there were several lockdowns, and also it meant that international student numbers declined as border closures took effect. This had a ripple effect as institutional budgets were redesigned to mitigate the shortfall in projected revenue.

The Impact

As an early career researcher with a freshly minted PhD, I was now in a strange Twilight Zone where I had completed the research, lived and breathed the topic I was now supposedly an expert in, but now had few physical in-person options in regards to being able to present this research to an audience, be it domestically or internationally. The effect of a lack of conference funding meant that there was now an unexpected barrier in place in terms of my ability to network face-to-face with others in my research area; sure, I could present my research online, but the real opportunities from research conferences arise in the more social aspects that such events embrace: the dinners, the chats in between presentations, the building of actual rapport between researchers who are otherwise just an avatar on an email.

Conclusion

It is easy to become disillusioned with how the last three years in a full-time academic position have panned out from my perspective. However, the well of optimism has not completely run dry; I still live in hope that the restrictions I have experienced around a lack of conference funding will reverse eventually. Obviously, the pandemic was not the fault of those who make the decisions around budgeting – but for early career researchers, I believe it is important to be able to provide some light at the end of the tunnel to boost morale in an era dominated by conferences which masquerade as just another MS Teams or Zoom meeting.

There needs to be the ability for tertiary institutions to be able to support the aspirations of their early career researchers in a way that is not dominated by numbers on a spreadsheet. Being able to network improves research profiles, gets researchers noticed, and ultimately helps to sow the seeds for future research projects. This then has a direct flow-on effect to the citations, bibliometrics, and professional development that an early career researcher can furnish their institution with. Building a name as a researcher is a challenging game in a post-pandemic world; however, such experiences can serve to build resilience within those who have lived through these events and remained within the academic field.

Remember, you are more than just a number on a spreadsheet – even if the circumstances and political forces within the tertiary education system dictate otherwise. Research is important in terms of critiquing society and provides a conscience in a world where such an idea seems like a foreign concept.

Feel free to send me that Christmas e-card.

ON BEING A POSTDOC

There is no doubt that being a postdoc can be a highly stressful experience. As a postdoc, I find myself often putting in long hours and working for relatively low pay. Unfortunately, this leaves me little time for healthy diversions and exercise, which could effectively mitigate stress and its adverse health effects. Moreover, my strong commitment to work often leaves me feeling isolated from friends and family, as I am far away from home and overwhelmed with stress, uncertain about where to turn for help. Despite these challenges, I have some strategies and responses to tackle the key pressures I face.

Job Market Competition

Postdocs often face intense competition when seeking faculty positions or other career opportunities in academia. The limited number of available positions compared to the number of qualified applicants creates significant pressure, especially as the hospitality and tourism industry has been significantly disrupted by the pandemic. Consequently, students may perceive the major as less promising in terms of future job prospects, leading to decreased interest in pursuing hospitality and tourism programs (Tiwari, Séraphin, & Chowdhary, 2021). This, in turn, results in colleges and universities offering these programs experiencing a decline in tuition revenue. Financial constraints may force institutions to reallocate their limited resources to sustain core programs and departments attracting more students and generating greater revenue, leaving less funding available for expanding faculty positions. The reduced availability of faculty positions in hospitality and tourism due to these constraints intensifies the competition among postdocs and early career researchers vying for those limited positions, exacerbating the challenges they face in securing academic positions within their field.

Strategies

Continually producing high-quality research, publishing in reputable journals, and presenting at conferences are key steps to enhance visibility and competitiveness. Actively engaging with peers, mentors, and senior researchers in the field not only establishes valuable connections but also increases awareness of job openings and potential collaborations. Securing teaching opportunities during the postdoc period can strengthen an application for faculty positions, as teaching experience is often a requirement for academic roles. Additionally, gaining practical experience through internships, part-time positions, or contract work can help build a strong professional network, develop industry contacts, and increase chances of securing full-time employment when the hospitality and tourism industry rebounds.

Work–Life Balance for Asian Women Postdocs

Juggling the demands of research, teaching, and personal life can be an arduous task for postdocs, leading to stress and burnout. Asian women in academia often face unique pressures to demonstrate their capabilities and excel in their field, surpassing gender biases and stereotypes. Additionally, they grapple with societal expectations regarding caregiving responsibilities and maintaining a harmonious family life.

Strategies
To navigate these challenges, I prioritize defining success on my own terms and establishing achievable milestones that align with my values and priorities. I proactively engage in discussions with my family members to establish shared understandings and distribute responsibilities effectively. Carving out dedicated time for self-care and well-being is essential, whether through exercise, hobbies, or quality time spent alone or with loved ones. Moreover, connecting with other women in academia or joining support groups allows for the sharing of experiences, concerns, and coping strategies, providing valuable validation and encouragement.

Pressure to Publish

The significant pressure to produce high-quality research and publish in reputable journals stems from the competitive academic environment and the need to establish a strong publication record for future job prospects.

Strategies
Actively attending academic research conferences to forge connections with other scholars has proven invaluable. Collaborating with established scholars not only provides guidance and access to resources but also opens opportunities for co-authorship. Seeking constructive criticism on my research and writing from mentors, peers, and colleagues helps enhance the quality of my publications.

Lack of Support from the School or College

Postdocs often rely on their mentors for guidance, feedback, and career advice. However, inadequate mentorship can hinder their professional development. Additionally, limited access to research facilities, equipment, data, or funding can impede progress. Insufficient career guidance and support make it challenging to transition into permanent positions or explore alternative career paths.

Strategies
I actively participate in professional associations and attend conferences to connect with scholars who can serve as mentors or offer valuable advice. Seeking grants, fellowships, or research funding from external sources supplements the resources provided by my current institution. I have taken the

initiative by organizing research seminars, workshops, and discussion groups to foster collaboration and knowledge exchange among fellow postdocs and researchers. Additionally, I reach out to alumni and former postdocs from my institution who have successfully transitioned into careers I am interested in, seeking their advice and insights.

Securing Funding

Obtaining research funding is crucial for conducting research, attending conferences, and networking. However, funding pressures arise due to limited grant opportunities in the field of hospitality and tourism research, increased competition, and long review cycles. For example, my research grant application to the American Hotel and Lodging Association (AHLA) Foundation was under review for three months, while another grant application to the FCSI Educational Foundation also took three months for the second review.

Strategies
I proactively search for grants, fellowships, and awards relevant to my research area. Collaborating with researchers from other disciplines or departments can provide additional funding opportunities and broaden the scope of my research.

RESISTING THE TREADMILL OF NEOLIBERAL ACADEMIA: READ AND TEAM UP!

For most people, pursuing a career in academic research is not motivated by accumulating monetary wealth but by an idealistic curiosity to know and explain phenomena based on sound theory, to help to solve societal problems, and to educate future generations to become critically but empathically thinking agents. As a novice scholar, one dreams about being part of a professional community that strives for self-correcting and evolving science through rigorous peer review. One imagines sharing exciting research findings and projects with colleagues during hours' long stimulating debates.

Yet, reality looks different. Who gets into academia and can professionalize their thirst for knowledge depends not so much on merit but on family finances and the right kind of intellectual support during childhood. An academic career is mostly reserved for middle-class offspring who had the freedom to develop their minds in a safe environment far away from precarious living conditions (e.g., O'Sullivan, 2023). Nevertheless, as in most social spheres and professions, job insecurities and anxieties of how to make a living in the future are increasingly plaguing most early career researchers as well. Economic restructuring in universities and the reduction of tenure track positions in social sciences enhances competition among an ever-growing number of PhDs. The negative effects of neoliberal university management on working conditions for researchers, culminating in austerity, individualism, and market-oriented performance measurement, are nowadays aggravated by the global rise of authoritarian populism, which fuels direct attacks on scientists with the goal to curtail academic freedom (e.g., Väliverronen & Saikkonen, 2020).

Within these neoliberal and politically hostile, albeit spatially variegated environments, the notions of publish or perish, impact factors, and other numerical scoring metrics vis-à-vis the pressure to produce "high-impact" research for a mainstream audience (and in some cases craft only politically non-offensive studies to avoid severe repercussions as Ersoy & Karakoç, 2021, report), are becoming the norm for early career scholars. The book *The lean PhD* (Kirchherr, 2018b) offers a vivid example for this contemporary rationality. The author recommends adopting a business startup mindset to a PhD dissertation and to aim for "good enough" or "minimal viable" outputs instead of getting lost in "reading obscure academic literature" and striving for excellence (Kirchherr, 2018a). In order to turn a mediocre research idea into an impactful study, one is advised to network with the most important figures in one's specific field, collect as much peer feedback as possible, and to latch onto a supervisor who is willing to grant the actual scientific expertise. Simply reacting to comments of people who are actually well read (see Kirchherr, 2018b) seems a bit like freeloading and leeching on a system built on recipro-cal peer review.

Such neoliberal utilitarianism diminishes not only the joy of research, dis-covery, and exploring the intellectual history of one's field or discipline but calls also for societally (but mostly business) relevant research whilst dismiss-ing studies which are (allegedly) only interesting for a small academic circle. No doubt, applied research is essential for human and technological advances but the grand domain of social sciences is to theorize and explain social phe-nomena, to answer abstract questions, and to engage in systemic critique (e.g., Lindroth, Sinevaara-Niskanen, & Tennberg, 2022). These research outputs are not readily commercializable objects but insights that facilitate societal emancipation and awareness of one's condition in the world. Indeed, in times of rapidly advancing language models, ChatGPT might easily outperform a human who relies on a "minimal viable paper" approach (Kirchherr, 2018b) and AI might synthesize commercially applicable solutions from existing studies within seconds. It is the said classical tasks of social sciences that ChatGPT cannot accomplish (yet?).

Furthermore, academic knowledge that could facilitate social, ecological, and economic transformations exists in abundance but it remains vastly underutilized. This is particularly evident regarding our profound scientific acquaintance with the life-threatening effects of anthropogenic climate change (e.g., Keskitalo, 2022). Yet, political actions are incremental at best. In that sense, critical social science research exposing the reasons for inaction and power structures is societally relevant. My favourite example of such critical but insightful examination in tourism geography is Hof and Blázquez-Salom's (2015) comparative analysis of touristic water consumption and land use patterns on the Balearic Island of Mallorca. Drawing upon spatial analysis, the authors show that residential quality tourism in Mallorca, fostered by sustainable tourism development policies, consumes significantly more fresh-water than conventional mass tourism and aggravates rather than solves the unsustainability of tourism (Hof & Blázquez-Salom, 2015). In addition to the policy relevance of this paper, a further merit lies in its connection between well-developed research methods, and theory-based and contextual explana-tions of the research findings.

Then there's the social dimension of neoliberal academia. A few years ago, a fellow PhD candidate told me that they participated in a career seminar where they were advised to strictly select acquaintances and professional contacts according to utility. The neoliberal credo is to compete and advance as an individual. Coupled with the quest for "mainstream market viability" and competitive individualism, this doesn't only blight the delight of working together with like-minded people in an inspiring atmosphere, but the erasure of solidarity and compassion also paves the way for further alienation and fortifies toxic hierarchies. As a good dissident, team up and read!

DISCUSSION AND CONCLUSIONS

There are a number of commonalities in the various perspectives of the new and emerging researchers who have contributed to this chapter. One of the most obvious being that there is clearly pressure to publish for young research-ers and that those pressures appear to be increasing. In particular, there appears to be more pressure to publish in high-impact or ranked journals, rather than in lower ranked journals or to produce book chapters, even if they may be appro-priate outlets, especially for more specialized research areas. Instead, such higher ranked journals appear to be desired by potential and current employers. As several of the contributors note, this raises issues not only with respect to journal selection and the length of time the publishing process takes, but also raises profound personal, ethical, and motivational issues as to where to publish and why. Such concerns are, of course, not just the domain of younger researchers but can apply at any stage as one goes through an academic career (Hall, 2004; Fanghanel, 2012), although may be particularly relevant for those researchers seeking to contribute to specific knowledge areas and communities (Fenelon, 2003; Hall & Sutherland, 2018; Walters et al., 2019; Kidman, 2020).

The contributors also point to some of the tensions that exist between academic life and career and personal lives, especially for women, minorities, or in the case of being of a different culture or nationality to the country one is studying or trying to build a career in. Women in universities, for example, "already face the pressure of having to constantly compete with their men counterparts. Women have centuries of exclusion from academia to catch up on after all; therefore they must *prove* them-selves harder" (Zarevich, 2021, p. 2). Despite some claims that social media may reduce isolation and improve connectivity at universities, we would also note that Indigenous and minority staff continue to experience isolation (Kidman, 2020; Culpepper et al., 2021).

While the academic labour market is international, it is still more accessible for some than others. Despite the "ivory tower" image still promoted by some media outlets, universities are as much places of stress, anxiety, and harm, as they are places of discovery, intellectual endeavour, and learning. Publishing stress, which has been reinforced by processes of marketization and commodification of the modern university, have only served to reinforce this. These stresses have served to bring attention to what Fleming (2021) described as "dark academia", which reflects the "widespread despair and even depression among faculty" (Fleming, 2020, p. 1305) in the contemporary university.

For many new and emerging researchers, the stress of publishing is only made worse by the process of finding university positions and the associated insecurities of growing casualization and extended tenure processes. Solitary work (researching, writing, publishing) is punctuated by performance work (communicating, supervising, teaching) occurring within an increasingly metricized institutional context, which makes it all the more difficult to cope (Hall & Sutherland, 2018). Nevertheless, several strategies are suggested, whether it be activism and keeping true to your personal goals and values, or whether it be ensuring you have appropriate mentors and support in place (both in the university and at home). Perhaps most importantly, the issue of support we cannot stress enough – while many universities increasingly provide formal mechanisms of support for new and emerging staff it is the informal connections that are just as important. It is therefore important to find others to talk to and work with to overcome some of the darkness of academia, and, of course, to publish with.

ACKNOWLEDGEMENT

C. Michael Hall and Tyron Love would like to acknowledge the support of the Marsden Fund.

REFERENCES

Australian Business Deans Council (ABDC) (2023). *2022 ABDC Journal Quality List released.* https://abdc.edu.au/2022-abdc-journal-quality-list-released/.

Culpepper, D., Reed, A.M., Enekwe, B., Carter-Veale, W., LaCourse, W.R., McDermott, P., & Cresiski, R.H. (2021). A new effort to diversify faculty: postdoc-to-tenure track conversion models. *Frontiers in Psychology*, 12, 733995. https://doi.org/10.3389/fpsyg.2021.733995.

Ersoy, D., & Karakoç, J. (2021). Political science in the age of populism: Perspectives from Turkey. *European Political Science*, 20(1), 204–217. https://doi.org/10.1057/s41304-020-00310-w.

Fanghanel, J. (2012). *Being an academic*. Routledge.

Fenelon, J. (2003). Race, research, and tenure. *Journal of Black Studies*, 34(1), 87–100.

Fleming, P. (2020). Dark academia: Despair in the neoliberal business school. *Journal of Management Studies*, 57(6), 1305–1311.

Fleming, P. (2021). *Dark academia: How universities die*. Pluto Press.

Grossmann, A., Mooney, L., & Dugan, M. (2019). Inclusion fairness in accounting, finance, and management: An investigation of A-star publications on the ABDC journal list. *Journal of Business Research*, 95, 232–241. https://doi.org/10.1016/j.jbusres.2018.10.035.

Gössling, S., Scott, D., & Hall, C.M. (2020). Pandemics, tourism and global change: A rapid assessment of COVID-19. *Journal of Sustainable Tourism*, 29(1), 1–20. https://doi.org/10.1080/09669582.2020.1758708.

Hall, C.M. (2004). Reflexivity and tourism research: Situating myself and/with others. In J. Phillimore & L. Goodson (Eds.), *Qualitative research in tourism: Ontologies, epistemologies and methodologies* (pp. 137–155). Routledge.

Hall, C.M. (2014). *Tourism and social marketing*. Routledge.

Hall, M., & Sutherland, K.A. (2018). He pī, ka rere: Māori early career academics in New Zealand universities. In K.A. Sutherland (Ed.), *Early career academics in New Zealand: Challenges and prospects in comparative perspective* (pp. 137–156). Springer.

Hof, A., & Blázquez-Salom, M. (2015). Changing tourism patterns, capital accumulation, and urban water consumption in Mallorca, Spain: A sustainability fix? *Journal of Sustainable Tourism*, 23(5), 770–796 https://doi.org/10.1080/09669582.2014.991397.

Keskitalo. E.C.H. (Ed.) (2022). *The social aspects of environmental and climate change institutional dynamics beyond a linear model*. Routledge.

Kidman, J. (2020). Whither decolonisation? Indigenous scholars and the problem of inclusion in the neoliberal university. *Journal of Sociology*, 56(2), 247–262.

Kirchherr, J. (2018a). A PhD should be about improving society, not chasing academic kudos. *The Guardian*. https://www.theguardian.com/higher-education-network/2018/aug/09/a-phd-should-be-about-improving-society-not-chasing-academic-kudos.

Kirchherr, J. (2018b). *The lean PhD: Radically improve the efficiency, quality and impact of your research.* Bloomsbury.

Lindroth, M., Sinevaara-Niskanen, H., & Tennberg, M. (Eds.) (2022). *Critical studies of the Arctic: Unravelling the North.* Springer.

McKercher, B., & Dolnicar, S. (2022). Are 10,752 journal articles per year too many? *Annals of Tourism Research*, 94(96), 103398.

O'Sullivan, K. (2023). *Poor*. Penguin Books.

Tiwari, P., Séraphin, H., & Chowdhary, N.R. (2021). Impacts of COVID-19 on tourism education: Analysis and perspectives. *Journal of Teaching in Travel & Tourism*, 21(4), 313–338.

Truong, V.D., & Hall, C.M. (2013). Social marketing and tourism: What is the evidence? *Social Marketing Quarterly*, 19(2), 110–135. https:// doi .org/ 10 .1177/ 152450041348445.

Väliverronen, E., & Saikkonen, S. (2020). Freedom of expression challenged: Scientists' perspectives on hidden forms of suppression and self-censorship. *Science, Technology, & Human Values*, 46(6), 1172–1200. https://doi.org/10.1177/ 0162243920978303.

Walters, K.L., Lukszo, C.M., Evans-Campbell, T., Valdez, R.B., & Zambrana, R.E. (2019). "Before they kill my spirit entirely": Insights into the lived experiences of American Indian Alaska Native faculty at research universities. *Race Ethnicity and Education*, 22(5), 610–633. https://doi.org/10.1080/13613324.2019.1579182.

Zarevich, E.R. (2021). The perils of "dark academia". *Women in Higher Education*, 30(5), 1–2.

Zhu, C., & Fong, L.H.N. (2022). Book review "contemporary research methods in hospitality and tourism". *Information Technology & Tourism*, 24, 435–437. https:// doi.org/10.1007/s40558-022-00232-x.

PART V

CONCLUSION

17. Publishing lessons, futures and emerging issues

Chris Cooper and C. Michael Hall

INTRODUCTION

In concluding this book, we want to briefly draw together a number of the themes brought up in the various chapters, and place them in the context of developing a publishing strategy and career as well as note emerging issues. We first try and synthesise some of the insights from the various contributions before discussing future concerns and issues.

STRATEGIES AND CAREERS

There are a range of things that people seek to achieve in publishing and developing an academic career, including advancing and conveying knowledge, personal fulfilment, career advancement and security, and/or developing a research profile. For most researchers in tourism the broader publishing context is the interrelationship between research and scholarship, teaching, and publishing. Publication outputs are one of the key elements in developing academic and research careers. In seeking to achieve your publishing goals, your publishing strategy should be tied to your broader research strategy as they are interrelated. There are several starting points for research and publication. Clearly it is important to be reading literature and talking to colleagues, but it is essential to be recording ideas. If teaching, every course should provide a basis for literature reviews and gaining insights into gaps in the literature. In addition, teaching may provide an opportunity to undertake teaching-related research and develop that for publication. Research grant applications are also a good starting point for a publication as a good research grant usually takes as long as an article to develop and write. Obviously, doctoral theses are also the basis of many publications, but, in addition, it is important to consider what you do after the thesis and/or after several publications have been taken from the thesis data.

In developing a research and publication strategy, it can also be extremely helpful to test ideas in a supportive environment. For example, some scholars have a stepping stone strategy in which they give a conference presentation of their work so as then to provide impetus to write a full paper. In some cases, conferences are also good occasions to connect with journal and special issue editors as well as find potential collaborators. However, it is important to recognise that conference presentations and proceedings publications by themselves are not a substitute for journal articles and other publications, with the possible exception of specialist areas in ICT. Conferences are therefore valuable for developing ideas, feedback, developing research networks and leveraging research contribution factors.

Journal articles, especially recent review articles, are good for leveraging ideas for publications. This may mean not only reading the journals in the tourism and hospitality areas but also those in cognate fields, especially as there are many tourism-related articles published outside of tourism journals. This can be extremely valuable for work in cross-disciplinary areas such as sustainability and resilience, as well as cross-over work in disciplines such as geography, management and marketing. However, just as important for idea generation is keeping up with media, policy issues, online research networks and newsgroups, and academic and professional associations. Reviewing for journals is also a valuable way of keeping up with ideas in publishing trends. In some cases, previous articles can be built upon to develop new interpretations and approaches, sometimes this may be to different audiences.

In considering where to publish, the starting point should be considering the nature of research that you want to publish. Sometimes research may even start with a journal in mind but most of the time this is not the case. Some of the points to consider include:

- Who will be interested?
- Who are your potential audiences?
- What is the most appropriate published source for your target audience?
- What is realistically achievable given the content of the material that you wish to publish?
- What are your time constraints in preparing and publishing the article?
- How easily can you adjust your writing style?

The most important thing is to identify the most appropriate publishing outlet as your paper is then more likely to be published, rather than just focussing on the highest impact factor or ranking. Knowing the library and journal options is therefore essential. In thinking about publication also consider how your work might provide:

- A new perspective on a subject;

- How it might bring new material and insights from one discipline into another;
- How it might bring new material and insights from one audience to another;
- New practical and theoretical contributions; and
- Rejoinders – is your work a response to what someone else has written?

In preparing a paper make sure that it is grammatically correct with no spelling mistakes and written according to journal guidelines. This is absolutely essential given the number of papers submitted to journals. If you have had a paper rejected from a journal do not just resubmit the paper to another without taking reviewer and/or editor comments on board as well as reformatting the paper. Ideally, give your paper drafts to colleagues to read and provide comments on. If you are fortunate, you may have a research circle that you are part of in which you can share material or even publish together.

Once the paper goes through the review process treat the editors' and reviewers' comments with respect. Even if you disagree with them, the comments need to be acknowledged and responded to in a careful manner. Always make it very clear how you have responded, especially if you disagree with a reviewer's comment. Editors do not expect you to necessarily agree with every comment, but they do want to see considered reasoned responses.

Finally, your paper gets published. Congratulations! But do not see your publications in isolation. Place them in the context of your career and your wider work–life balance. This is arguably one of the biggest lessons of all. There is more than just publications. For those in higher education there is a nexus between teaching and research that should be valued. Teaching and research should work off each other as they create ideas and new applications in both directions and provide for more efficient use of time as well. University teaching is meant to be research informed (and it's even better if it's your research!).

FUTURES

There are a number of issues that are on the horizon for journal publishing. Artificial intelligence (AI) has become a major issue given its potential influence on the publishing process with respect to the generation of text. Undoubtedly, AI may be useful, especially for second language scholars, however at this stage at least it is clearly a tool and not a substitute for the hard work that goes into the manuscript writing process.

AI is clearly just one factor that is affecting the publishing landscape. There remains considerable pressure in some jurisdictions to be producing open access publications. However, at the same time there remain substantial pressures to publish in certain journals because of their ranking and/or impact.

Given the focus of universities around the world in terms of their ranking, of which publications (in specified journals) remains a major part, it is extremely unlikely that pressure to publish in particular journals, especially if incorporated into promotion and accreditation processes, will change in the foreseeable future. One implication of this is that the demands to publish in the top tourism journals will clearly not disappear, although there are likely to be new issues that emerge, and potentially new interpretations of impact beyond just citations, with research assessments in a number of countries demonstrating the impact on business, welfare, policy or the environment as well.

The publishing and higher education policy environment is also affecting research culture. Nevertheless, while governments and universities put substantial emphasis on international and national rankings, and students are influenced by them in their university selection, it is likely that publishing pressures will influence the trajectory of the research culture with respect to expectations. This affects established scholars, but especially those starting out on their careers. As several chapters in this book have noted, this will also influence research integrity and the formal and informal systems by which it is maintained. Importantly, it will likely also reinforce the dominance of medical and health science approaches to research and publishing integrity over more social science-oriented perspectives as well as English remaining the dominant international language for academic journals.

CONCLUSION

Pressures from the institutional and external environment, as well as one own's desire to develop a career, mean that publishing is about more than just writing. This book has tried to inform on some of the factors that help research and writing eventually turn into a publication. It is not an easy process and provides many personal and professional challenges. However, publication should feel rewarding. It provides recognition for the hard work that goes in to developing a good paper. It is also your contribution to knowledge. Hopefully, the insights provided in this book will assist you in making such a contribution.

Index

absolute confidentially 137
abstract 58, 110, 111
abstraction 99
academic career/s 177, 185, 199, 220,
    233, 240
academic dissemination 168
academic emotional labour 206
academic hiring processes 219
academic job openings 225
academic journal paper 96
academic journals 6
  expansion of 6
academic knowledge 72, 95, 234
academic labour market 236
academic landscape 177
academic lingua franca 168
academic notoriety 215
academic paper
  as storytelling 109
academic publications 151, 152, 153,
    155
academic publishing 122, 156, 159, 179
academic publishing system 26
academic reality 177
academic review paper 98
academic super-hero 199
academic thinking 71
academic tourism papers 122
academic workload 73
academic writing 45, 173
accreditation bodies 110
accuracy 85
AC/DC positioning grid/matrix 116, 119
Acta Turistica 22, 23, 24
actors 110, 118
Adu-Ampong, E. A. 68
Alrawadieh, Z. 184
Altmetric scores 208
Alvesson, M. 69, 73
American Economic Association 153
American Hotel and Lodging Association
    (AH&LA) Foundation 233

American Psychological Association
    (APA) 86
Andersen, K. 152
Anglophone journals 21
Anglophone writers 174
Annals 25, 26, 27
Annals of Tourism Research 25, 26, 27,
    65, 74, 155, 157, 177
*Annals of Tourism Research Empirical
    Insights* 74
anonymity 137
article processing charges (APC) 185
artificial intelligence (AI) 31, 82, 144,
    170, 242
art of writing 169, 173
Asian women post-docs 231
aspirational values 141
Aubert Bonn, N. 135
Australasia 216
Australia 16, 189, 191, 193, 199
Australian Business Deans Council
    (ABDC) journal 156, 183, 216
authorship 44, 51, 142, 143

Barney, J.B. 57
behaviour change 38
behaviourism 100
Bianchi, R. V. 69
bibliographic review 101
bibliographic study/ies 102, 103
bibliometric analysis 154, 155, 158, 181
bibliometric databases 144
bibliometric mapping 22
bibliometrics 102, 220
biomedical journals 21
Black feminism 149, 162, 164
Black feminist epistemologies 159
Black women 159, 161, 164
Blázquez-Salom, M. 235
Boettcher, J. C. 129
Bottrell, D. 198
Bramwell, Bill 125

Brazil 6, 7
British colonialism 151
Britton, S. G. 160
Brundtland Report 12
Buckley* 185
budget allocations 191
budget constraints 16
Buhalis, Dimitrios 212
Byrne, J. 102

Canada 7
Canadian female professors 153
career 211
career advancement 4, 178
career development 203
career growth 186
career guidance 232
career impacts 214
career planning 189
Cerne 116
Cetina, K. 141
Chambers, D. 159
Chan, I. C. C. 178, 182, 183, 184
Chapman, C. S. 96
ChatGPT 212, 216, 234
Cheng, C. 13
China 7, 29
Chou, L. 156
citation metrics 220
citation/s 182, 183, 204, 208, 220
CiteScore 183
CiteScore rankings 204
CIT Research Letters/Notes 28
CIT Reviews 28
Clarivate Web of Science 143, 204
clear and concise language 88
co-authorship 72, 102, 153
co-citation analysis 23, 24
code frame 100
coding 100
cognitive theory 100
cognitivism 100
Cohen, E. 16
Cole, J. R. 155
Coles, T. 94
collaboration/s 163, 181, 182, 233
collaborative approaches 65
collaborative consumption 30
collaborative research 224
collaborative ventures 181

Collini, S. 72
colonialism 151, 161, 162
coloniality 159, 160, 162, 164
Committee on Publication Ethics 51
communication method 109, 110, 111
compact but sophisticated
    introduction 46
competitive journal landscape 21
competitiveness 224
completeness 85
complex networked systems 82
conceptualization 99
conclusion 60
conference papers 179
conferences 241
confidentiality 136, 137
conscience 230
consistency 85
contribution 96
contribution, paper 56
contribution strategies 68
co-occurrence network 23
Cooper, H. M. 113
Copy Cats 31
Cornell Hospitality Quarterly 7
*Cornell Hotel and Restaurant
    Quarterly* 7, 12
corporate accountability 30
corporate social responsibility 30
Couch, G. 6
Covid-19 31, 44, 155, 229
Crang, M. 13, 67
creativity 81
credibility 82, 88, 178, 181, 186, 206,
    214
credit 51
critical thinking 221
critical tourism 66, 69
critical tourism scholarship 69
Croatia 22, 23
cross-faculty collaboration 182
Crouch, G. 13
cultural heritage 12
culture of integrity 140
Cunil, O. M. 183
currency, academic life 2
*Current Issues in Asian Tourism
    (CIAT)* 29
Current Issues in Tourism (CIT) 27, 28,
    29

cutting edge conceptual research 50

Dallen Timothy Best Paper Award 35
dark academia 236
data analysis 114
data analysis procedures 87
data analysis process 85
database 7
data collection 26, 45, 84, 114
data collection methods 87
data digitisation 82
data display matrices 100
data gathering 81
data handling process 87
daunting challenge 75
debriefing 138
decision-making 136, 178
decolonial theory/ies 162
departmental leadership 9
destination marketing 21
developed economies 6
Díaz-Carrion, I. A. 158
differentiated context strategies 68
discussion section 59, 60
disruptive tourism 69
dissemination 178
diversity 9
doctoral candidates 66
doctoral thesis literature review 93
doctoral thesis review 98
Dolnicar, S. 17, 72, 215
Doran, A. 68, 69
dramatization 108, 111, 118
Duval, D. 94

early career academics 129, 130, 213
early career researcher/s (ECR) 213,
        217, 218, 220, 228, 229, 230,
        231, 233
EarlyCite 40
Echtner, C. M. 67, 160
ecosystem 50
editing 3
Editorial Advisory Board 40
editorial board 27, 43, 205
editorial process 24
editorial team 38
editors 126, 129, 171
Editors-in-Chief 35, 48, 74, 124, 159
Edwards, M. S. 125, 128

Einstein, Albert 79
Elsevier 126, 130, 152, 154
Emerald Publishing 39
emerging academics 211
emotionalization 108, 111, 112, 118
emotions 117
emotive peace tourism 73
employment opportunities 225
encyclopaedia 99
England 150
English language 4, 12, 169, 170, 171
English language journals 9, 16, 169,
        171, 173, 174
English language tourism 15
English tourism journals 173
English writing 173
epistemology 84
Ertaş, M. 179, 181, 185
Erwin, J. 73
ethical considerations 86, 87, 138
ethical governance procedures 135
ethical issues
    macro and micro 135
ethical responsibilities 133
ethics 4, 72, 134, 135, 136, 138, 144
    regulatory scope of 134
ethics creep 134, 140, 144
ethics frameworks 135
European Tourism Futures Institute
        (ETFI) 39
evaluation process 24
events journals 7, 8, 11
Excellence in Research for Australia
        (ERA) 193, 194
expert panels of reviewers 194

fabrication 51, 140, 142
falsification 51, 140, 142
familiarization 98, 99
family finances 233
FCSI Educational Foundation 233
feminist participatory action research
        methods 149
fictionalisation 108, 111, 114
Figueroa-Domecq, C. 150, 155, 157, 158
financial responsibility 74
Financial Times Top 50 Journals
        (FT50) 183
five strategy typology 68
Fleming, P. 236

Font, X. 37
fourth-wave feminism 149
Franklin, A. 13, 67
full-time equivalent staff (FTE) 194, 196
funding 190

gastronomy 13
gatekeepers 174
gender 149, 151, 159, 161, 162, 164
gender differences 153, 154
gendered politics/issues 153
gender gap 155, 162
gender imbalance 152
gender (in)equality/ies 151, 155, 162
gender intersectionality 159, 164
gender parity 154, 162
  in tourism publishing 163
  in tourism research 164
gender research 149
gender work 150
generalist journals 12
generalist titles 9
general tourism journals 12
Generative Artificial Intelligence 51
generic method 104
geographical focus 12, 51
geography 12, 13
geography of submissions 29
geotourism 12
ghost authorship 143
gift authorship 143
Gilbert, D. 110
Global North 71, 160
global scientific community 22
Global South 36, 70, 71, 123, 149, 160
good abstract 58
good conclusion 60
good mentors 48
government funding 191
Grant, B. M. 198
Grant, L. 153
greater agency 74
Griffies, S. M. 172
Griffith, T. L. 129
Grit, A. 69
groundbreaking research 31
guest authorship 143
guest editing 125, 127, 128
  benefits of 127
guest editors 124, 126, 127, 129

guest-edit SIs 127
Gursoy, D. 15

Haggerty, K. D. 134
Hall, C. M. 14, 94, 139, 163, 212
Hall, D. R. 155
Hargens, L. 17
harm 138
Hay, I. 198
herculean challenges 65
heritage tourism 35, 123
Hicks, D. 191
hierarchical publication system 207
higher education 6
higher education policy
    environment 243
higher metrics 125
highest impact factor 241
high-IF journals 204
high-impact research 234
high-quality journals 226
high-quality research 231, 232
H-index 219
Hof, A. 235
honesty 137
Hong Kong 189, 191
Hosany, S. 110
hospitality 6, 8, 9, 11, 12, 13, 14, 15,
    17, 22, 30, 31, 32, 80, 81, 82,
    86, 112, 113, 118, 171, 177, 212,
    213, 214, 231, 241
hospitality journals 112
hospitality management 12, 29
hospitality service providers 44
Huang, J. 154
Huber, J. 123
Hull, G. 172
human–robot interaction 30
Humber 123
Hunziker, Walter 49
Hu, T. 179

ICMJE 143
impact 229
impact factors 214, 215
impactful publication 227
impactful research 214, 215
Imperial Eyes 160
implications 60
inadequate mentorship 232

inconsistencies 88
independent journals 9
indigenous communities 108
individualism 224
Indonesia 13, 189
information technology journals 12
informed consent 136
innovation 12, 31, 36, 66, 204
Innovators 31
institutional ethics 133, 138, 141
instrumental foreign language 169
integrative literature review 103
intellectual discourse 80
intellectual enquiry 16
intellectual productivity 72
intellectual stagnation 13
internationalisation 22
*International Journal of Hospitality
    Management (IJHM)* 29, 30,
    31, 32
international language 243
international publishers 8
international scientific community 168
introduction 58, 112
introspectionism 100

Jamali, R. 9
Jamal, T. 15, 204
Jamal, T. D. 67
Japanese 7
job market competition 231
job prospects 232
journal articles 241
Journal Citation Indicator (JCI) 33
journal cultures 56
journal editor/s 37, 96
journal growth 8
journal guidelines 242
journal impact factors (JIFs) 204, 208
journal landscape 3, 21
journal metrics 21, 195, 214
*Journal of Destination Marketing &
    Management (JDMM)* 32, 33,
    34, 35
Journal of Ecotourism 123
Journal of Heritage Tourism 35, 125
*Journal of Sustainable Tourism
    (JOST)* 37, 38, 125
Journal of Tourism Futures (JTF) 39,
    40, 41

Journal of Travel Research (JTR) 41,
    42, 43
journal orientations 208
journal paper 96
journal publishers systems 3
journal publishing landscape 4
journal rankings 202, 203, 205, 206, 207
    use and abuse of 205
journal requirements 57
journal review paper 95, 98
journal review system 205
journal special issues 122
journal's requirements 227
journal submission platform 62
journal themes 11
journal titles
    evolution of 9
justification 88

Kachru, B. 169
Khoo-Lattimore, C. 156, 159
King, Stephen 60
Kinnaird, V. 155
knowledge 2, 3, 6, 38, 65, 66, 81, 91,
    95, 98, 99, 118, 125, 128, 217,
    224, 243
knowledge dissemination 79, 177
knowledge exchange 233
knowledge production 169, 171
Korean 7
Koseoglu, M. A. 158
Kozak, M. 8, 16, 179, 181, 185
KPIs (Key Performance Indicators) 228
Krapf, Kurt 49

labour intensive tourism 14
language barriers 21, 51
large language models (LLM) 170
Latin American tourism gender
    scholarship 159
Law, R. 15, 178, 182, 183, 184
Law, Rob 212
leadership 156
Leahey, E. 154
learning new skills 228
legitimacy 16
legitimacy issue 14
Leigh, J. S. 125, 128
"Letters to the Editor" 42
Liburd, J. J. 67, 69, 73, 74

literature review/s 46, 58, 92, 93, 95, 96, 98, 101, 103, 104, 112, 113, 115, 116
  skills needed for completing 93
Lloyd, S. 16
Lugones, M. 161
Lusch, R. F. 116

machine learning 82
Malaysia 13, 189
managerial implication 115
Manathunga, C. 198
Māori cosmologies 71
'Marketing' 9
mass tourism 67
Mathews, A. L. 152
Mayer, S. J. 153
McClintock, A. 161
McDowell, J. M. 153
McKercher, B. 14, 17, 72, 80, 94, 170, 177, 182, 184, 215
medicine research 102
mentorship 181, 182
meta-analyses 118
meta-ethical issues 135
Metaverse 212
methodology/ies 59, 80, 81, 82, 83, 84, 85, 86, 87, 88, 89, 98, 114, 115, 123, 149
metrics 214, 218, 219
metrics-driven tourism academy 65
Mewburn, I. 198
micro-ethical scale 136
Mika, J. P. 71
mixed-methods 47, 82, 85, 109, 114
Mohanty, Chandra 163
moral theory 73
Murky stories 111

Nakhaie, M. R. 153
name recognition 127, 129
narrative review/s 101, 102, 103, 104, 113
narrative thread 224
national research policies 189
native language 172
Nature 71
neoliberal academia 233
neoliberal approaches 190
neoliberal credo 235

neoliberal metrification 15
neoliberal utilitarianism 234
nepotism 128
netnography 137
New Zealand 189, 191, 192, 195, 217
Nichols-Casebolt, A. 140
non-Anglophone author/s 168, 169, 171, 172, 174
non-Anglophone tourism scholars 170
non-English writers 172
North America 7
North Cyprus 222
Norway 191
novelty 81
Nunkoo, R. 157
Nylenna, M. 143

Oceania 7
Olk, P. 129
online ethnography 137
ontology 83
Oosterhaven, J. 17
open access journal 206
open access model 115
Open Access publications 242
openness 137
Orientalism' 160
overtourism 39
ownership 136

Palmer, C. A. 160
paradigm funnel model 4, 97
peer review 29, 35, 45, 79, 185, 202, 203, 205
peer-reviewed journals 178
peer-review model 192
peer-review process 186
peer-review systems 205
Perdue, R. 6, 13
Performance Based Research Evaluation 195
performance-based research funding systems (PBRFS) 5, 189, 190, 191, 192, 193, 198
performance evaluation 203
Perrie, W. A. 172
personal ethics 144
personalisation 108, 111
perspective papers 50
PhD process 65

PhD program 226
PhD student/s 212, 213, 214, 218, 221, 222, 223, 227
Phillips, E.M. 96
Pickering, C. 102
Pinxten, W. 135
Pitt, R. 198
plagiarism 51, 140, 142
plagiarism software 3, 21, 29
platforms 62
Platinum Open Access journal 39
pluriversal approaches 71
Poland 7
polishing, paper 60
Pomfret, G. 68
Portuguese 12
Portuguese language journals 170
positioning 57, 108, 111
positioning of papers 55
positioning, paper 2
postdoc/s 230, 231, 232
post-war economic development 49
potential journal contributors 47
potential stress 199
poverty 67
practicalities 55
practical limitations 87
practical suggestions 60
Prasad, P. 160
predatory conferences 179
predatory journals 17, 184
Prideaux, B. 94
Priem, R. 128
primary challenges 225
Pritchard, A. 158
privacy 136
procrastination 224
productivity 186
professional academic publishing 62
professional associations 232
professional ethics 133
professional learning 213
professional listservs 124
Profilers 31
proofing 60
psychological well-being 220
psychology 97
publication outputs 240
publication strategy 241
public policy 197

public policy narratives 190
publishing 177, 186
publishing ethics 133, 134, 139
publishing houses 9
publishing pressures 243
publishing strategy 240
publish-or-perish culture 221
Pugh, D. 96

qualitative approaches 81, 86
qualitative research 85
qualitative studies 115
quality assurance 6
quality writing 2
quantitative approaches 81
quantitative research 84, 85, 114
Quebec 7
quest for legitimacy 7, 14

race 161
RAE2008 193
Ram, Y. 139
Rankin, E. 173
ranking methodologies 203
Rathman, J. M. 153
readability 21
readership 44
recognition 178, 225, 243
refereed journal/s 2, 55, 62, 63, 122, 179
refereed journal articles 6
refereed paper/s 57, 63
refereeing process 6, 128
referees 29, 59, 61, 80, 125
reflective writing 223
reflexivity 151, 164
regulation/s 134, 136, 137
rejection letter 49
reliability 203
replicability 88, 118
replication studies 112, 117
replicatory strategies 68
reproducibility 118
reputation 206
Research Assessment Exercise (RAE) 189
research authorship 152
research-based submissions 42
research career 75
research design 83, 87
research environment 196

researcher integrity 144
research ethics 51, 134, 136
research evaluation 190, 191
Research Excellence Framework
         (REF) 189, 196, 197
research funding 189, 190, 196, 206, 233
research governance 137
research grant applications 240
research innovations 50
research instruments 84
research integrity 133, 135, 140, 141,
         243
   macro and micro ethical issues 135
research method 80, 81, 212
research metrics 134
research misconduct 51
research objectives 47, 88
research outcomes 88
research papers 50
research performance 189, 191, 192,
         193, 194, 195
research policy 189, 190, 191, 192, 198
research problem 84, 86
research process 59, 110, 114, 115, 118
research quality 191, 194
research question 59
research value 213
research work 81
resilience 110
resilience theory 116
resubmission 45
revelatory approaches 68
review 48
review articles 181
reviewer/s 80, 95
reviewer reports 41
review paper 96
review process 42, 139, 242
right to withdraw 137
rise and fall of journals 6, 7
risk 138
Ritchie, J. 100
Roberts, C. 14
rules, for writing 63
Ryan, M. 80

Said, Edward 160
sampling techniques 87
sanctionable values 141
Sandberg, J. 69, 73

Sandstrom, J. K. 15
scheduled issues 127
Scheyvens, R. A. 71
scholarly contributions 75
scholarly publishing 173
ScholarONe platform 62
scholarship 202, 226
science 79
   modern communication of 79
scientific article
   structuring 171
scientific communication 24
scientific knowledge 168, 174
scientific language 169
scientific method 80
scientific research 23
scientific terminology 22
scientific writing 173
scientometrics 102
SCImago Journal Rank 204
scoping review/s 99, 101
Scopus CiteScoreTracker 51
Scopus database 152, 155
Segovia-Perez, M. 158
self-imposed zero-sum game 207
senior academics 184
service quality discourses 108
servicescape/s 30
sex trade 159
sexual dimorphism 161
Shanghai ranking 190
Shani, A. 14
Shea, L. 14
Sheller, M. 161
short communications 44
short titles 57
shotgun approach 124
Sismondo, S. 141
slow scholarship 73
small speciality publishing houses 8
small tourism journal 21
smart tourism 12, 212
Smith, B. 204
SNIP (Source Normalized Impact per
         Paper) 204
social capital theory (SCT) 116
social justice 151, 164
social media 16, 21, 124, 126, 218
   humble brags on 218
social norms 140

social responsibility 213, 214
Social Science Citation Index (SSCI) 14,
    158
social science perspective 27
social science readership 26
social science research 101, 135
social sciences 118, 144
societal impact 178
sociology 97
software development 15
solitary-work 236
sophisticated journal metrics 29
sound methodology 47
so-what question 116
Spanish 6, 7, 12
Spanish language journals 170
special issues (SIs) 122, 123, 124, 125,
    126, 127, 128, 129, 130, 183, 184
  benefits of publishing 126
  critiques and challenges 128
specialist journals 13
specialist titles 12
Spencer, L. 100
SSCI journal 223
Stack, S. 153
staff well-being 30
state-of-the-field articles 67
Steinberg, R. 129
Story Tellers 31
storytelling 45, 108, 109, 110, 111, 113,
    114, 117, 118, 212
  academic paper as 109
  positioning academic papers 111
structural aspects 172
Strunk, E. B. 60
Strunk, Jr. W. 173
Sturm, T. 73
style 2
style guide 61
submission 29, 42, 44, 45, 47, 55, 61,
    62, 193
submission guidelines 42
submission process 60
submission protocols 55
success in publication 48
supervisor 181
sustainability 21, 37, 38
sustainability titles 12
Sustainable Development Goal/s
    (SDG) 22, 152

sustainable tourism 37, 212
sustainable tourism journalists 38
Swain, Margaret Byrne 155
synthesis 101
systematic literature review/s (SLR)
    101, 102, 103, 104
systematic qualitative literature review
    (SQLR) method 99
system-wide ranking lists 16

target audience 37
target readership 182
Taylor and Francis 29
teaching opportunities 231
teaching-oriented academics 199
technological developments 82
technology 15, 16, 21, 31
tenured employment 65
Tesch, J. 66, 73
test hypothesis 103
Thailand 13
The Gender Gap in the Tourism
    Academy 156
The Lean PhD 234
thematic journals 8
thematic title 9
themed issues 122, 123, 124, 126, 129
theoretical implications 60
The Tourism Review 7, 49
Thomas, R. 198
Thompson ISI index 154
timeliness 85
timing 229
titles ceased publication 8
top-tier tourism journals 151
Torraco, R. J. 103
tourisation 67
tourism 6, 8, 9, 11, 12, 13, 14, 15, 16,
    17, 21, 22, 28, 29, 37, 44, 49,
    57, 65, 74, 80, 81, 82, 86, 91,
    94, 104, 112, 113, 118, 150, 151,
    160, 162, 171, 182, 193, 212,
    213, 214, 215, 225, 231, 241
  diverse and pluriversal knowledges
    in 70
  full-time permanent lecturing roles
    in 217
  knowledge binaries of 68
  scholarship of 67
tourism academia 73

tourism academics 55, 156
tourism ecosystem 50
tourism emotion 100
tourism gender research 150, 155, 157, 158, 159
tourism journal landscape 6
tourism journal/s 3, 20, 55, 95, 150, 177, 183, 205, 217
tourism knowledge 67, 72, 149
tourism knowledge production 158, 163
tourism literature 94, 97, 103, 116
tourism management 67, 202
Tourism Management (TM) 44
tourism publishing
  gender parity in 163
Tourism Recreation Research (TRR) 46, 48
tourism research 197
  gender parity in 164
Tourism Review (TR) 49, 50, 51, 53, 182
tourism scholarship 66, 113, 169
tourism social science 25
tourism studies 66, 67, 68, 69, 70, 71
tourism theory development 26
Tower, G. 154
Tranfield, D. 101
transformations 70
Tribe, J. 67, 69, 73, 74
Trimble, J. R. 172
truism 150
Tseng, H. 156
Tung, V. W. S. 184
turns in tourism 70

UK 7, 16, 169, 191, 192, 196, 197
Ulrichssweb 56
uncontrollables 229
uniqueness 85

United Nations Sustainable Development Goals 37
university teaching 242
UN World Heritage listing criteria 35
Uriely, N. 14

validity 82, 85, 88
Valkenburg, G. 133, 141
Vargo, S. L. 116
Veijola, S. 69, 73
visibility 214
Vizcaino-Suárez, L. P. 158
volunteer reviewer 48

Ward, K. B. 153
Ward's method 114
Watson 100
Watson, E. 204
web-based submission process 62
Web of Science (WoS) 185
Webster 100
Western hegemony 70
White, E. B. 173
White, W. 60
Williams, J. M. 172
women 154
work–life balance 5, 206, 231
world-leading tourism 193
World Leisure Journal 71
World Tourism Organization 22
writing 222, 243
writing a review 101
writing styles 174

Yang, F. 156, 159
young academics 182

Zapitista movement 71
Zhao, X. 178, 182, 183, 184
Zinsser, W. 173
Zuckerman, H. 155